Designing Care

Designing Care

ALIGNING THE NATURE
AND MANAGEMENT OF
HEALTH CARE

Richard M. J. Bohmer

HARVARD BUSINESS PRESS
Boston, Massachusetts

Copyright 2009 Richard M. J. Bohmer
All rights reserved
Printed in the United States of America

13 12 11 10 09   5 4 3 2

No part of this publication may be reproduced, stored in or introduced into
a retrieval system, or transmitted, in any form, or by any means (electronic,
mechanical, photocopying, recording, or otherwise), without the prior permission
of the publisher. Requests for permission should be directed to
permissions@hbsp.harvard.edu, or mailed to Permissions, Harvard Business
School Publishing, 60 Harvard Way, Boston, Massachusetts 02163.

978-1-4221-7560-6

Library-of-Congress Cataloging information forthcoming.

The paper used in this publication meets the requirements of the American
National Standard for Permanence of Paper for Publications and Documents
in Libraries and Archives Z39.48-1992.

For

my wife

Lynette Smith

My children

Asher Bohmer

Isobel Bohmer

And my parents

Augusta Bohmer

1914

Olomouc

Hugo Bohmer

1910–1996

Podivin Wellington

Contents

Acknowledgments

Writing a book has much in common with being a doctor. On the surface, it has the appearance of being an individual pursuit, but in fact it is a team enterprise. I have been very lucky to be surrounded by a group of people without whom this book would never have been.

First, and most importantly, among these is my wife Lynette Smith. She has supported, cajoled, accommodated, listened, critiqued, and especially loved for the many years I have been working on the ideas contained in these pages. This book is for her.

Next are my children, Asher and Isobel, who not only tolerated their father's absences but also actively supported the enterprise. It is they who gave me the title and the cover.

In my editor, Barbara Feinberg, I have been particularly fortunate. Insightful, patient, passionate, and relentless in pursuit of clarity, Barbara is a remarkable intelligence, and it has been a privilege to work with her.

This book also owes a great deal to the support I have received at Harvard Business School. As the only doctor on the faculty of a general management school, I am grateful for the unwavering support of two deans, first Kim Clark and then Jay Light. Both believed in the project and provided me with the resources to support my research and the freedom to pursue my particular interests. Of my many colleagues at HBS, two in particular have helped me on the intellectual journey that this book summarizes. Gary Pisano and Amy Edmondson, who started as colleagues and became friends, taught and debated me, critiqued my ideas and encouraged their pursuit. I am also grateful to Rob Austin, Carliss Baldwin, Steve Bradley, Clay Christensen, Arthur Daemmrich, Frances Frei, David Garvin, Richard Hamermesh, Bob Hayes, Rob Huckman, Marco Iansiti, Dorothy Leonard-Barton, Alan MacCormack, Warren McFarlan, Mike Roberto, Stefan Thomke, Anita Tucker, David Upton, Jonathan West, and Steve Wheelwright.

For many years, I have been fortunate and privileged to be a member of a remarkable community of health care academics and practitioners in Boston, as notable for its collegiality and selflessness as its intellect. They have all given me their time, critiqued the ideas, and read and reread drafts patiently and generously. More, they have given me their friendship. Foremost among these people are David Blumenthal, Jim Conway, Rushika Fernandopulle, Stan Finkelstein, Bob Hanscom, Jeanette Ives Erickson, Jerry Kassirer, Sheridan Kassirer, Raju Kucherlapati, Lucian Leape, Tom Lee, Robert Mandel, Gregg Meyer, Al Mulley, Heather Palmer, Meredith Rosenthal, Peter Slavin, Charlie Safran, Luke Sato, and David Torchiana. I have also had the privilege of working with a number of talented doctoral students over the past few years, including Julia Adler-Milstein, Ingrid Nembhard, Ann Winslow, and Darren Zinner, and, of course, many MBA students.

Finally, there are many friends and colleagues around the world, both academics and practitioners, who have listened to and discussed my ideas and helped me clarify and crystallize them. In particular I am grateful to David Lawrence. Others include Roger Bohn, Laura Esserman, Carlos Ferrer, Tom Flynn, Brent James, Gary Kaplan, Arnie Milstein, Luciano Ravera, Jaume Ribera, Mark Smith, Ralph Snyderman, and Dan Wong.

Of course, in spite of all these peoples' very best efforts, the remaining errors are all mine.

Introduction

My current illness began in 1972 with symptoms of urinary infection. A subsequent exam and biopsy revealed that I had cancer of the prostate that had spread a little . . . About three years ago, however, I developed a narrowing of the urethra, resulting in a series of complications leading to infection and renal failure. I became very, very ill and was admitted to the hospital. The problems were compounded because the urologist and the nephrologist didn't agree on the nature of my problem or the best treatment for it. Since there was no meeting of the minds, they left it to me to decide what to do. To me! In the end, they discharged me.

—Avedis Donabedian[1]

The litany with which many professional and lay articles on health care begin has a depressingly familiar ring to it. Health care is in crisis. Nations all over the world face unprecedented challenges to their health care systems. At a time when health care is demonstrably expensive, uncertain, unreliable, and sometimes even unsafe, both the demand for health care and the technological capability to do extraordinary things for patients are rising. And while policy makers, payers, and employers have been confronted with relentless cost increases, health care practitioners' lives have been defined by the conflicting (and irreconcilable) forces of increased patient demand and simultaneously constrained resources, causing many to leave the caregiving professions.

How to address the simultaneous problems of lack of value—expensive health care of inconsistent quality—and increasing demand is the focus of active debate among politicians, civil servants, practitioners, and the public. This debate largely centers on the financing of health care: how, and by whom, it should be paid for. Most recently in the United States, defined contribution insurance and high-deductible plans have been proposed to replace more traditional managed care insurance plans in an attempt to make patients more aware of, and more responsible for, their own discretionary health care spending in the hope that they will be able to control costs where others have failed. Payment reform has included every conceivable variation of hospital and physician payment scheme: prospective payment, global fees, fee-for-service, discounted fee-for-service with withholds, salary, capitation, and most recently "pay-for-performance."

Less attention has focused on the "it" for which we are paying; not simply which tests and therapies should or should not be available or covered, but how those tests and therapies are deployed—that is, how health care is delivered. With a few notable exceptions—those working on process improvement in delivery organizations—much of the current debate takes as a given the current structure and functioning of health care delivery systems, at both a national and a local level. Less attention has been focused on the design and management of the processes and organizations that compose a health care delivery system.[2]

THREE PROBLEMS WITH DELIVERY

Concerns about the performance of the health care delivery sector typically focus on one or more of its usual outcomes—cost, quality, and the patient experience of care—or the clinical behaviors associated with these outcomes—underuse, overuse, and misuse.[3] But, as later chapters will argue, many health care delivery organizations fail to address a deeper set of problems that underlie these issues—problems that derive from the state of medical knowledge and the uncertainty that continues to dog much medical and nursing practice.

The first of these is that in many clinical circumstances, we don't know what to do. Although estimates of the exact percentage of day-to-day medical practice for which there is a sound underlying evidential basis vary, uncertainty about what to do in any given clinical situation remains a fact of life for most practitioners and, as the above quote from Avedis Donabedian implies, for patients too. And it is not simply that these practitioners are uninformed. Rather, the medical science to inform a particular clinical choice or strategy for a given patient simply does not exist. No one knows.

Beyond an absolute lack of certainty lies a second, equally troubling problem. When the science does exist, it is often not applied. That is, we don't do what we know. Health care is either over- or undersupplied, contrary to the recommendations of medical science. Interventions demonstrably without benefit continue to be delivered, and known beneficial therapies are underprescribed, both resulting in measurable patient harm. For instance, in spite of consistent evidence that optimal medical therapy is as effective as percutaneous coronary interventions in preventing death and reducing the risk of myocardial infarction, the latter continues to be used in patients with stable coronary artery disease. Moreover, only 44 percent of patients receiving a percutaneous intervention had a prior stress test—a simple, cheap, and noninvasive test that would identify those most eligible for medical therapy only.[4]

Finally, there is the question of fidelity of execution. Even when we know what to do, and do what we know, we don't do it right. Health care delivery remains fraught with errors, of commission and omission. Estimates of harm resulting from medical error place it as a leading cause of death, ahead of motor vehicle accidents, breast cancer, and AIDS.[5] The very basics of health care—for instance, hand hygiene and medication accuracy—cannot be relied on in twenty-first-century health care institutions, performance that is orders of magnitude behind that in other complex, high-risk science-based industries.[6]

All three of these problems relate to the creation and application of medical knowledge to solve individual patients' health problems, the most fundamental activity of care. The question often not explicitly considered by current health care reform debates is exactly how proposed interventions will improve the performance of this basic activity. Moreover, many of the interventions that specifically target health care delivery focus on the static problem, doing what we know, and not on the bigger question of knowing what to do. That is, they address static, but not dynamic, efficiency. The challenge left to managers, long after the reform debate is over, is the design of more effective and efficient approaches to this basic task: the creation of a system for delivering health care.

COMPONENTS OF A SYSTEM FOR
DELIVERING HEALTH CARE

Patient relief—here defined as the cure or prevention of disease and the relief of physical and emotional suffering—is the primary goal of health care. Relief is the outcome of interaction among four core elements of a system for delivering health care: medical knowledge, care processes, practitioners, and health care delivery organizations. Practitioners, supported by health care delivery organizations of various types, apply medical knowledge through care processes to individual patients, with the aim of solving those patients' health problems and relieving their distress. The knowledge for care includes both the medical knowledge about a health problem and what to do about it, and the organizational knowledge about how to best execute that medical knowledge for the relief of the patient. And the application of this knowledge to individual patients is supported by different organizations that deliver all or a component of a patient's health care, including a hospital, a group practice, a physician's organization, and a disease management company—either for-profit or not-for-profit, private, state or foundation owned.

But current systems for generating patient relief—widely considered out of control, inefficient, unsafe, and of poor quality—are often not "systems" at all. They are a patchwork of poorly connected—or entirely unconnected—constituent parts that don't work well together. Typically, they have not been explicitly designed for their purpose. Rather, their four components and the relationships among them have simply developed over time.

In recent years, however—at the same time that policy makers' and managers' primary focus has been on the economics of health care—important changes have occurred to each of these four components. These changes can be observed in health care systems all over the developed world and have occurred irrespective of how specific national or local health care systems are organized, regulated, and financed. Some are the result of deliberate decisions, some of happenstance, and some are unintended consequences of decisions elsewhere. Regardless of their cause, these changes have the potential to redefine the way health care is delivered. And, more importantly, they are forcing us to consider how systems for delivering health care should be designed in the future to effectively and efficiently achieve their goal of patient relief. The purpose of this book is to examine these changes and explore their implications for the deliberate design and management of care processes and health care delivery organizations.

> *Knowledge.* Of these four core elements, one is more fundamental than the others. Inasmuch as clinical practice is the operationalization of medical knowledge—the application of a general body of clinical science to the health needs of a specific individual patient—changes to the knowledge base on which clinical medical and nursing practice is based have had powerful influence on the other three components of the care delivery system. And medical knowledge has undergone a quiet but important change over the last two decades. Not only has medical knowledge become increasingly, dizzyingly, voluminous— nearly thirty thousand new citations are added to Medline, the online medical journal database, each month—but it has also become much

more specific. Hence health problems for which, only a few years ago, there was no unequivocal solution can now be addressed by applying a detailed algorithm that may be explicitly embedded in a clinical guideline, the software of a medical device, or implicit in a modern biopharmaceutical. In effect, the nature of medical knowledge has changed—from the general to the specific.

Processes. For most of medicine's several-thousand-year history, care knowledge was anything but specific, and care itself anything but specifiable or standard. Quite the contrary, from earliest recorded history, health care has been a largely experimental process. Of course, well-accepted general knowledge about how to characterize and resolve health problems—typically in the form of exemplars and descriptions of idealized cases—has long existed. The oldest known medical text, the Edwin Smith papyrus, dating from 2000 to 1500 BCE, bears a striking resemblance to a modern medical text inasmuch as the knowledge for care is organized and presented similarly in both. However, what to do for an individual patient with a specific problem could only be determined in the moment through trial-and-error tests of the match between the specific patient and the known pattern of the disease. The care process—that sequence of clinical decisions and tasks that result in patient relief—was iterative and emergent, consisting of multiple feedback loops and cycles of testing and retesting, and unique to each patient or each patient's health problem. The uncertainty surrounding care was reflected in the very language doctors used to communicate with one another—one study of pathology and radiology reports found thirty distinct "expressions of probability."[7] This uncertainty was proposed as the primary explanation for the geographic variation revealed in a series of studies in the 1980s.[8] In recent times, however, as in other industries, increasingly specific medical knowledge has made it possible to approach improving outcomes in the health care industry through the introduction of standardized decision algorithms and care processes. So now there exist two ways in which health problems are solved: by applying a preformed and pretested solution to a well-understood problem, and by crafting a unique solution to a less well-characterized problem in real time. These two approaches utilize very different processes: the former a sequence of specified steps, and the latter an iterative process of trial and error with multiple feedback loops and branches in the logic.

In this way, changes in medical knowledge have had an impact on care processes.

Practitioners. Changing medical knowledge has also had an impact on the third element of health care systems. Both who can be a "practitioner" and how practitioners practice are influenced by changes in knowledge as well as regulation. At the same time as medical knowledge has become more specific, it has also become more widely available and more easily accessible. So those without formal medical or nursing training—in particular, patients—now have easy access through the Internet to the same knowledge base that was a generation ago the exclusive domain of the clinical professions. And with this increased access to medical knowledge have gone decision rights. Patients are doing to, and for, themselves things that were not previously in their domain, and entrepreneurs are rushing to provide new goods and services to support the "empowered" patient. Moreover, knowledge increases have fueled increasing specialization, both within the established professions (where reimbursement considerations have also been an important driver) and in the creation of entirely new medical care delivery roles such as care coaches.[9]

Organizations. Finally, the role of the health care delivery organization has undergone important change. Until recently, there was a fairly distinct bifurcation between medicine and management. Doctors predominantly decided what was wrong with the patient and what was to be done about it, and managers ran the organization in which those professionals undertook this work. The role of the health care delivery organization was to deliver the resources that practitioners used when they delivered care. Over the last century, the most important of these was the "nursed bed": the site of patients' treatment and convalescence. In the early twentieth century, health care delivery organizations (principally hospitals) also began centralizing the expensive resources, such as laboratory and radiological services, that were essential to the practice of "scientific medicine."

Although delivery organizations were traditionally responsible for some of the most important aspects of health care—for example, nursing care and the resources for scientific medicine (the tests, and therapies deployed by physicians that together helped create patient relief)—they were not responsible for the selection or sequencing of those tests and therapies or the way in which these activities were organized. The doctor determined the optimal care process for a given patient—drawing from the menu of tests and therapies the organization made available—and the health care delivery organization provided the resources for the execution of the care process.[10] Throughout the twentieth century, the health care delivery organization's role was largely supportive. In fact, a clear separation of the doctor and the organization was regarded as essential for ethical practice. Doctors could not be expected to make decisions in the best interests of their patients if they were preoccupied with the business concerns of the hospital.

These four components, acting together, create patient relief, in the way represented in figure I-1. Yet the way they work together to accomplish the basic task of providing patient relief typically has not been deliberately designed. Moreover, each component has changed significantly over the last two decades, as has the way in which they interact. Most significantly, changes in the knowledge for care have both forced and allowed changes in the other three.

FIGURE I-1

Components of health care

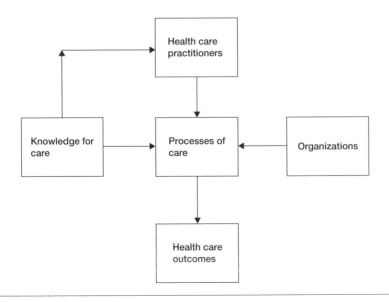

KEY THEMES

The book is built around four key themes.

1. The Management of Care

Over the last two decades, the practices of medicine and management have become increasingly conflated. Expanding medical knowledge has allowed doctors and nurses to determine the right thing to do in many clinical circumstances (evidence-based medicine). However, it has also been the basis for an approach to measuring, holding accountable, and improving the performance of doctors and hospitals, a use for which it was not initially intended. In particular, improved medical evidence has facilitated the development of detailed performance measures that have been applied to both individual doctors and to health care delivery organizations: both risk-adjusted outcomes measures and process measures. The latter allow clinicians and managers to evaluate the fidelity with which practitioners and organizations execute generally accepted "best care" processes. Improved ability to specify and measure "the right thing to do" (i.e., to define the care process) has facilitated the application to health care of managerial tools and approaches developed in other industries in which standard operating procedures (SOPs) are the norm.

This represents a subtle but important shift in management thinking. Now not only is the institution in which clinicians deliver care a focus of management attention, but so too is the actual care itself. That is, care is managed. This shift toward care management is distinct from "managed care," primarily an insurance arrangement focused on incentives and resources, although some of the tools synonymous with managed care did indeed attempt to manage the care.

Recent evidence suggests that how care is managed matters a great deal. Improved performance measurement has revealed the extent to which organizational performance—in particular, how care processes are approached, supported, and managed—is an important determinant of individual patient outcomes. Put simply, in the technologically complex environment of modern health settings, patient relief is as much determined by organizational as by individual physician performance. It is no longer sufficient to credential and colocate great individual clinicians. This insight, and the improved ability to measure performance, has inclined policy makers, regulators, and the general public to hold both individual practitioners and organizations accountable for care itself, both its effectiveness and its efficiency. National and local, public and private, for-profit and not-for-profit organizations all rate both physicians' and organizations' performance in the provision of care. And both regulators and consumers of care use these ratings to hold organizations accountable.

The change in management focus toward the management of care has paralleled a change in the perceived role of the health care delivery organization: from clinician support to the delivery of care. The mission of health care delivery organizations is gradually shifting from the provision of services to the generation of outcomes. That is, health care delivery organizations deliver relief to patients as well as resources to clinicians. In fact, organizations have increasingly marketed themselves to patients as key determinants of patient outcomes, and, accordingly, patients have come to view both physicians and the organizations to which these doctors admit their patients as important for their own well-being. Patients facing a health crisis seek care from an organization as well as an individual doctor, be it a nationally recognized institution such as the Mayo Clinic, Massachusetts General Hospital, or M. D. Anderson Cancer Center, or their local hospital. Thus, increasingly specific medical knowledge has enabled the application of both a set of process management tools and an accountability system drawn from other industries to the health care setting, and in so doing has caused a shift in the role of the organization: from physician support to partner. Inasmuch as they structure and execute care processes in concert with doctors, delivery organizations are taking an ever-larger role in providing patient relief and are sharing accountability for providing this relief. In effect, to the extent that delivery organizations participate in the design and execution of care processes, they are managing care.

2. *The Experimental Nature of Care*

The second key theme is the nature of care. In order to manage care, it is essential to understand the nature of what it is that is being managed. Many current approaches to managing care make some fundamental assumptions about the certainty of care and the extent to which it can be prescribed as a linear sequence of known actions. Increased managerial knowledge accrued over the last century—about how to design and run production organizations that create high-quality products cost-effectively—has been developed in industries such as car assembly, airline service, and steel and paper production. In these industries standardization of production processes and work practices has been a central component of performance improvement. In health care, too, reductions in variation and uncertainty in the outcomes of care have been achieved by the rigorous and effective application of "evidence-based" medicine. Together, improvement in the evidence base of medicine and an increased managerial understanding of how to effectively and reliably apply that evidence in daily patient care have propelled improvements in health care practitioners' and health care delivery organizations' outcomes.

But many of the approaches and tools drawn from industrial settings fail to adequately account for the residual uncertainty in medical care or explicitly address the experimental nature of much care. Patients predominantly present to caregivers and health care delivery organizations with health problems to be solved. In some cases these problems are well structured and the solution well known, and thus the work of health care is predominantly the reliable execution of a known solution. But in other cases the problem is more ambiguous, and what to do about it much less clear. To solve these problems, clinicians and patients engage in a joint process of iterative search, initially for a diagnosis and subsequently through trials of possible treatments—in effect, small-scale experiments, each a turn of the scientific method. Thus health care is a problem-solving and experimental process. When problems are well characterized, care has the appearance of being more certain and less experimental—the execution of a well-known solution. But this is a special case: only one iteration of the scientific cycle underlying all care. In the final analysis, this, too, is an experiment: a test of the therapy's capability to fix the problem in that patient.

Because some problems are well characterized and others are not, the work of health care is highly variable, not only from patient to patient but also within a single episode of care for an individual. The work of diagnosis is often different from the work of treatment, and the work of decision making is often different from the work of decision execution. Furthermore, different diseases may require different work for their clinical management or cure because medical knowledge about how to solve the problems they present is more or less well developed.

Operations management and evidence-based medicine both tend to focus on standard practices and the reduction of variance. In so doing, both make assumptions about what is certain and what is not. Because of this similarity, the two bodies of knowledge have been assumed to be entirely consistent. However, standard operating procedures as conceived of in production environments may not directly apply to health care, and therefore how they are used as a management tool may not be assumed to be the same in both environments. Although standardized care processes (embodied in clinical pathways) exist for the clinical management of the major chronic diseases in adults, ambiguous problems or less well-characterized interactions among multiple problems predominate in day-to-day practice. Such may not be covered by an SOP. Thus management tools drawn from other industries based on standardization of processes and practices may not be universally applicable to all problems or patients. Instead, they most likely will have to coexist with tools and approaches to care processes and the creation of patient relief that make no assumptions about certainty and standardizability.

In sum, modern health care managers are facing a morass of standard and nonstandard processes, certain and highly uncertain patient circumstances and approaches to disease, and a large and varied set of managerial tools and philosophies from which to choose.[11] And in this context, their task is to transform general-purpose care delivery organizations that developed organically during an era when the state of medical knowledge did not permit clinical standardization and physicians' and managers' roles were more distinct. Given the variability in patient problems and the processes by which providers address them, no one design of a health care organization will likely be sufficient.

3. Evidence-Creating Medicine

The third broad theme of the book derives from the experimental nature of health care. If routine health care is by its nature experimental, then we might expect that these experiments occasionally generate new insights. Although institutionally funded basic science research and formal clinical trials are usually thought of as the source of the knowledge base used in the solution of patients' health problems, routine care is also an important source of innovation. When each patient interaction is a potential test of an evaluative or therapeutic strategy, day-to-day care generates as well as uses medical knowledge. Breakthroughs come from the clinic as well as the lab. Not all innovations will be scientific—that is, new ways to investigate or treat a particular problem. Some will be organizational, inasmuch as they will be new ways of executing on that knowledge. Not only is medical care based on evidence. It creates evidence.

The need for new knowledge in health care, both scientific and organizational, is ongoing. We still know too little, not only about what to do, but also about how to do it. Furthermore, new science that informs clinicians' approaches to solving a particular problem often demands new knowledge about how to go about applying that science in practice. Health care delivery organizations are sociotechnical systems in which technology influences social order.[12] And without organizational change, technological change often falters.[13]

As the medical knowledge base continues to grow and evolve, albeit inconsistently and sporadically, care processes, practitioner roles, and organizational forms are in constant flux. A patient's health problem solved in one way this year may be solved in an entirely different way five years hence. Who solves the problem, in which setting, using which technology, by which process, and drawing on the resources of what kind of organization, are all subject to change. New knowledge creates a need for new learning.

However, much of the learning deriving from the experiments of routine care will be lost without deliberate efforts to capture it. We cannot presume that the current system for delivering care, not specifically designed or optimized to deliver any particular type of health care, can learn and absorb changes in knowledge, processes, roles, and organizations, adapting organically. Learning must be deliberately designed into an organization's norms and routines.

4. The Central Role of Operating Systems

The foregoing—that clinical performance has become an organizational as well as an individual attribute, that both institutions and care are the manager's purview, and that the process being managed is an experimental problem-solving process that both draws on and creates medical and organizational knowledge—raises the question of how managers might best approach managing care. What are the parameters under their control, and how might these be used to most effectively and efficiently create patient relief? The fourth key theme is the central role of the operating system: that set of business processes, technologies, policies, and organizational structures that supports the core process of care.

Historically, health care delivery organizations were not specifically designed and optimized for the roles of delivering care or learning from day-to-day experience; they were designed to centralize essential resources. In the case of an inpatient facility, the key resource initially was the nursing service, and later in the nineteenth century, surgical facilities. With the advent of scientific medicine at the turn of the twentieth century, the resources grew to include laboratory and radiology technology. From the very beginning, health care delivery organizations provided care for a diverse set of problems; so while these resources were colocated, they were not usually configured to specifically address the needs of any particular patient group. Instead, general-purpose resources were organized as a job shop.

To adapt to their new role, modern health care organizations have looked to industry for management tools and models that would allow them to exercise some measure of operational control over the delivery of care. Some of these tools aim to influence what doctors and nurses do, predominantly through the use of guidelines, measurement, and incentives. Others have a more industrial flavor: standard operating procedures and compliance measurement. The two most common tool sets for managing care have been clinical guidelines and financial incentives for practitioners to comply with those guidelines. Sometimes such tools have been packaged with a managerial philosophy to create a global management model—for example, Total Quality Management (TQM) or the Toyota Production System (TPS).

But most often care management tools have been used as stand-alone interventions with the aim of improving a particular clinical or financial outcome, one project at a time. They have not necessarily been integrated into a coherent operating system deliberately designed to support the care of a particular population of patients or the solution of a set of health problems. Yet for an organization that manages care, lasting performance improvement requires the coherent configuration of a set of interdependent resources (both human and technical), care processes, and management policies covering such issues as incentives and production control, into an operating system. Moreover, learning systematically by exploiting the evidence-creating nature of care depends on the integration of multiple learning activities and supporting structures into an operating system for learning. Processes and operating systems are crucial points of leverage in organizations that manage care. Creating internally consistent designs that specifically add value for patients by solving their health problems effectively and efficiently is the essential work of health management.

DESIGNING CARE

As already noted, little of the current discussion of health care reform centers on the design and management of the health care delivery system. The reforms most commonly proposed, often by those at a distance from the work of patient care, are structural and financial—predominantly focusing on the financing of health care by governments and consumers, alternative payment systems for physician and hospital services, and specialized delivery organizations. Such discussions implicitly assume that reform of the design of, and management approach to, the delivery system will naturally follow from changes in the incentives for health care delivery organizations and health care providers. Politicians, policy makers, and managers are usually silent on the reforms to delivery system design and management that are necessary if care providers are to respond appropriately to new incentives.

Motivating individuals to do better, through either financial or nonfinancial incentives, will never be sufficient on its own to guarantee better health outcomes. Rather, the work of care and the operating systems that support that work must be explicitly designed for this purpose, and not left to accrete by chance and happenstance. The question for managers is thus not only, should we build new institutions, and if so, what kind? But more importantly, how do we reform the thousands of existing health care delivery organizations (hospitals, skilled nursing facilities, physician group practices, etc.) we already have in order to improve their performance? This book will argue that the reform of existing delivery organizations (as well as the design of future ones) requires the configuration of operating systems internal to the organization, with the aim of accommodating and exploiting changes in the knowledge for care and its impact on processes and practitioner roles.

The work required to solve a patient's health problem and provide relief—given the current state of knowledge about that particular disease and therapy, the processes by which this work is undertaken and the ideal result realized, the roles of the various workers involved, and the organizations in which they work—is the "it" for which national health systems pay. Without thoughtful design of these components of local health delivery systems and their relationships to one another, lasting improvements in health system performance may elude us. Much of the day-to-day work of performance improvement and reform in health care delivery is operational, comprising the deliberate design of the four components described above and their interrelationships.

Managers undertaking this work, whether clinically trained or not, face several dilemmas. Importantly, they must reconcile the inherent uncertainty and variability of much patient care with increasing but still incomplete standardizability, and decide how to make best use of modern industrial management tools and approaches that center on standardization. In wrestling with this dilemma, managers will be challenged to determine exactly what constitutes "value" for each of the many populations they serve, and delineate exactly by what processes is such value created and by which is it not. Unlike in other industries, most health care managers usually cannot exercise input control. They must serve all, turn none away, and create processes and operating systems capable of addressing the diverse needs of many patient populations, needs that cannot necessarily be determined *ex ante*. With this constraint, increasing medical knowledge has in fact made the manager's job harder, not easier. Because much still remains unknown, operating systems must now cope with patients whose care can be managed by a predetermined clinical pathway and those whose management emerges iteratively through a series of focal experiments. And new scientific knowledge has exposed the paucity of application knowledge—knowing what to do is not the same as reliably doing what you know. Ironically, the more we know, the harder is the work of applying this knowledge. Finally, these knowledge bases will continue to shift, demanding not only design, but redesign. As the cover of this book suggests, the work of reforming health care delivery is still a work in progress.

FRAMEWORK FOR THE BOOK

This book attempts to develop a contingent approach to the design and management of systems for delivering health care predicated on an understanding of the nature of the work required to care for an individual patient suffering from disease. Figure I-2 illustrates the book's conceptual framework.

The book falls broadly into two sections, the first focusing on the knowledge for care and the processes of care, and the second on health care practitioners and operating systems (see figure I-2). Before I discuss specific approaches to addressing the challenges described above, it will be important to develop a detailed understanding of the nature of medical care—that which we are attempting to manage. Without such an understanding, it will

FIGURE I-2

Conceptual framework

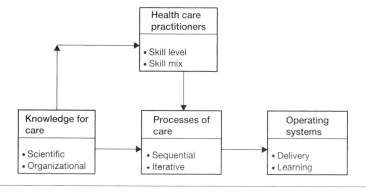

be difficult, if not impossible, to design processes, organizations, and systems of care capable of delivering the level of performance that health care's many constituents are coming to expect, let alone ones capable of accommodating, adopting, and exploiting coming generations of promising new technologies. Hence the first four chapters explore the nature of care and our current approaches to care management, and the latter four chapters discuss approaches to designing care delivery processes and organizations.

Chapter 1 begins by describing the transition from managing resources and institutions to managing care, and the growth of industry-based care management tools with their focus on the standardization of care and their underlying presumption of certainty in medical practice. Chapter 2 then discusses a fundamental problem with these approaches: the parlous state of much of the evidence upon which evidence-based medicine (and by implication evidence-based care management) is based. Although it is clearly attractive to presume a level of medical certainty when designing health care processes and organizations, it may be neither justified nor realistic. Medical care is often (although not always) much more complex than applying a standardized guideline, quite simply because in many circumstances either a guideline does not exist or the guideline that does exist is not applicable to that particular patient. With the goal of framing an approach to designing health care processes and organizations discussed in later chapters, chapter 3 examines the process of medical care in detail to clarify its fundamental nature. It examines the way in which care frequently, but not always, comprises a set of iterative focused experiments, rather than a linear sequence of steps. Chapter 3 identifies two broad classes of care process: iterative processes comprising multiple small-scale focused experiments, and sequential processes consisting of an orderly set of well-defined steps. Finally, as chapter 4 discusses, even when it is possible, as it is with many common diseases and procedures, to rely on a standard sequence of steps, the evidence base of medicine is constantly shifting and evolving. Thus not only must managers design processes that accurately apply current knowledge to individual patients; they must also design systems that are capable of constant change and learning.

Chapter 5 begins the second section of the book by introducing the concept of an operating system—the organizational infrastructure and set of processes and policies that support a production process—and discussing the importance of aligning its design with the type of care process. Experience from other industries indicates that the organizational designs and the managerial tools to manage sequential and iterative care processes are very different. This chapter describes the different operating systems required by these two processes and concludes by discussing approaches to supporting sequential and iterative care processes simultaneously. Chapter 6 continues this theme by discussing the design of operating systems capable of capturing and using learning from routine care—evidence-creating medicine.

Chapter 7 takes up the issue of the roles practitioners play in the operating systems described in previous chapters and discusses the ways in which old roles are changing and new roles are emerging in response to changes in medical knowledge—in particular, roles for the doctor and the patient. This chapter concludes by discussing the impact of these changes on the broader market for health care services and the creation of yet more new roles. Finally, chapter 8 concludes by presenting a conceptual model for the design of health care delivery organizations that integrates the various components discussed in the preceding chapters. It describes six essential capabilities required by health care organizations if they are to effectively manage care and share accountability for generating patient relief.

In summary, what follows is an attempt to integrate the sciences of medicine and management to frame an approach to managing the act of caring for a sick patient, by starting with an understanding of the work of health care. In developing principles for the design and management of health care, this book deliberately avoids discussion of reimbursement and regulation, two powerful influences on any system for delivering health care. Managers' choices are routinely governed by such factors as local reimbursement policies and price contracts, network structures, scope-of-practice regulations and assessments of community needs, not to mention the lobbying power of physician organizations and nursing unions. These factors will obviously strongly influence how care is delivered and by whom in any individual locale. The components and relationships described above, however, are universal and fundamental. To a large extent, they determine the basic options managers and clinicians have available to them for designing a system for delivering care. How individual nations, states, or regions pay for and regulate health care will influence how managers chose among these options, but it is primarily the state of medical knowledge that determines what the options are. And how the four components of a system for care delivery are configured is a matter of design.

1

Managing Care and the Allure of Certainty

Long-term observers of the health care delivery sector will have noted that many reforms have been developed in isolation from each other. Systems for financing and delivering health care are so complex that professional and lay discussions of health care problems and solutions, quite naturally, tend to address each in isolation and one at a time. But in so doing, they risk missing important interdependencies and interactions among the key elements of a care delivery system. Moreover, focusing on the latest problem or solution also risks distracting us and preventing us from noticing the longer-term trends of which each isolated issue may be a part.

One trend in particular, the move toward the increasingly explicit management of medical care, is the impetus for this book. Most of the recently proposed solutions to problems of health care costs and quality have an important factor in common. Financial incentives inherent in new financing or payment models, such as "consumer driven" insurance plans and capitation or pay-for-performance, presume that caregivers and care delivery organizations have the requisite capabilities to deliver care in ways consistent with the new incentive. That is, they treat medical care as a manageable activity. They presume that processes of care and care delivery organizations can respond flexibly to changed incentives, and that the delivery systems in which care takes place function as systems. And of course, they presume that the tools in common use for care management are effective and sufficient. "Managed care," primarily a set of insurance and reimbursement arrangements, presumed that care could be managed. This chapter will examine how such presumptions came to be so deeply entrenched in the minds of both health care policy makers and managers, how care came to be managed, and where the tools for care management came from; and it foreshadows chapter 2's evaluation of whether these presumptions and the choices they engendered are in fact reasonable.

To begin, it is important to note that such presumptions are new. For all but the last twenty years of the long history of medicine, medical care was not treated as manageable and was not the focus of management attention; and systems, to the extent that they were "developed" at all, were developed without deep analysis of clinical processes. The predominantly lay directors of the emerging hospitals of the late nineteenth and early twentieth centuries focused on the buildings and later the technologies they housed, not the care they delivered.[1] Indeed, the practice of medical care providers—the decisions they made about individual patients, or the ways they executed those decisions—was largely independent of the institutional setting in which care was delivered, and not subject to any management design or control. Only recently have physicians' decisions and skills come under close scrutiny.

Of course, practitioners were never entirely free of scrutiny and free to do whatever they wanted. Their discretion has long been constrained by the professional expectations, explicit and implicit, that guided medical and nursing practice, expectations that were embedded in the routines of daily practice, the unspoken rules of professional courtesy, and occasionally in guidelines published by professional societies. When an adverse patient outcome occurred, physicians' preceding decisions and actions were evaluated in a "morbidity and mortality" meeting. But by and large, managers were neither responsible for nor focused upon the details of the medical care delivered to individual patients. Quite the contrary, professional independence has long been a basic tenet of medical practice, the sine qua non of high-quality care. For years physicians' individual responsibility and ethical commitment to the patient was seen as "obviating the need to assert the public interest through prescriptive rules," and the management and oversight of medical practice remained the "purview of the profession."[2] Payers, policy makers, managers, and patients had a somewhat passive role as it was left to physicians to determine both the supply and the demand for medical services.[3] The role of the managers and the policy makers was to manage the institution (and industry context) in which independent-minded physicians practiced their profession. For instance, the response, in the 1960s, to growing concerns about the costs of medical care was not to constrain the decisions doctors made in delivering that care (most of which implied the consumption of somebody else's resources) but to train more doctors, on the presumption that an increase in physician supply and competition among physicians would reduce the unit price. Prior to the 1970s, managers' primary focus was on the resources of health care. Policy makers were concerned with ensuring an adequate supply of well-trained professionals and hospital beds and that adequate insurance coverage guaranteed patients' access to services. And hospital managers ran the institutions in which doctors practiced their profession, in turn ensuring a supply of that key resource of health care delivery: the nursed bed-day. But all this began to change in the 1970s, when these groups' attention turned to the actual care that was delivered to patients within these institutions, and subsequently to the notion of managing that care.

THE IMPETUS FOR MANAGING CARE:
VARIATION, INAPPROPRIATENESS,
UNDERSUPPLY, AND ERROR

Several factors created an impetus for a shift in management focus and changes in care processes and management tools. First and foremost was the increase in the societal costs of medical care. Physician autonomy, fee-for-service physician reimbursement, cost-plus hospital reimbursement, and an explosion in medical technology were a potent cocktail driving a rapid rise in health care costs, leading in turn not only to the development of new ways of paying for health care (Medicare and Medicaid in 1965, the growth of health maintenance organizations in the 1980s), but also to an examination of the quality of care bought with that increased spending. For all its spending, the United States performed badly on standard indexes of health care quality such as infant mortality and life expectancy.[4] To the prevailing professional model of individual responsibility and peer oversight was added a layer of bureaucratic oversight both external and internal to the health care delivery organization. By the 1970s, hospital accreditation by the Joint Commission on Accreditation of Healthcare Organizations (JCAHO) became "virtually mandatory" for a hospital to receive Medicare payment; and professional standards review organizations (PRSOs) were established by federal legislation in 1972, with the mandate for cost and quality oversight of the care delivered to Medicare and Medicaid patients.[5] In 1974 the JCAHO required that hospitals operate an internal quality assurance program in which problems in care delivery were identified and solved, usually by monitoring and addressing the causes of sentinel events such as health care–associated infections.

More-recent roots of this change in attitude can be attributed to a series of research results in the 1980s and 1990s, although the idea that medical care should be monitored and practices compared and explicitly and rigorously evaluated is of course much older than this. For example, in her landmark work, *Notes on Hospitals* (1859), Florence Nightingale compared hospital mortality rates and attributed their variation to differences in physical design and the through flow of air. At the turn of the twentieth century, Ernest Codman, a Boston surgeon, proposed that the surgical outcomes of individual surgeons at Massachusetts General Hospital be collected, compared, and published (the "end results idea").

Starting with an important paper in 1982, health services research began homing in on several important insights. First, the work of Jack Wennberg and his colleagues revealed the extent of geographic variation in health care service delivery rates.[6] Wennberg, an epidemiologist, used the statistical tools of his profession not to analyze the incidence rates of diseases, but to examine the incidence rates of therapy. What he found has influenced managers' and policy makers' thinking ever since. Wennberg identified significant variation across populations of patients in the use of common surgical procedures.[7] Moreover, this variation was not explained by characteristics of the population—such as its demographics (age, sex, race profile) or disease burden (type and severity of disease)—that might suggest that there was variation in the need for the procedure. In fact, adjacent geographic areas in which there was no conceivable difference in medical need—for example, for procedures such as hysterectomy or tonsillectomy—nonetheless received very different rates of these operations. Further, this variation was more marked for some procedures than for others. Although the rates of inguinal hernia repair did not vary much from one area to another, there was a sixfold variation in tonsillectomy rates among the areas that Wennberg studied.[8]

Only two reasons could possibly explain these observations; either there was indeed some, as yet unmeasured, difference in medical need between contiguous areas, or doctors had wide discretion in whether or not to recommend these procedures and varied in their prescriptions. Wennberg's work prompted two further lines of inquiry into the latter explanation.[9] One followed the argument that physicians were responding to both their own natural risk aversion and the incentives inherent in a fee-for-service reimbursement system by overproviding medical care. If this was so, then physicians might be providing services to patients for which the clinical benefit did not clearly outweigh the risks for that patient—in other words, care that was "inappropriate."

A somewhat controversial series of studies by the RAND Corporation in the 1980s investigated rates of "inappropriate" care. In comparing—case by case—the procedures individual patients received with the best current evidence about whether that patient would benefit from that procedure, the RAND researchers demonstrated that many invasive procedures—for example, coronary artery bypass surgery and carotid endarterectomy—were not clearly necessary.[10] Using retrospective chart review of previous cases, expert reviewers concluded that many procedures were, at best, undertaken on equivocal clinical grounds and, at worst, frankly inappropriate.

The second line of inquiry followed the hypothesis that the observed variation in rates of care reflected professional uncertainty about the "right" thing to do in any individual patient circumstance. If there was no clear consensus among physicians about the best course of care for many common health problems, then physicians would naturally pursue different clinical management strategies. A landmark paper in 1984 by David Eddy made this case as an explanation for the observed variation. Eddy described a simple experiment in which attendees at a national meeting of experts in colorectal cancer screening were asked to estimate the "overall reduction in colorectal cancer incidence and mortality that could be expected if men and women over the age of fifty were tested with fecal occult blood tests and 60cm flexible sigmoidoscopy every year." This group of experts gave estimates ranging from just above 0 percent reduction in incidence and mortality to just below 100 percent.[11] Eddy proposed that in fact much medical care was uncertain. Moreover, the more uncertain the indications for a particular procedure were, the wider the variation in use rates would be, helping explain the differing rates of variation for inguinal hernia repair (the clinical indications for which were less uncertain) and tonsillectomy (the indications for which were highly controversial).

But this explanation only applied to those medical problems or therapies for which there was no clear consensus about the best practice. What about those situations in which there was general agreement? Presumably, where there is a clear consensus, doctors would all follow the same practice, and rates of therapies for these conditions should not vary significantly. Yet another body of work has investigated the problem of undersupply and found that this is not the case. Even for interventions unequivocally known to lead to better outcomes (i.e., a "right thing to do"), there was variation in delivery. Studies in the 1990s found rates of delivery of warfarin in atrial fibrillation, beta-blockers after acute myocardial infarction, and ACE inhibitors in congestive heart failure to be 32 percent, 21 percent, and 31 percent, respectively.[12] Moreover, such underuse clearly resulted in patient harm; the underuse of warfarin in atrial fibrillation, for example, was estimated to result in forty thousand additional strokes per annum.[13] A recent large study that used 439 indicators to assess quality of care found that, overall, patients appear to be receiving a little over half of the recommended care.[14]

Finally, another important paper in 1991 alerted the community to the issue of medical error.[15] This initiated another stream of troubling research into medical error and especially drug error, in which it has become clear that health care institutions are not safe places. Not only are dangerous infective agents concentrated there, but so are unreliable processes and fatigued and overburdened caregivers.

Thus, not only did the evidence suggest that doctors did not always know what to do, but when they did know, they didn't always do it; and when they did do it, they didn't always do it right. Taken together, these insights into variation, uncertainty, inappropriateness, undersupply, and error have chipped away at the notion that doctors were all-knowing and should be left unencumbered by oversight to deliver care to their patients. In fact, these findings have resulted in not only a much greater scrutiny of physicians' practices (and outcomes) by policy makers, payers, and managers, but also an increased willingness by these groups to actually direct these practices. Where medical care was previously the exclusive domain of medical and nursing staff, it then became the explicit focus of managers and policy makers, who for the first time felt entitled to measure and manage the details of the care itself. Although in the 1990s the term *managed care* predominantly connoted particular structures for care delivery (restricted care delivery networks comprising owned physician practices and inpatient facilities), payment methods and incentives for physicians (capitation or discounted fee-for-service), and an insurance arrangement (defined benefits and a restricted set of preferred providers), it also meant "managing care" (using such techniques as guidelines and utilization management). Thus the last two decades have seen a gradual evolution from a management focus on the institutional context of care (i.e., managing the institution in which the physician delivered care) to a focus on the management of the care itself. And a key player in this evolution has been what would become an essential mechanism of care management—the clinical practice guideline, widely seen as a remedy to the three different classes of uncertainty surrounding medical care and its management: clinical uncertainty (we don't know what we need to do), execution uncertainty (we don't do it even when we know what to do), and quality uncertainty (when we do it, we do it wrongly).

THE CENTRAL ROLE OF THE GUIDELINE
IN MANAGING CARE

One implication of the research on variation, uncertainty, appropriateness, underuse, and medical error seemed clear: performance could be improved if the best care processes were specified and we ensured that these processes were followed. Doctors needed both help to know what the standards of the day were, and control to ensure that they were in fact practicing in accordance with those standards.

The mechanism that would achieve both goals was the guideline. Simply defined as "systematically developed statements to assist practitioner decisions about appropriate health care for specific clinical circumstances," guidelines have been imbued with multiple goals.[16] First, of course, they were aids for decision makers. Second, guidelines were intended to be educational. Because they encapsulated the current understanding of "best practice," they served to educate physicians about the appropriate care they were expected to deliver, and thus the guideline was intended to direct physicians' treatment choices. Third, they were also the basis for quality and performance measurements. Because the guideline stipulated the optimal choice of test or treatment for a patient with a given condition, the rate at which an individual physician actually made these choices could be used as a measure of the quality of care (guideline compliance rate), and thus one provider could be compared with another. And they were de facto tools of control; they were the basis of criteria sets intended to control medical care through the authorization of tests and therapies that physicians ordered. Finally, it was hoped that by following the published best practice, a physician would be less vulnerable to medicolegal action in the event of a bad patient outcome.

Guidelines, which are by no means a new phenomenon, were not initially intended to fulfill all these roles. For many years, guidelines were simply general statements, often full of conditional language, intended to do what their name suggested: guide. For example, a guideline published in 1812 in a circular to Boston dispensing physicians stated, "The strictest economy is recommended in the distribution of Medicines and Wine; one quart only of the latter shall be ordered at one time, and that to be Lisbon, or Sherry, or some other not exceeding their value. Port may sometimes be directed, if thought to be peculiarly beneficial; giving preference to the cheapest that will suit the case."[17] However, in the last two decades, guidelines have increased not only in number, but also in specificity, to the point that some authors now make a clear distinction between a guideline and a protocol.[18] Whereas the former outlines general principles that should be taken into account by a professional providing care in a specific situation, the latter provides explicit and specific instructions about exactly which steps should be taken.[19]

It is these specific instructions—always intended to be flexible and leave room for clinical judgment—that form the basis of many modern performance assessment and management systems. Most tools for managing care are in some way derivatives of a guideline. Tactics primarily aimed at influencing physician decision making—such as criteria sets, utilization management, preauthorization, mandatory second opinions, outcomes and process measurement and "report cards," and pay-for-performance incentives—all derive from an underlying guideline to some extent.

Underlying this approach to medical management is the notion and practice of *evidence-based medicine* (EBM). Clinical decisions should, to the extent possible, be based on the best currently available scientific evidence (and by implication, not on anecdote or habit).[20] However, guidelines are complex inasmuch as they encompass many steps in a patient's care and may synthesize the results from many individual randomized controlled trials. Such trials are often highly focused, and the evidence they contribute to the guideline nuanced and sophisticated. Hence, if the guideline is to be the mechanism by which the evidence is translated into appropriate care, then an additional process is required to distill and consolidate large volumes of medical research into usable recommendations for practitioners. Thus EBM has come to mean not just the principle of applying science to individual patient decisions, but the practices of evidence assessment and guideline development using epidemiological (e.g., meta-analysis) and organizational (e.g., consensus development) tools.[21] Through the ongoing processes of rigorous evidence evaluation and distillation, clinical practices and decisions that were once uncertain and vague have become increasingly certain and specified. The evolving state of medical knowledge made it easier to manage care through specification of the care process.

EVOLVING MEDICAL KNOWLEDGE

Since the 1970s the amount of medical knowledge has exploded. Not only has the volume of knowledge increased exponentially, with over three hundred thousand new citations being added to Medline every year, but the specificity of that knowledge has increased.[22] Although this number includes publications of all types—for example, the results of observational studies, case reports, policy analyses, and letters to the editor—over ten thousand of these citations per year are drawn from randomized controlled trials: trials that result in specific recommendations for the care of patients with a particular disease or the use of a particular therapy.[23] This number is up from about one hundred per year in 1966, and fully 49 percent of these articles were published in the last five years of the interval between 1966 and 1995.

While the increase in the volume of medical knowledge over the last three decades has created a need for evidence-based medicine, it is the increase in the specificity of that knowledge that has enabled the use of managerial tools (discussed in detail below) that specify, measure, and provide incentives for the application of clinical guidelines to day-to-day physician practice. This increase in specificity can be seen in the evolution of the guidelines that serve as the basis for these tools. The guideline for hypertension management—first published in 1977 by the Joint National Committee on Prevention, Detection, Evaluation, and Treatment of High Blood Pressure (JNC) and republished six further times—provides an example of this evolution.

Over the twenty-six-year period between 1977 and the publication in 2003 of the seventh update (known as JNC-7), the basic structure of the guideline has remained largely constant, but both the language and the content of the guideline have become more specific (see table 1-1). A good example of this

TABLE 1-1

Weight control and salt restriction recommendations for hypertensive patients

Edition	Recommendation	Expected effect
JNC-1 (1977)[a]	For some patients, weight control and a reduced salt intake may lower blood pressure, . . .	
JNC-2 (1980)[b]	In general, weight reduction in obese subjects and sodium control . . . (85mEq sodium daily) in all patients should be considered adjunctive to the management of hypertension.	A few studies on the effects of dietary intervention suggest that weight reduction or moderate control of sodium intake may lower BP in some patients.
JNC-3 (1984)[c]	. . . weight reduction should be an integral part of therapy for all obese patients (>115% ideal weight) with hypertension. Moderate dietary sodium restriction to a level of 70 to 90 mEq/day may reduce elevated BP.	Weight reduction by caloric restriction often results in a substantial decrease in BP, even if the ideal body weight is not achieved.
JNC-4 (1988)[d]	. . . all obese hypertensive adults should participate in weight reduction programs, with goal body weight being within 15% of desirable weight. . . . proper counseling is necessary to achieve moderate sodium restriction. This counseling should include reference to sodium labeling of canned, frozen, and other processed foods, . . .	Weight reduction may reduce arterial pressure in overweight hypertensive patients; . . . . . . some patients with mild or moderate blood pressure elevation may achieve control through moderate sodium restriction to 70 to 100mEq/d. There is no easy way to identify those patients who will benefit from sodium restriction.
JNC-5 (1993)[e]	. . . an increased waist-to-hip ratio above 0.85 in women and 0.95 in men, has also been correlated with hypertension, . . .	A reduction in blood pressure usually occurs early during a weight loss program, often with as small a loss as 4.5kg.

TABLE 1-1 (CONTINUED)

Edition	Recommendation	Expected effect
	. . . all hypertensive patients who are above their ideal weight should initially be placed on an individualized, monitored weight reduction program involving caloric restriction and increased caloric expenditure.	. . . a 100mmol/d [or] lower average sodium intake was associated with a 2.2mm-Hg lower SBP in 10,000 people and a 5-to-10 mm Hg lower SBP in several other studies . . .
	Reduce sodium intake to less than 100 mmol/d (Table 6).	
JNC-6 (1997)[f]	. . . body mass index . . . of 27 or greater is correlated closely with increased blood pressure . . . A waist circumference of 85cm or greater in women or 98cm or greater in men, also has been associated with the risk for hypertension	Weight reduction, of as little as 4.5kg, reduces blood pressure in a large proportion of overweight persons with hypertension.
	. . . all patients with hypertension who are above their desirable weight should be prescribed an individualized, monitored weight reduction program involving caloric restriction and increased physical activity.	An analysis of 17 published RCTs involving patients 45 years or older with hypertension found an average decrease of 6.3/2.2 mm Hg with a urinary sodium reduction of 95 mmol/d.
	Reduce sodium intake to no more than 100 mmol/d (Table 7).	
JNC-7 (2003)[g]	Maintain normal body weight (BMI 18.5 to 24.9) [Table 3].	Approximate systolic BP reduction, range: 5–20 mm Hg/10kg weight loss [Table 3].
	Reduce dietary sodium intake to no more than 100 mEq/L. [Table 3]	Approximate systolic BP reduction, range: 2–8 mm Hg [Table 3].

Sources:

a. The Joint National Committee on Detection, Evaluation, and Treatment of High Blood Pressure, "Report of the Joint National Committee on Prevention, Detection, Evaluation, and Treatment of High Blood Pressure: A Cooperative Study," *JAMA* 237, no. 3 (1977): 255–261.

b. The Joint National Committee on Detection, Evaluation, and Treatment of High Blood Pressure, "The 1980 Report of the Joint National Committee on Detection, Evaluation, and Treatment of High Blood Pressure," *Archives of Internal Medicine* 140 (1980): 1280–1285.

c. The Joint National Committee on Detection, Evaluation, and Treatment of High Blood Pressure, "The 1984 Report of the Joint National Committee on Detection, Evaluation, and Treatment of High Blood Pressure," *Archives of Internal Medicine* 144 (1984): 1045–1057.

d. The Joint National Committee on Detection, Evaluation, and Treatment of High Blood Pressure, "The 1988 Report of the Joint National Committee on Detection, Evaluation, and Treatment of High Blood Pressure," *Archives of Internal Medicine* 148 (1988): 1023–1038.

e. The Joint National Committee on Detection, Evaluation, and Treatment of High Blood Pressure, "The Fifth Report of the Joint National Committee on Detection, Evaluation, and Treatment of High Blood Pressure (JNC V)," *Archives of Internal Medicine* 153 (1993): 154–183.

f. The Joint National Committee on Prevention, Detection, Evaluation, and Treatment of High Blood Pressure, "The Sixth Report of the Joint National Committee on Prevention, Detection, Evaluation, and Treatment of High Blood Pressure," *Archives of Internal Medicine* 157 (1997): 2413–2445.

g. The Joint National Committee on Prevention, Detection, Evaluation, and Treatment of High Blood Pressure, "The Seventh Report of the Joint National Committee on Prevention, Detection, Evaluation, and Treatment of High Blood Pressure: The JNC 7 Report," *JAMA* 289, no. 19 (2003): 2560–2572.

phenomenon is the recommendations for lifestyle modification—for example, weight reduction and salt restriction—in the treatment of hypertension. In 1977 these recommendations were brief: "For some patients weight control and a reduced salt intake may lower blood pressure." By 1980 the recommendation had evolved to "weight reduction in obese patients and sodium control (85mEq sodium daily) in all patients should be considered adjunctive to the management of hypertension." The recommendation in JNC-3 (1984) was that "moderate dietary sodium restriction to a level of 70 to 90 mEq/day may reduce elevated BP," but by 1993 JNC-5 stated curtly, "Reduce sodium intake to less than 100 mmol/d" (article table 6). Similarly, the definition of *overweight* evolved. Initially undefined, it changed from 15 percent above "ideal" (JNC-3, 1984), to "an increased waist-to-hip ratio above 0.85 in women and 0.95 in men" (JNC-5, 1993), to "body mass index of 27 or greater" and "a waist circumference of 85cm or greater in women or 98cm or greater in men" (JNC-6, 1997).

Moreover, the impact of controlling weight and salt intake was more clearly articulated in later editions of the JNC guidelines. For example, JNC-2 (1980) noted that "a few studies on the effects of dietary intervention suggest that weight reduction or moderate control of sodium intake may lower BP in some patients." The same section of JNC-3 (1984) stated that "weight reduction . . . often results in a substantial decrease in BP, even if the ideal body weight is not achieved"; and in 1993 JNC-5 defined the amount of body weight reduction necessary: "A reduction in blood pressure usually occurs early during a weight loss program, often with as small a loss as 4.5kg." The same is true of salt restriction. JNC-5, and subsequent editions, specified the amount of blood pressure reduction that could be expected from a low-salt diet. By JNC-6 (1997), the weight of evidence was clear: "An analysis of seventeen published RCTs involving patients forty-five years or older with hypertension found an average decrease of 6.3/2.2 mm Hg with a urinary sodium reduction of 95 mmol/d." And in JNC-7 (2003), the expected effects of lifestyle modification were presented in a table listing the approximate systolic blood pressure reduction: "5–20 mm Hg/10kg weight loss" and "2–8 mm Hg" for a diet of less than 100 mEq/day.

The kind of evidence that is distilled into modern guidelines also serves as the basis for quality measures. For example, in the recent RAND study of quality of care in the United States, quality was assessed by measuring the rate at which care that should have been delivered (the "indicator") was actually delivered.[24] What should have been delivered was derived from the kind of guidelines of which JNC-7 is an example. The RAND study indicators that track the quality of a hypertensive patient's evaluation and treatment include "initial laboratory tests should include serum potassium" and "first line treatment for patients in risk groups A or B is lifestyle modification. The medical record should indicate counseling for at least 1 of the following interventions prior to initiating pharmacotherapy: weight reduction if obese, increased physical activity if sedentary, or a low sodium diet."[25]

Over the years the language of guidelines has changed—from conditional to declarative—and the recommendations have become more specific and detailed. The same has occurred to the measures of clinical performance (quality) that are based on such guidelines. For example, the HEDIS clinical performance measures show a similar pattern of increasing specificity. When first published in 1994, the Health Effectiveness Data and Information Set (HEDIS) included twelve effectiveness-of-care measures—for example, the cervical cancer screening rate and the rate of eye examinations for diabetic patients. Since then, many more effectiveness-of-care measures have been added (and some have been retired). Of the sixty-eight measures used by the HEDIS quality measurement system at some point in the last thirteen years, only ten have been outcome measures. Most of the growth in quality measures in this measurement set has been in process measures: rates of compliance with specified process steps in the recommended care for patients with particular clinical conditions.[26]

These kinds of performance measures are similar to those used to assess the performance of individual doctors and reward performance through such incentive schemes as pay-for-performance. In a recent study over half of the 252 health maintenance organizations (HMOs) surveyed had a pay-for-performance contract with their providers, predominantly targeting physicians.[27] And a previous study of thirty-seven pay-for-performance programs found that clinical process measures dominated, mostly being drawn from the HEDIS measurement set.[28]

In light of this increase in the volume and specificity of medical knowledge and the increasing clarity and directness of the documents that guide the actions a clinician is expected to take, it is not surprising, therefore, that in the last two decades managerial interventions aimed at moving clinicians and organizations toward "doing the right thing"—the tools of process and decision management—have become more prominent. Whereas in times past the "right thing" was an ethical construct enshrined in the values of the caregiving professions, it is now a particular drug, test, or strategy supported by the burgeoning medical literature.

MANAGING CARE

If the last two decades have seen a gradual increase in willingness to manage care, how has this been achieved? How is care "managed," and who manages it? Because, even when salaried employees, physicians remain to a large extent independent professionals—whose behavior is guided as much by their peers as by managers of the organizations in which they practice—and health care is a social good; it was payers and regulators who played the central role in "managing care," if only indirectly. The tools these two groups used—physician and hospital licensure, tort law, payment systems, and the publication of outcome data—mostly operated at a distance from where medical care takes place: the interaction between an individual care provider and an individual patient. The key components of medical care—the tests ordered, diagnoses made, therapies used, and outcomes achieved—are only indirectly influenced by these interventions. The day-to-day managers of the care process were, of course, the doctors.

For much of the modern era of medicine physicians have managed the process of care through the mechanism of "orders." That is, the physician evaluated the patient's problem, ordered and interpreted diagnostic tests, and then prescribed the treatment and the details of its execution. Until the nineteenth century most patients were cared for at home, and it was left to the family to carry out the prescribed care; and in many parts of the developing world it is still the role of the patient's family to procure and render the prescribed treatment, as well as to provide basic nursing care and feed the patient. As inpatient institutions gained prominence—first as places of shelter, quarantine, and confinement and only later as sites of (largely surgical) intervention—professional nurses implemented the physician's orders.[29] The senior physician not only managed the care by prescribing the tests and therapies the patient was to receive (that is, writing the orders), but he also maintained ultimate oversight of how it was executed by the nursing and junior medical staff, usually during the ritual of morning ward round.[30] And no one managed the senior physician; with the exception of egregious instances of neglect or malfeasance, neither the physician's orders nor the outcomes of his care were subjected to scrutiny or direction.

In recent times, however, these components of medical care have been subject to active and deliberate management, not only in minute detail by the individual physician rendering the care at the bedside or at a distance by regulators and insurers but also by managers (who may be physicians themselves) working either for a physician group or for a hospital. Like regulators, they have the goal of managing patient care by shaping the choices made by individual physicians, but unlike regulators, they are also concerned with how these choices are executed. They have the power to shape both the local context in which physicians undertake their work and the details of the work itself. That is, the locus of care management has shifted from being predominantly outside of the care delivery organization to within it. And as the management of care has moved from action at a distance to becoming much more intimately involved with the details of an individual patient's care, it has made use of a widening set of tools—in particular, the tools of process management. The evolution of the medical knowledge base has been paralleled by an evolution in the tools available to managers that allow them to manage the care delivered with ever more precision. And at the root of this changing approach to managing care and the tools used to achieve this end, has been an increasing expectation of certainty.

A CHANGING TOOL SET FOR MANAGING CARE

Broadly speaking, only a finite set of tools and techniques are available to manage medical care, or indeed any production or service process. These tools—some used by both regulators outside and managers within care delivery organizations, and some predominately tools of the internal manager—vary in the extent to which they directly influence a worker's activities, and they fall into five broad classes (see table 1-2):

- Shaping the *values* of medical and nursing professions and the values and culture of the organization in which they deliver care

- Constraining the *resources* they have available to them in their work

- Monitoring *outcomes* of care (retrospectively) and comparing these with actual or theoretical standards (benchmarking)

- Defining and monitoring the exact *process* by which the patient's health problem is to be solved (which tests and therapies are to be used, how, and in which sequence)

- Specifying the exact *decisions* an individual professional should make in individual circumstances

Each of these five classes of tools can be used in association with an incentive (positive or negative) for the physician. For example, capitation

TABLE 1-2

Tools for managing care

Tool set	Time period	Tools used
Values	First 3,000 years	Tacit and explicit professional and organizational norms
		Disciplinary procedures
Resource availability (types, absolute amount, utilization, and productivity)	1960s to 1970s	Staff hiring (including licensure and credentialing)
		Technology assessment and purchasing
		Financial control
		Bed and OR utilization (referral stream, LOS [length of stay], scheduling)
Outcomes monitoring	1980s to 1990s	Benchmark basic outcome measures Report cards (public or private)
Process management	1990s	Guidelines
		Critical paths
		Operations management techniques
		Flow mapping
Clinical decisions	2000s	Criteria sets
		Highly specified protocols
		Electronic prescribing (CPOE)
		Decision support systems

contracts provide an incentive for doctors to realize specific outcomes (such as low costs per case or low referral rates), and pay-for-performance bonuses include incentives to perform specific process steps, such as ordering mammograms and HbA_{1C} tests, and performing Pap smears.[31]

Values

The age-old values of the caregiving professions include people devoting themselves to service and thus placing individual and public health above other social goods; placing the needs of the patient above all else; doing no harm and delivering all the care that is necessary and none that is not; and training juniors in the arts and tenets of the profession.[32] These values are made explicit in caregivers' professional oaths of dedication, inculcated into nurses and doctors by their mentors through the socialization that occurs during training, and reinforced by their peers and professional societies over the course of a career. Individual organizations augment these with their own culture and value set, again making them explicit through mission statements, codes of conduct, or credos and reinforcing them through specific policies and procedures. Codes of conduct usually define the boundary conditions of behavior (what should not be done), while mission statements articulate the organization's or professional's aspirations (what will be done).[33] However, although these values powerfully shape professionals' choices and actions on behalf of their patients, ultimately the control they are capable of exerting over the care of any specific patient is relatively weak.

Resources

In industry, specifying—often in minute detail—the resources used in production is a way of determining performance of a process, even in the absence of a complete understanding of how the process causes a good outcome and which process steps are the most influential. Intel, for example, uses the principle of "copy exactly"—allowing no changes—when it transfers semiconductor manufacturing to new production facilities.[34] In health care, however, managing resources usually means constraining them. In contrast to values, control over the inputs to medical care—the number and nature of staff (and their competency through basic licensure and board certification); their scopes of practice; the number and types of inpatient beds and specialized care locations, such as delivery suites, catheterization laboratories, and operating rooms; capital assets such as MRIs and CT scanners; and the drugs available—directly influences the way care is rendered. For many years this has been a preferred technique of regulators and insurers. The care process can be managed by managing the supply of its essential resources, the most important of these being the inpatient bed. In 1994, for example, Wennberg and colleagues showed that the readmission rates within three years for Medicare beneficiaries initially hospitalized in Boston, Massachusetts, for myocardial infarction, stroke, hip fracture, gastrointestinal bleeding, and cancer surgery, were on average 64 percent higher than for patients with the same conditions living in New Haven, Connecticut, even though the two populations did not differ in their severity of illness.[35] What did differ between the two cities was the per capita number of available hospital beds (although bed occupancy rates were similar); bed numbers were lower in New Haven than in Boston.[36] Noting, as Roemer had a generation earlier, that demand tended to fill the available supply, Wennberg termed this *supply-sensitive care.*[37] Since the 1970s, regulators and insurers have used control over the supply of the inputs to care as one of their primary mechanisms of controlling costs.[38]

Specific tools by which resource availability may be controlled include Certificate of Need (CON) regulations, limited drug formularies, and technology assessment, all of which restrict what physicians have available to use in their work. Similarly, utilization management, in which a physician must obtain specific authorization from the payer before ordering a costly test or therapy for an individual patient, is another example of managing care by controlling access to the resources consumed during care. Finally, of course, one of the most costly resources is the physician. Primary care delivery models in which the human resource of a physician is replaced with a nurse-practitioner can reduce the costs of care without compromising quality.[39]

Outcomes Monitoring

A third way to manage a production operation is to monitor its output. Monitoring and publishing (either internally or publicly) the outcomes of medical care have also proved to be effective mechanisms for managing care. However, public reporting of data about the outcomes of medical care ("report cards")—for example, by the Pennsylvania Health Care Cost Containment Council and New York Cardiac Surgery Reporting System (CSRS)—has continued to be controversial. Whether, and how, outcomes monitoring and reporting works has been the focus of some debate. The CSRS has been collecting hospital- and surgeon-specific data since the late 1980s, making public only the hospital data. In 1991 New York's *Newsday* newspaper famously sued, and published risk-adjusted cardiac surgery mortality rates—by institution and by surgeon. During the period 1989 to 1992, the cardiac surgery mortality rate in New York State dropped by over 40 percent (from 4.17 percent to 2.45 percent), with the largest reductions occurring at those hospitals with the highest initial mortality. However, in the same period, although they did not publish outcomes data, the states of New England saw a similar drop in mortality.[40] Hence the reason for the decline in mortality in New York State is disputed. Did the benchmarking improve outcomes by precipitating a change in the population of surgeons—some individual surgeons with low procedure volumes or high mortality rates either exited the practice of cardiac surgery or left New York State[41]—or by motivating hospitals to undertake process improvement activities, and could such improvement work be stimulated without public reporting? Some observers even suggested that New York surgeons were gaming the system, either by referring high-risk patients out of New York or by gaming the risk adjustment data, although these explanations have been disputed.[42]

In production industries, outcomes monitoring improves performance by acting directly on the production process, through an "inspect and reject" process. Product quality is improved by identifying products or parts that do not meet preset standards and removing them from the supply chain. In health care, however, outcomes monitoring (particularly, public reporting) does not act directly on the "production process" of care. Rather, it acts to improve performance by motivating health care delivery organizations to change their internal processes. Providers are motivated to change either because they are naturally competitive and want to outdo each other, or because they fear a loss of market share if they do not improve.[43] And they improve performance either by changing individual doctors' clinical behavior, selecting out poorly performing staff, or by improving internal organizational processes. Of course, the limitation of outcomes monitoring as a management tool is that it is prone to perverse effects; physicians measured only by outcomes may be motivated to eschew high-risk patients in order to preserve their performance records.[44]

Regardless of whether it is used externally as public report cards—comparing individual clinicians or delivery organizations with each other or with previously established benchmarks—or internally as audits, outcomes monitoring makes no assumption about the way in which a given outcome should be achieved. Overseers make no assertions about how best to go about realizing superior performance. In using outcomes monitoring as a tool to manage care, the manager does not even have to know exactly how to realize superior performance; this tactic implicitly presumes that the hospitals and their staff would either know how or be able to learn. The situation is very different with process management, which presumes that the manager and the physician know, and can articulate, exactly what the process of care should be, and can thus manage toward it.

Process Management

Today the importance of processes internal to the care delivery organization in determining the ultimate cost and medical outcome of care is well established. Outcomes previously attributed to the behavior of individual physicians or nurses—their judgment and expertise—or organizations, are now seen to be determined by the performance of intraorganizational processes, both care processes and business processes. Not only do process failures cause medication errors, but the performance of key processes differentiates higher- from lower-performing institutions.[45] A recent survey of those institutions that were the highest performers on the list of "America's Best Hospitals," for instance, found that cardiac patients with acute myocardial infarction admitted to the top-ranked hospitals had lower thirty-day mortality, and that "a substantial proportion of the survival advantage may be associated with these hospitals' higher rates of use of aspirin and beta-blocker therapy."[46] That is, the key determinant of medical outcome was the reliability with which specific processes of care (including the key steps of prescribing and delivering aspirin and beta-blockers) were executed.

Two types of processes exist in care delivery organizations. At the core of any care delivery system is the *process of care*. This is the fundamental "production process" of medical care: the sequence of clinical decisions and tasks (tests and therapies) that together result in the solving of a patient's health problem and the creation of patient relief. It is the process that is often represented on a care path. The process of care encompasses problem identification, diagnosis, treatment selection, treatment delivery, and post-treatment monitoring. This care process is supported by (and provides the demand function for) a myriad of *business processes*, some supplying essential resources to the care process (such as information, drugs, clinical personnel and supplies, and time slots in specialized areas like the operating room, delivery suite, or an inpatient bed) and some relating to the execution of tasks, such as the placement of a central line. The term *process management* applies to the management of both of these types of processes.

Although business processes have long been the focus of health care managers, the notion of defining, measuring, and improving the core process of medical care is relatively new. One contributor to this change was the introduction of Total Quality Management (TQM) and the tools of industrial quality management science into health care. In their early application in the health care sector, the tools and techniques of TQM were used to improve the performance of business processes such as patient transport and laboratory turnaround.[47] But in making the case in 1989 for the application of "industrial quality management science" to health care, Laffel and Blumenthal implied that the method's tools could be used to manage any process in a health care organization, including those that pertained to clinical decision making.[48]

Numerous process management tools are now in common use. They tend to be focused either at a high level—managing (i.e., expediting) the flow of the patient from one stage of care to the next (for example, from preoperative preparation to the operating room to the postoperative recovery unit)—or a lower level, managing (i.e., specifying in detail) what is supposed to occur at each stage. Managing the progression of patients from one resource to the next utilizes the tools of queuing theory and supply chain management, whereas managing the activities undertaken to and for patients at a stage of care uses such tools as protocols and care paths.[49] Other tools—for example, human factors analysis—help with the accurate execution of a process.

To manage a process means not only to specify it and codify that specification as a standard operating procedure, but also to measure and adjust key process parameters. Statistical process control (and the common tool, the control chart), long used in industry, has been applied to health care since the early 1990s to identify when key process parameters (such as time to thrombolysis in the emergency room) are meaningfully out of control. More recently, pay-for-performance systems have tied process (and outcome) measurements to financial incentives for doctors. For example, General Electric's Bridges to Excellence incentive system rewards doctors who order appropriate blood tests for their patients (such as HbA_{1C} for diabetic patients) and achieve preset targets for those tests (e.g., $HbA_{1C} < 8$ percent).

Managing Decisions

Finally, managers can manage care by exactly specifying all that should happen to a patient—predominantly the decisions caregivers make about and for the patient—even going so far as to specify when and where these actions should be taken. Physicians have long been recognized as imperfect decision makers, incapable of computing more than a few variables simultaneously.[50] Moreover, it is also well recognized that algorithms, even simple linear ones, outperform humans. Psychological research from the 1950s demonstrated that statistical predictions are more accurate than global judgments by experts, even when the experts and the statistical models use the same variables.[51]

Similarly to process management, physician decisions can be managed at various levels of detail. The simplest intervention in medical decision making is to ensure that all of the patient's data—including past and active problems, allergies, drugs being taken concurrently, and the results of previous tests—are available to the clinical decision maker at the moment a decision is being made. Of course, such is the role of the medical record and the promise of the modern electronic medical record; some estimate that in 27 percent of visits to the doctor, the paper medical chart is unavailable, and so presumably decisions are made in the absence of the complete medical record.[52] A second set of interventions aim to make knowledge—for example, about the utility of a particular test for evaluating a symptom, or the value of repeating a test—available to the decision maker when needed. This knowledge can be presented to the decision maker either as a recommendation when the test is ordered or in the form of a review article.[53] Finally, systems can recommend (or even mandate) certain decisions. Computerized physician order entry (CPOE) systems, for example, not only allow a doctor to write a prescription electronically (thereby simply replacing the prescription pad), but also allow the prescription to be compared with preset rules that specify an appropriate dose given that particular patient's other medications, diseases, or even symptoms. Such information technology–based decision support can be less or more invasive, suggesting a preferred dose, alerting the physician when she or he has ordered a dose or drug other than that preferred, or even going so far as to not allow any other dose or drug to be ordered. Not all decision management involves information technology, of course. Utilization management techniques—popular among insurers in the 1990s—made use of written lists of criteria to determine whether expensive tests or therapies would be reimbursed.

The five classes of managerial tool described above differ on several dimensions. Most importantly, they vary in the tightness of coupling between a managerial action and the actual care an individual patient receives. For instance, the basic role of values and culture is to shape physician and nurse decision making in situations where there is no recognized "best practice" or organizational policy to guide decision making. They are general principles rather than specific "if-then" statements and don't necessarily result in a particular element of care being delivered or denied. These general principles are nonspecific inasmuch as they are applied similarly to all patients in the care of a professional, and to all professionals, regardless of the specifics of the patient's disease. In effect, they are applied before the patient's care has begun. The socialization of nurses and doctors begins in training (and maybe even before that in the selection process for entry to professional schools). Similarly, resource constraint acts globally, influencing all patients, practitioners, and delivery organizations similarly, and is applied before a particular patient enters the care delivery system.

In contrast, tools such as disease-specific care paths, protocols, criteria sets, and electronic decision support systems—all of which in some way manage clinicians' specific decisions—target specific patients, diseases, clinicians, and actions. These tools tend to be much more local and specific to a patient's encounter. They are applied once the patient's care has begun and while the patient is in the care delivery system. They are much more specific in that they depend on the specific disease being treated or medical resource being used, and result in specific predictable clinician actions. And because they are much more specific to the patient, the disease, and the context in which care is being provided, they depend on knowing which specific choices and actions cause a preferred outcome. These tools presume that a known best practice—with which the practitioner's specific choices can be compared—actually exists, and can be articulated. They all make use of (and presume) the increasing specificity of medical knowledge.

In sum, increasing specificity of medical knowledge has made available tools that allow explicit management of the details of medical care for the purpose of increasing both quality and efficiency. In effect, as medical knowledge has improved, the possible (and preferred) approaches to managing care have moved down the rows in table 1-2. Over time, managers have been able to reach more deeply into the care process and influence it in greater detail. The tools in table 1-2 all lie on a spectrum of increasing control over patient care.

The availability of these tools not only allows many more aspects of the care process to be "managed" but also implies two important design decisions. The first of these relates to the match between the tool and the clinical circumstance. That is, the tools are likely to be most effective when highly specific tools are applied to highly certain care (an issue taken up in detail in chapter 5).

The second design decision relates to the integration of this set of tools into a coherent approach to the management of health care processes and organizations (see chapter 8). To this end, increasing specificity of medical knowledge and clinical recommendations, and the assumption of certainty, has not only been associated with a change in the available tool set; it has also been associated with the (somewhat sporadic) adoption into health care of management metaphors and models drawn from production industries.

INCREASING SPECIFICITY AND THE
ADOPTION OF CARE MANAGEMENT MODELS
FROM INDUSTRY

Many popular broad managerial approaches and philosophies, including Total Quality Management, the Toyota Production System (TPS), and Six Sigma (and specific tools and methodologies such as critical paths, protocols, and associated pay-for-performance schemes), have their roots in production industries where the quality of the product is determined by the extent to which it meets its design specifications. In these industries the performance of the final product, the equivalent of a medical outcome, can be ensured by exactly specifying how the product is to be produced. The product's design specifications and production parameters are knowable, known, and announced in advance. Takahiro Fujimoto, a scholar of the Toyota Production System, has pointed out that information about a car, and how it is supposed to work, is embodied in both the car's design specifications and the car itself. He views the production process as converting the information stored in the design into information "stored" in the physical form of the product.[54] The more precise this conversion and the better the design executed the better the car. The cost and quality of the product are therefore managed by measuring and managing the steps in the production process. The predominant mechanism by which these approaches and tools realize better product performance is through ensuring precision and accuracy in the execution of production parameters; all presuming the pre-existence of a production specification.

Importantly, these tools and these approaches to management do not presume that frontline workers are simply automatons executing on the prescribed rules (although this was a central idea in Frederick Taylor's model of "scientific management" at the beginning of the twentieth century). Exactly the opposite—although the codification of technical knowledge and increasing automation that has occurred over the last two decades has largely made the tacit knowledge that workers are needed to run production machinery obsolete, it resulted in a premium being placed on workers who could solve complex high-level problems.[55]

These approaches and tools have become increasingly attractive in health care in part because improvements in medical knowledge meant that the steps that cause a desired medical outcome could be specified in an analogous fashion to the production specifications of a product or service.[56] The outcome could therefore be guaranteed by ensuring that those steps were executed accurately and reliably. In the early 1990s the tools and techniques of Total Quality Management began to be applied to health care delivery, and a decade later the Toyota Production System was employed as an organizing framework for hospital operations.[57]

The decision of whether to draw on management models from production industries as a way of organizing a set of individual tools into a coherent management approach in health care has been a vexed one, however, in part because the recent history of Total Quality Management in health care has been mixed. Despite initial enthusiasm, promised widespread improvement in performance did not materialize. A national survey of health care managers found that none could identify a health care institution that had fundamentally improved its performance using these methods.[58] Moreover, evidence of improvement was particularly lacking in clinical journals.[59] Reasons offered for TQM's lackluster performance differ. Some have argued that it was a failure of implementation, because, for example, senior leaders were uncommitted, or physicians were not adequately involved in hospital governance;[60] or because although early adopters customized the model specifically to realize gains in quality and efficiency, later adopters were motivated more by the prevailing fashion than by a sincere desire to improve. Others have argued that, on the contrary, TQM itself, with its emphasis on top management's hierarchical control over work processes and its presumption of rational decision making, was conceptually ill suited to the health care environment.[61] Perhaps not surprisingly, most health care delivery organizations that make use of some or all of the tools described above do so without making reference to an integrated organizing framework, either of their own design or one imported from other settings such as TQM or TPS. That is, they adopt the tools piecemeal without necessarily designing the way in which multiple tools, organizational structures, and processes should work together, in part because they have not been conceived of as elements in a system that interact with each other. Nonetheless, health care delivery organizations have begun to focus more on the details of the care they deliver.

EVOLVING APPROACHES: FROM MANAGING INSTITUTIONS TO MANAGING CARE

Although the guideline and its derivatives have become available as specific tools for managing care (either as independent interventions or as part of the kind of broader approach to production management described above), the way in which these tools are used in practice (and in fact the extent to which they are used, if at all) varies substantially among care delivery organizations. That is, health care delivery organizations differ in the extent to which they deliberately manage care. Five broad approaches can be observed, differentiated by the tools organizations use and the way in which they use them to manage care: manage the resources used, manage decision-maker values, monitor (and reward) outcomes, manage flow, and manage decisions themselves (see table 1-3). Although the approaches discussed below overlap somewhat, and no one institution represents a pure form of any one approach, the management of care in any single care delivery organization tends to lie

TABLE 1-3

Approaches to care management

Focus	Control exercised over	Managerial approach	Tools used
Asset	Inputs	Resource provision	Staff hiring and credentialing Technology assessment and capital purchasing
		Optimize capacity	Financial controls Operations management (scheduling, length-of-stay management)
Disease	Outcomes	Performance monitoring	Benchmark basic outcome measures
	Processes	Flow management	Flow (and value) mapping and critical pathways
		Decision management	Highly specified protocols Electronic prescribing (CPOE) Decision support systems

on a spectrum, from virtually no explicit care management at all to highly managed care. At one end of the spectrum, managers' predominant focus is on the assets of health care delivery—the beds, staff, operating room, and MRI slots. The managers run the institutions that provide these resources for care, and the clinical staff manages the care process itself. At the other end of the spectrum, managers focus on the patients' diseases and create processes and systems that execute protocols clinicians have created ahead of time. Surgeons at Canada's Shouldice Hernia Centre all perform a herniorrhaphy the same way. In the former approach, care is a property of the clinician, and in the latter, a property of the care delivery organization.

As we have already seen, the prevailing model of the last several centuries was for the care delivery organization to provide the essential resources of care but exercise no or little management oversight on how these resources were utilized to cure disease and relieve suffering. To the extent that care itself was managed, it was at a distance through choices about which resources would be made available: the physicians who were hired or granted admitting privileges, the number and skill levels of nursing staff and thus the types of beds (general medical versus specialized), and the technologies offered. For many American community hospitals (with a voluntary medical staff), even some of these care management tools are effectively unavailable; the physician, as

much as the patient, is the institution's primary customer, and hospitals that
compete for physicians' patient referrals are not inclined to restrict resources
available to the physicians or manage the care they provide within the hospital's walls.[62] Quite the opposite—they make resources available (equipment,
operating rooms, etc.) as a way of attracting physicians and encouraging them
to refer their patients there.

In more recent years, as the cost of each resource has increased and
budgets have become constrained, managers have employed the tools of operations management—queuing theory and scheduling, staffing to demand,
benchmarking—to optimize the utilization of each resource and the productivity of staff. These tools have the twin effects of limiting the downtime of expensive capital equipment or specialized care areas and improving the access
of doctors and patients to those resources. Some institutions, typically those
in which physicians are salaried employees, have extended resource management to include managing the utilization of the doctor's time through the
measurement and management of physician productivity (usually defined as
the number of patient visits per unit time, and often tied in some way to physician payment) and more recently through open access scheduling.[63]

Few institutions aggressively manage processes and decisions. Some—
for example, Seattle's Virginia Mason Medical Center—have recently employed the tools of the Toyota Production System to manage the flow of
patients, materials, and information. Toyota's "lean" production principles
are used at Virginia Mason to remove waste in all its forms from the care of
the patient, thereby smoothing the flow of the patient through the care system and expediting care. Waste in Virginia Mason's terms includes not only
unnecessary tests and procedures but also unnecessary patient delays, unnecessary writing, and unnecessary distance traveled by staff. By removing
these "non-value-added" activities, Virginia Mason seeks to create an effective increase in capacity. But it also de facto manages care, sometimes by
specifying what care any particular patient is to receive (e.g., sending patients with uncomplicated back pain directly to physical therapy without an
MRI), but mostly by smoothing and speeding the patient's transitions from
one phase of care (investigation, diagnosis, preparation, treatment, etc.) to
the next.[64]

If few hospitals or physicians organizations are managing patient flow, even
fewer are managing the details of physician decision making. Although increasing numbers are implementing computerized physician order entry systems
to standardize and error-proof prescription writing and drug dispensing—by implementing high-dose limits and checking for drug–drug, and sometimes

drug–disease, interactions—few try to manage the doctor's decision of which drug should be prescribed to which patient. A recent survey of large physician organizations (POs) found the use of "care management processes" (including case management, physician profiling, disease registries, use of clinical guidelines, and the teaching of patient self-management skills) to be low. Only one-third of the 1,040 POs surveyed used a disease-specific guideline with an associated reminder system for patients with asthma.[65] One institution that does try to manage physician decision making is Salt Lake City's Intermountain Healthcare (IHC). As will be discussed in later chapters, IHC has created multiple detailed protocols specifying specific investigation and treatment choices and patient disposition.

THE CURRENT STATE OF CARE MANAGEMENT: THE EXAMPLE OF DIABETES

Perhaps more than any other disease, diabetes provides an example of the trend to increasing management of care and the use of increasingly specific care management tools that is based upon increased knowledge and an associated presumption of medical certainty. In fact, diabetes has become the apotheosis of care management. Discussions in the literature and at conferences of reminder systems, patient registries and at-risk lists, report cards, and pay-for-performance systems all use diabetes as their primary (and sometimes, only) example. Of the 113 plans with physician-oriented pay-for-performance programs, 98 (86.7 percent) targeted diabetes. The next most common clinical indicators targeted were mammography (75.2 percent) and asthma medication (70.8 percent).[66] And in the survey of POs' care management processes (described earlier), the most common guideline in use was the one for diabetes, used by 38.5 percent of the POs surveyed (compared to asthma, 33.9 percent; congestive heart failure, 27.7 percent; and depression, 12.5 percent).

So why diabetes? For over two thousand years, diabetes was a recognized, but ill-understood and untreatable affliction of the young.[67] The term *diabetes mellitus* was first used by the Greek physician Aretaeus in the second century BCE. Patients afflicted with this disease were diagnosed by the symptoms of excessive thirst, weight loss, and sweet urine (hence the disease's name). And for most of the subsequent two thousand years, the disease was incurable. In fact, those cures that were available were often worse than the original disease. In the early twentieth century, diabetic patients were hospitalized and treated with calorie reduction. Patients with type 1 diabetes (or juvenile-onset diabetes, the most severe form, in which the patient has no natural insulin) had a life expectancy of less than one year after diagnosis.

But in 1921 all that changed. Although pancreatectomized dogs were known to become diabetic, and the dogs were cured when injected with a solution of crushed pancreas, the responsible chemical was not isolated until 1921. The discovery of insulin (named for the pancreatic islet cells from which it came) revolutionized the care of this disease. Insulin, initially horribly impure—the treatment could cause severe local and systemic reactions—had several important characteristics. It was short acting (even the longer-lasting insulins have a duration of action of less than twenty hours), it had immediate and easily recognized effects, and, as a protein, it had to be injected. Thus, from the beginning, therapy had to be community based, and the patient had to be deeply involved in its delivery. Further, measuring the concentration of sugar, initially in the urine and subsequently in the blood, could be used to monitor the short-term effectiveness of the treatment. For example, the Benedict's test, introduced in 1914, allowed the urine sugar concentration to be measured simply, at home and in five minutes.

Since 1921, new insights into the disease and technological developments have further refined this treatment, although the basic pattern of treatment—repeated self-injection and dietary control—has not changed. Purification of insulin reduced side effects and allowed more accurate dosing. New types of insulin with longer durations allowed patients to self-inject less frequently. Better needles and delivery systems eased the burden of self-injection. Initially, patients delivered insulin in the doses prescribed by their doctors. If there was a problem, they returned to the doctor for review and redesign of the insulin regimen. However, between the 1950s and 1970s the significant impact of patients' diet and exercise regimen became better understood, and dietary guidelines became more detailed; and sliding scales were developed, allowing patients to modify their insulin doses according to the results of their blood glucose tests. Hence the instructions for care became more specific. The development of new blood glucose measuring devices made it easier for patients to individualize therapy and to titrate the therapy to their own life patterns.

The results of the ten-year Diabetes Control and Complications Trial (DCCT), published in 1993, brought about another big change. This trial clearly demonstrated that tight glucose control (maintaining blood glucose levels as near normal as possible through at least four-times-per-day testing and three-or-more-times-per-day insulin dosing) significantly reduced the long-term complications of diabetes, such as blindness, kidney failure, and stroke.

In response, the American Diabetes Association (ADA) revised its guidelines in 1994, laying the foundation for detailed care management. Diabetes has all the requirements for detailed management. The exact steps required to achieve a good outcome—in terms of treatment with insulin and dietary modification, and long-term surveillance for early signs of complications—are well understood and documented. An intermediate outcome variable (e.g., HbA_{1C}) exists that allows tracking of how well these steps are being carried out. Early negative effects of therapy (hypoglycemic episodes) are easily diagnosed and characterized. And long-term outcomes of treatment (e.g., renal failure) are also easily measured. Hence, for the majority of diabetics, the "ideal" process and expected outcomes of care can be specified, measured, and managed.[68] And accordingly, the performance of physicians, delivery organizations, and health plans can be assessed by measuring compliance rates with this ideal process, and improved through the use of interventions that increase the compliance rate.

THE ALLURE OF CERTAINTY

Facilitated by changes to the knowledge base of medicine, care processes, management tools, and approaches to the management of care delivery organizations have all undergone significant change over the last two decades. For many, the signs point to medical science ultimately vanquishing uncertainty. Science and precision triumph. The medical care of patients is an increasingly certain process, ever more highly specified; and accordingly, managerial tools drawn from production and assembly industries are ideal to manage the activities of health care delivery. As science advances and we identify more clinical variables of importance, along with the actions that influence those variables, we will increasingly be able to codify the optimal care a patient should receive in any circumstance. Armed with this knowledge, health care management increasingly becomes an exercise in managing the execution of the known best practice—putting the protocol into action.

Increasing certainty in health care is very attractive, with its potential to reduce patients' anxiety and increase the efficiency with which care delivery organizations can meet the increasing demands of a growing population of patients needing increasingly sophisticated care. Dramatic advances in medical and managerial sciences appear to put it within reach. Certainty is both sought and rewarded because it is assumed to be possible; over time medical science reduces the uncertainty about what action to take in any given situation and what the impact of those actions will be, and managerial science reduces the uncertainty surrounding the execution of those actions. And as the care and business processes become more specifiable, their output, patient relief, has become progressively more the outcome of a production organization as well as of an individual.

The common chronic diseases of adulthood, such as diabetes, congestive heart failure, and hypertension, have received a lot of attention from health care managers in large part because they represent such a large proportion of the burden of disease and the costs of health care. But they have also lent themselves to the management tools described above and thus seem to provide support for the presumption of increasing medical certainty that underlies the growing reliance on these managerial tools.

However, is it fair to assume that all diseases behave like diabetes? Because of the prominence of these diseases, we risk being lulled into thinking that every disease and its treatment can be so clear cut that all care processes are, or can be made to be, equivalent to car processes—that care, in the last analysis, can be captured in standard operating procedures. The allure to managers of certainty in health care is based on a number of assumptions: that medical knowledge about a disease is becoming, and can become, complete and flawless, that this progression in knowledge is the same for all diseases, that this knowledge can be perfectly applied to any individual patient, and that the act of bringing this knowledge to bear on the health problem of that individual patient can be executed reliably, effectively, and efficiently.

But do managers' assumptions of certainty fit with the day-to-day experiences of practitioners? For practitioners, care is always probabilistic. The paucity and fragile state of the evidentiary base of clinical practice, which will be discussed in the next chapter, means that the knowledge upon which practitioners and patients base individual health care decisions and actions is always incomplete. And where robust medical science does exist, it frequently furnishes practitioners only with probability distributions, not deterministic certainties—probabilities that are often conditional and constantly changing. Moreover, in their daily work, clinicians are engaged in problem solving for individual patients, each of whom has her or his own unique biology, value set, and preferences. The rapid growth in external quality monitoring, pay-for-performance reimbursement, and the widespread use of standardized clinical guidelines all seem to treat care as a manageable "procedure."

Given the above uncertainties in patient care, however, to what extent is it reasonable to rely on managerial tools predicated on standard operating procedures? When are such management tools applicable, and when are they not? How should managers approach care management in the face of varying levels of uncertainty? Before discussing an approach to care management and the design of processes, organizations, and systems of health care, the next chapters will examine the above assumptions about medical science and clinical care. Chapter 2 discusses the state of medical knowledge about diseases and their treatments in more detail. Chapters 3 and 4 will then examine the process by which scientific and clinical knowledge is used to solve specific patient health problems, given varying levels of certainty about patients and their health problems. And subsequent chapters will look at the problem of execution.

2

Certainty, What Certainty?

The trend outlined in the previous chapter—from uncertain, idiosyncratic care to increased certainty, predictability, and repeatability—has many attractions for the health care manager. A world in which health care delivery is more "production-like" is easier to model financially and allows the use of well-developed operations management approaches and tools drawn from production industries. The tools in the top rows of table 1-2, chapter 1, are often harder to use than those at the bottom rows. Changing culture, shaping values, and mobilizing diverse teams can be more managerially challenging than measuring individual compliance with a written protocol and paying individual compensation accordingly, especially with today's information technology.

Unfortunately, however, this world is not always recognizable to practicing doctors and nurses. Their day-to-day reality is not one of certainty and predictability. Just the opposite—the clinical practice environment can seem chaotic, capricious, even random. And this chaos is not simply a result of poor design, of a delivery system comprising fragmented, distributed, and poorly coordinated processes, practitioners, and organizations. Nor is it the result of poor management, although, to be sure, health care delivery settings could certainly use improvements in both design and management. For practicing clinicians health care is just not as certain as the tools of process measurement and management, decision management, and pay-for-performance would imply. Two primary sets of factors contribute to this, one relating to the nature of the medical evidence, and the other to the nature of patients to whom this evidence is being applied. To apply, unmodified, tools from production and assembly industries—tools that imply certainty in production— is to ignore two basic facts: medical knowledge (of cause and effect) remains incomplete, and patients vary in multiple ways.

THE STATE OF THE EVIDENCE

As chapter 1 described, underlying the progression in managerial tools and approaches is one important driver: the increasing robustness of medical evidence. Predominantly a collection of anecdotes in the nineteenth century, the medical evidence that guides modern clinical practice comprises the accumulated results of decades of rigorous scientific studies—as the term *evidence-based medicine* implies—each study building on previous knowledge. This knowledge base is the foundation of the guidelines and performance measures that facilitate the management of medical care and the measurement of the quality of that care. Such tools presume a level of certainty.

However, if medical care is to be managed by making reference to the underlying evidence and asking how often the individual or organization complied with the accepted ideal process, then the question arises, how good is that evidence upon which such determinations are made? Does the state of the evidence justify the presumption? One way to answer this question is to conceive of medical evidence itself as a product of a process in which evidence is created, tested, distributed, and used. Recently, each stage in this "production" process—trial design and conduct, results analysis and reporting, and results use—has been the subject of study. That is, evidence has been collected about the creation of medical evidence. And the results of these studies have identified a substantial problem, calling into question the quality of the evidence and the ways in which it is used.

Trial Design and Conduct

Several recent reviews have pointed to the frequency of significant methodological errors in the randomized controlled trials (RCTs), and the journal articles that report on them, that are the bedrock of medical science and clinical practice.[1] Such errors include RCTs without an identifiable statistical design, studies in which there was inadequate specification of the patient eligibility criteria, the method to generate random numbers, the method to allocate interventions, and study reports that failed to state whether blinding was used. These failures are surprisingly common, being found in 25 percent to 89 percent of the RCTs reviewed, and widespread, occurring in obstetrics, dermatology, surgery, general medicine, and rheumatology.[2]

Such errors do not represent omissions of little consequence. Quite the opposite—they bias the results. Although positive findings were reported in 48 percent of designed studies, they were reported in 70 percent of studies with no reported design, of concern because positive studies are more likely to be published than negative ones.[3] Furthermore, even studies without serious methodological flaws are likely to be contradicted by future studies, or the initially strong effects found to be less strong. A review of forty-nine highly cited studies—ones with substantial influence on clinicians' thinking—found that 16 percent were contradicted by subsequent studies, and a further 16 percent reported effect sizes that were stronger than those reported by subsequent studies.[4] Moreover, this occurred in five of the six nonrandomized studies reviewed but in only nine of the thirty-nine randomized trials. Among the randomized trials, the greatest predictor of contradiction or initially stronger effects was small sample size.

Regrettably, recent high-profile exposures of research fraud, such as the case of Korean stem cell researcher Dr. Hwang Woo Suk, suggest that some errors are not unintentional slips or oversights. Scientists themselves not only confirm the existence of poor trial designs but admit to questionable conduct. In an anonymous survey of over three thousand mid- and early-career research scientists (reported under the title "Scientists Behaving Badly"), 13.5 percent reported using inadequate or inappropriate research designs.[5] In the same survey, 15.5 percent of respondents reported changing the trial design in response to pressure from the trial's sponsor, and 6 percent admitted to failing to report results that contradicted the results of their own previous research.[6] Given the reporting bias likely in such a survey, it is possible that many more investigators have knowingly been involved in poorly designed research.

Results Analysis

Flaws have also been found in the statistical analysis of even well-designed trials. Not only are clinical researchers often not trained statisticians, but statistical analytic techniques have been growing steadily more sophisticated and complex, making it harder for untrained researchers to correctly apply newer methods.[7] As a result, statistical errors are common in published papers. For example, one study found statistical errors in 40 percent of 164 publications in a psychiatry journal, an error rate that had not changed over time. Although many of these were not serious, "some were serious enough to cast doubt on [the] conclusions."[8] Other studies have found similar results.[9] The use of inappropriate comparators (placebo rather than an existing efficacious drug), composite end points (e.g., combining death, end-stage renal disease, and a doubling of serum creatinine into a single end point), and subgroup analysis (highlighting the results for a small subgroup of the study population when the study was not specifically designed to investigate an effect in this group) are examples of poor statistical analysis applied to well-designed trials in ways that may influence how the trial is interpreted.[10] Of note here is the fact that most of these published papers passed peer review. Many readers, especially those without statistical training, may assume that a paper published in a reputable peer-reviewed journal is methodologically sound and therefore not critique the paper's methods.

Results Reporting

In any complex scientific study there are many intellectual streams, results, and possible points of discussion. Which of these the authors of a study chose to highlight—and which editors chose to publish—can be a matter of some discretion. And therefore, not surprisingly, bias can creep into results reporting. Not only are studies with statistically significant results more likely to be published, but favorable results within trials are selectively reported.[11] Moreover, incomplete reporting of outcomes is greater for harm outcomes (65 percent incomplete reporting) than for efficacy outcomes (50 percent incomplete reporting). This same report noted that in 62 percent of the trials reviewed, at least one primary outcome was "changed, introduced or omitted."[12] What this means is that negative trials—an important potential source of learning—are less likely to be published, and those trials that are published are likely to overestimate the benefits and underrepresent the risks of an intervention.

The risk of incomplete and biased reporting extends beyond the journal publication. It can be compounded by media reporting, a significant issue because the media can be an important source of health information for doctors as well as patients. Unfortunately, media reporting of newer therapies can be not only incomplete but also potentially biased. A recent review of 207 television and newspaper reports of three medications used to treat major diseases found that 40 percent did not report the quantitative results at all, and only 15 percent reported both relative and absolute benefits. Moreover, only 47 percent of the stories mentioned potential harm.[13] This tendency to overenthusiasm and optimism extends to the reporting of the scientific conferences at which new and promising results are presented. Such conferences are of great interest to the lay public, practicing physicians, and the venture capital community and often result in front-page stories. However, in the three years after the publication of 252 news stories, reporting on 147 abstracts, fully 25 percent of the abstracts presented remained unpublished, and a further 25 percent were published in low-impact journals.[14] Thus, extensive prepublication attention—before rigorous evaluation through peer review—of studies that are small or may have weak designs disseminates potentially misleading results.

Results Use

Finally, the risk of biases coloring the way physicians interpret scientific studies and compromising their objectivity is ever present. In particular, physicians' financial conflicts of interest, and the potential they have to induce bias, have been of increasing concern recently. Through educational and research grants, speaker's and consulting fees, and even free pizzas, drug, biotech, and device companies seek to provide important support for medical research and clinician education and, either tacitly or explicitly, influence physicians' clinical and policy decisions.

Although financial relationships between product developers and physicians do not in and of themselves create bias, a growing body of evidence suggests that bias may well result.[15] For example, a review of articles examining the controversy surrounding the safety of calcium-channel blockers related the conclusions of each study to the author's self-reported financial relationships with manufacturers of calcium-channel blockers or competing products. The reviewers found that "authors supporting the use of calcium-channel antagonists were significantly more likely than neutral or critical authors to have financial relationships with manufacturers of calcium-channel antagonists."[16]

Such findings are all the more significant because the opinions of lead researchers (often those physicians most likely to have financial ties to industry) are very influential in determining which technologies become available and in setting the standards of clinical practice. An example of the former is provided by the case of the Cox-2 inhibitor Vioxx. The FDA uses panels of experts drawn from the ranks of researchers and clinicians to provide advice on such issues as whether a drug should be allowed onto, returned to, or withdrawn from the market. These panels often contain members with ties to industry, if for no other reason than those researchers focusing on the drug under review are the ones more likely to receive industry funding for their work. However, in the case of the Cox-2 inhibitors, of the thirty-two members of the advisory panel reviewing the return to market of Vioxx and withdrawal of the related drug Bextra—a panel that ultimately endorsed continued marketing of both drugs—those ten advisers with ties to industry voted overwhelmingly in favor of the drugs. If those with ties to industry had not voted, the panel would have voted twelve to eight that Bextra be withdrawn, and fourteen to eight that Vioxx not be returned.[17] These ten panel members voted nine to one to keep Bextra on the market, and nine to one to return Vioxx to the market.

Researchers with ties to industry have also been suspected of influencing the development of practice guidelines and associated performance measures. In 2004 the journal *Critical Care Medicine* published guidelines for the management of severe sepsis.[18] A large portion of the funding for the development of this guideline was provided by drug maker Eli Lilly, maker of a recombinant human activated protein C (Xigris). Although the evidence supporting the use of this drug was controversial—when Lilly applied for approval of the drug in 2001, half the members of the FDA's advisory panel voted to require a further trial before approval was granted—the guideline included a recommendation for recombinant human activated protein C.[19]

IMPLICATIONS

In aggregate, results such as these suggest that the "medical evidence" underpinning medical practice is not a set of facts or an absolute, but instead might better be viewed as an emergent construct, in constant evolution. It is of varying quality and trustworthiness and therefore of varying utility to the practicing clinician. Flawed research reports are not always intercepted by the peer review process; biases coloring consensus-based medical standards are not always apparent; and ultimately only the reader of an article or guideline can judge what value she or he draws from any piece of research. In other words, much clinical research is open to interpretation—with ample room for varying viewpoints and biases—and is not always the clear statement of "the right thing to do" that managers and policy makers would like it to be (and upon which some of the management approaches discussed in chapter 1 depend). Systematic reviews of the literature using statistical techniques such as meta-analysis attempt to redress some of these flaws. These reviews evaluate an entire body of research on a particular issue and combine multiple small studies to search for consistent effects. However, the utility of these techniques is ultimately limited by the quality of the underlying research.

One way to manage this problem for practicing physicians has been to rate the quality of the evidence supporting a particular clinical intervention. One rating system is that of Muir Gray, who proposed the five-level system shown in table 2-1. Systems such as these have increasingly been used to make explicit the strength of evidence supporting a particular recommendation (either in the

TABLE 2-1

Muir Gray scale for rating the level of medical evidence

Rating	Description
1	Supported by strong evidence from at least one systematic review of multiple well-designed randomized controlled trials
2	Supported by evidence from one properly designed randomized controlled trial of appropriate size
3	Supported by evidence from well-designed trials without randomization
4	Supported by evidence from well-designed nonexperimental trials
5	Based on opinions of respected authorities, or on clinical evidence, descriptive studies, or reports of expert committees

Source: Adapted from J. A. Muir Gray, *Evidence Based Medicine* (Edinburgh: Churchill Livingstone, 1997).

form of a guideline or implied by a quality measure). For example, researchers rated the level of evidence supporting each of the 439 quality measures used in the RAND study of the quality of care delivered in the United States using a three-point scale: (1) randomized trial, (2) nonrandomized controlled studies (e.g., case control), and (3) observational studies/expert opinion.[20] Similarly, a recent review by the Office of Technology Assessment (OTA) of patient safety practices rated the strength of the evidence supporting each practice and assigned the practices to five categories—greatest, high, medium strength of evidence, "lower impact and/or strength of evidence," and "lowest impact and/or strength of evidence"—using a similar hierarchy of study designs as the Muir Gray scale.[21]

What is initially striking about these examples of rating the quality of the evidence is how few generally accepted practices are backed by evidence considered of the highest quality—in other words, drawn from randomized controlled trials. Of the 439 quality measures in the RAND study, 92 were rated as level 1 (21 percent), and 291 (66 percent) were rated as level 3. In the OTA study of patient safety interventions, of the 63 practices rated in the report, 11 were given the rating of "greatest strength of evidence regarding their impact and effectiveness," a further 14 rated "high," and 22, 15, and 11 rated "medium," "lower," and "lowest," respectively. However, such an observation may not be as surprising as it first seems. Many of the measures or interventions are difficult to subject to randomized testing, either because such trials would be difficult to construct or not worth undertaking, or because it would be unethical to deny the test or intervention to those patients in the control arm in any RCT. Examples of quality measures ascribed a level of evidence rating of 3 (observational studies/expert opinion) by the RAND researchers include "patients with atrial fibrillation started on warfarin should have an INR checked within one week of the first dose," and "patients over age 65 should be asked about hearing difficulties at least every two years." Such measures assess examples of what is generally accepted to be good medical practice.[22]

However, in spite of the data about poor-quality evidence, it is important to remember that many medical practices are supported by very robust evidence. In these cases there is a clear, well-supported best course of action, or at least a course of action for which the benefits unequivocally outweigh the risks and therefore that can be recommended as standard treatment for all patients. The examples are well known; they appear in common quality measurement sets such as HEDIS and the RAND quality measures, and collections of best practices such as the Institute for Healthcare Improvement's "bundles" that list well-supported treatments for common diseases: pediatric immunizations, beta-blockers after acute myocardial infarction, ACE inhibitors in congestive heart failure, warfarin in atrial fibrillation, inhaled steroids in asthma, mammographic and cervical cancer screening for women, eye examinations for diabetics, and so on. There are also practices that should be applied to all patients, regardless of disease, that make care safe and reliable—for example, caregiver hand washing, monitoring for patients on persistent medications, medication reconciliation, smoking cessation advice and programs, and interventions to prevent ventilator-acquired pneumonia. (Distressingly, although these best practices are supported by robust evidence, nationwide compliance with them is often far from complete.)

Hence clinicians daily face situations and choices where the evidence upon which they can rely for guidance is of varying quality—sometimes rigorous and robust, sometimes inconclusive and in flux, and sometimes simply nonexistent. Thus in many clinical situations, appropriate care is a range, not a point.[23] There is simply no clear "right" course of action.

The fact that the medical literature is often open to interpretation has very real consequences on the substance of the interactions between doctors and their patients. It allows wide discretion in physician decision making; makes room for biases, heuristics, and personal preferences to drive medical decisions instead of the evidence; and even affects the very language physicians chose to communicate with each other and with their patients. The simple 1980 survey of radiology and laboratory reports mentioned in the introduction revealed the extent of the language of uncertainty in routine medical practice.[24] The authors catalogued thirty expressions of probability, "ranging from terms such as 'pathognomonic' and 'classic,' which imply a probability near unity, to expressions of intermediate or low probability such as 'consistent,' 'compatible,' or 'excludes.'" These are the terms with which doctors routinely communicate to each other and to their patients: *likely, possible, suggests, supports,* and *cannot be excluded.* And interestingly, while individual doctors were consistent in the numeric probabilities they associated with each term (assigning the same probability at different points in time), there were dramatic differences between doctors. For example, among the sixteen radiologists, pathologists, respiratory physicians, and general internists, the probabilities assigned to the term *classic* ranged from 0.65 to 0.92. In only nine of the expressions of probability did the sixteen physicians indicate a range of probability less than 0.5.[25]

Doctors' varying interpretations of the medical literature (and their confidence in it) is one of the (many) reasons that doctors frequently ignore guidelines. In surveys, doctors say they don't follow guidelines because they don't agree with them, either because their interpretation of the literature differs from that implicit in the guidelines, or because the guideline does not apply to their population, or because they perceive that the guideline's recommended course of action is not worth the risk, benefit, or cost.[26] Given the state of the evidence, it is perhaps not surprising that physicians are dubious about the standard operating procedures that are so central to many approaches to managing care.

And of course, differing interpretations of the science and discretion in decision making shape physicians' recommendations to their patients, as was elegantly demonstrated in a recent survey of urologists and radiation oncologists.[27] In this study, a random sample of members of these two specialties—who have access to the same body of scientific literature—were asked about the treatment of prostate cancer. First, both specialties believed that radical prostatectomy, external beam radiation therapy, and brachytherapy (placing radioactive rods directly into the prostate) offered a survival advantage to men with an expected life expectancy of ten or more years, in spite of the absence of any published evidence from RCTs supporting such therapies at the time. More importantly, members of each group overwhelmingly recommended the therapy that they themselves delivered. "For men with moderately differentiated, clinically localized cancers, and a more than 10-year life expectancy, 93 percent of urologists chose radical prostatectomy as the preferred treatment options, while

72 percent of radiation oncologists believed surgery and external beam radiotherapy were equivalent treatments."[28] For the treatment of prostate cancer, 82 percent of radiation oncologists thought that radical prostatectomy was overutilized, while only 34 percent of urologists thought the same. Conversely, only 13 percent of radiation oncologists thought that external beam radiotherapy was overutilized, compared to 37 percent of urologists.

WHEN THE EVIDENCE MEETS THE PATIENT

The state of the medical evidence is not the only issue influencing the utility of those production management tools based on the specification of tasks and decisions. Another set of issues—all of which make it hard to define the best course of action for a patient *ex ante*—arises when the medical evidence meets an individual patient. First, medical evidence is collected at the level of a population of patients and makes predictions about the "average" member of the study population, not about any individual patient, so it can only provide the clinician with general guidance in a specific situation. Second, most evidence is collected about single health problems, but many real patients have multiple, potentially interacting health problems, thus reducing the usefulness of recommendations contained in single-disease guidelines. And third, what the scientific evidence suggests might be the best course of action in a given situation may or not be what the patient values and wants.

Population-Based Clinical Research

Medical care deals in probabilities. Any symptom or sign, such as a cough or a swollen lymph node, can be associated with multiple possible diseases or health outcomes. Medical tests, used to make diagnoses or prognoses, only provide a probability estimate. And most treatments are effective in only a portion of the patients to whom they are applied. The fact that a patient's medical condition, response to therapy, and prognosis can only be guessed at ahead of starting therapy cannot necessarily be rectified by more and better research. Even if clinical trial methods were flawless, and reporting unbiased, the fact that these studies are by design undertaken in populations of patients—and therefore some amount of patient-to-patient variation is irreducible—means that clinical trials result in distributed outcomes and can only offer clinicians probabilities to inform their decisions. More and better research will certainly provide better probability estimates and tighter confidence intervals, but it may not result in unambiguous predictions.[29]

The somewhat controversial prostate-specific antigen (PSA) test provides an illustration of the problem. Like all diagnostic tests, the PSA test (used to predict the presence of prostate cancer in men) has a false positive and a false negative rate. This means that the positive predictive value—the probability that, given a positive test result, the patient actually has the disease being tested for—will be less than 1.0. In practice, a test result increases the probability that a disease is, or is not, present, but does not absolutely confirm that fact. As a screening test, the PSA is usually regarded as positive when the blood concentration of PSA is above 4.0 nanograms per milliliter. At this level the positive predictive value of the test is in fact only 21 percent. When the blood concentration of PSA rises above 10 nanograms per milliliter, the positive predictive value is 42 percent to 64 percent.[30] Thus a raised PSA increases the likelihood that the patient has prostate cancer but in no way makes it certain. Similarly, many diagnostic tests do not have the power to uniquely distinguish one cause from another.

The same problem arises for therapies. A therapy found to improve outcomes in a population of patients enrolled in a clinical trial is not guaranteed to improve the outcome in an individual patient to whom it is applied. In fact, a drug known to be efficacious in the general population is not known to be so in a particular patient until it is actually tried. Ex ante, all that can be said about a treatment is that it will change the risk of a given outcome in a population of patients with a given likelihood. This is particularly apparent in oncology, where the same treatment for a group of patients with similar stages and grades of the same cancer will have a range of outcomes.[31] For example, in only 15 percent of women with estrogen-receptor-positive breast cancer localized to the breast who are treated with the antiestrogen drug Tamoxifen will the cancer spread in the next ten years—a great achievement in the war against breast cancer.[32] However, what this also means is that some individual women will nonetheless suffer from spreading breast cancer in spite of having been treated. Similarly, drug efficacy is distributed such that any given dose of a drug works optimally in some percentage of the patient population, but not equally in all. For some patients the standard dose may be an overtreatment, perhaps resulting in toxic effects, and for some it may be an undertreatment, resulting in a lack of therapeutic effect.[33]

The causes of such variations in response to therapy are complex—for example, relating to individual difference in the rates of drug uptake, metabolism, and excretion, all of which are driven by underlying variation in the genes that code for the protein involved in each step, and all of which will influence the eventual blood level of the drug when taken. A second cause of variation is unidentified biological variation resulting in varying sensitivity of the cancer to the drug. Differential response of breast cancer cells to Tamoxifen, for example, has recently been shown to correlate with the levels of expression of sixteen tumor-related genes.[34] In addition to biological variability, patient behavior also varies. When treatment effect depends on the patient executing the treatment, by taking the prescribed drug at the correct dose and frequency, uneven patient compliance introduces a further source of variation. Because of the multiplicity of genetic and environmental factors that influence the ultimate effectiveness of a therapy in an individual patient, it is still impossible to predict a treatment's effect on an individual before actually trying it.

Finally, diseases are highly variable in the way in which they progress. Returning to the prostate cancer example, even knowing for certain that a man has cancer of the prostate does not mean that we can accurately predict the outcome of his disease. Not all cancers of the prostate are equally aggressive. Not only does the risk of prostate cancer increase with age, but so too do the chances that a man with cancer of the prostate will die of something other than that cancer. Early detection may not necessarily increase the chances of survival, because many cancers are slow growing, and treatments for fast-growing cancers are not universally effective. So the outcomes of a group of men with prostate cancer will vary. Some will have slow-growing cancers, and no treatment will be necessary. Others will have tumors so aggressive that no treatment will prevent death from the cancer.

Multiple Conditions

These problems are compounded when a patient has more than one disease concurrently. Inherent in the design of any randomized controlled trial is the principle that patients in the control and the experimental arms should differ only with respect to the treatment condition. Populations in RCTs are as homogeneous as the issue under study will allow. In practice, this means that patients participating in medical research often have only one disease: the disease under investigation. However, the patients who populate the waiting rooms of medical offices, clinics, and hospitals all over the world often suffer from more than one medical condition. Nearly two-thirds of all Americans over sixty-five suffer from two or more chronic diseases concurrently, and one-quarter have four or more.[35] Moreover, these patients are on complex treatment regimens; 50 percent of all Americans over sixty-five are taking five or more medications (an estimate that does not take account of over-the-counter and alternative medicines).

However, RCTs, the predominant source of knowledge about the treatment of patients with these diseases, typically focus on patients with one or few afflictions and, to the extent possible, without complex treatment regimens. The guidelines and protocols based on these studies focus on the evaluation and treatment of the single disease. Where the guidelines do acknowledge coexisting diseases, these are those diseases that "increase the risks associated with the target disease."[36] But the patient sitting in front of the doctor or nurse typically does not resemble the patient in the randomized trial to which the clinician is looking for guidance. And the coexisting diseases they may present need not be those primarily associated with the index disease covered by the guideline. Hence the care of this real patient is some amalgam of the care recommendations for each disease from which that patient suffers; it may or may not be the arithmetic sum of the treatment recommendations of multiple single-disease guidelines. And at least in theory, the recommendations of the several relevant guidelines could interfere negatively with each other.[37] The evidence, even if it is not flawed in any of the ways discussed above, therefore may not necessarily support anything resembling a "standard operating procedure" for that particular patient.

Patient Preferences

The application of medical evidence to real patients presents at least one other practical problem, even when that evidence is very robust. In some cases the evidence does not clearly support a single superior course of action. Not only does no action clearly trump all others, but different courses of action lead to different outcomes (including side effects), and patients vary on which, of multiple possible outcomes, they consider "better." Consider the case of breast cancer treatment. Both mastectomy (removal of the entire breast) and lumpectomy plus local radiation are associated with the same long-term survival. However, the latter is also associated with an increased risk of local recurrence of the tumor. For an individual woman, there is no "right" choice. Each patient must chose for herself and in so doing make her own personal trade-off—in this example, weighing her feeling about loss of a breast with her appetite for the small risk of a local recurrence of the cancer.

Wennberg and his colleagues at the Foundation for Informed Medical Decision Making term examples such as these *preference-sensitive care*: conditions where two or more medically acceptable options exist and choice should depend on patient preferences.[38] In fact, there are many situations where patients must make a choice for themselves based on their own preferences—not only choices among competing treatment options but also choices regarding how aggressively to pursue investigations for symptoms. Table 2-2 lists some examples of surgical procedures the foundation classifies as preference sensitive.

The pivotal role played by patients' values, rather than the science, in choices of medical therapies and patient care strategies also has profound impact on the way care can be managed. Any two consecutive patients with the same medical problem may disagree not only with each other, but also with their caregivers. Patients with the same disease may value their symptoms, or the potential benefits of intervention, very differently. For example, in a sample of men with prostatic hypertrophy, 24 percent of those with symptom scores indicating severe disease said they were not bothered by their symptoms, while 44 percent of those with scores indicating mild disease said that they were.[39]

Not only will the way in which patients value their symptoms determine whether or not they will seek an intervention, but their values may put them

TABLE 2-2

Preference-sensitive surgical conditions

Preference-sensitive surgical condition	Procedure
Osteoarthritis: knee	Knee replacement
Osteoarthritis: hip	Hip replacement
Herniated disc or spinal stenosis	Back surgery
Coronary artery disease	Percutaneous coronary intervention (PCI)
Coronary artery disease	CABG
Carotid stenosis	Carotid endarterectomy
Peripheral vascular disease	Lower extremity bypass
Benign prostatic hyperplasia	Transurethral resection of the prostate (TURP)
Early-stage prostate cancer	Radical prostatectomy
Chronic cholecystitis	Cholecystectomy
Early-stage breast cancer	Mastectomy

Source: Foundation for Informed Medical Decision Making, Al Mulley, personal communication with author, March 2007.

at odds with their doctors and nurses (and thus at least theoretically with the guideline that these practitioners are using to guide their clinical decisions). Where patients may see benefit in an intervention, clinicians may not, and vice versa. A telling study of parents and clinicians recently put this in perspective. Neonatologists, neonatal nurses, and parents were asked to rate five different health states for extremely low-birth-weight babies that ranged from being pain free, independent in the activities of daily living, and happy to being in pain some of the time, dependent for toileting and dressing, and occasionally worried, angry, or sad.[40] Overall, the doctors and nurses tended to ascribe the same utilities to the various health states, and value some equivalent to or even lower than death. However, the health care professionals also rated the health states significantly lower than the parents—an effect that was most pronounced in the two most severely disabled health states—raising the possibility of conflict between patients and professionals in the development and execution of treatment strategies.

The existence of medical decisions that depend largely on patients' values rather than medical science and the significant variation in patients' values and preferences means that in situations where care is predominantly patient sensitive, the plan of care and its execution must be developed and even negotiated one patient at a time—not prescribed by a standard operating procedure.

AN ESSENTIAL TENSION

This chapter has described two major challenges to the notion of managing care through specifying, and then managing toward, a preferred care process: variation in the quality of evidence upon which protocols are based, and significant patient-to-patient variation in response to disease and treatment, disease burden, and personal preferences. Both contribute to the significant uncertainty clinicians routinely face in providing care for individual patients. And although in some circumstances an individual clinician may not know the right thing to do (individual professional clinical uncertainty), in others the right thing to do may simply not be known by anyone (collective professional clinical uncertainty) or even knowable.[41] For most of the history of medicine, uncertainty was the natural order of things.[42] Without an extensive and well-developed body of science to guide clinical and personal decision making, health outcomes in the sick were predominantly determined by the skill and experience of the individual treating clinician. And care delivery systems and care processes reflected this reality; care was predominantly delivered by individual, isolated, and autonomous practitioners distributed throughout the community.

Over the last thirty years, the growing sophistication of our medical knowledge base and the associated development of guidelines, protocols, and criteria sets have brought considerable predictability and reproducibility to medical care. But they have also introduced a tension between two starkly different views of medical care. One holds that medicine is a specifiable, gradable, and ultimately manageable activity and that not only is certainty possible, but also, given more research, more and more care will become manageable. The other viewpoint sees medical care as an abidingly unpredictable, uncertain, and ultimately human enterprise. Both opposing views are associated with their own approaches to organization design and management, their own preferred sets of managerial tools, and their own proponents. And both views have their merits. The care of many diseases, notably the chronic diseases of adulthood, has progressed from quixotic to highly protocolized, and this trend will certainly continue as medical science slowly unravels the complexity of human biology. At the same time, knowledge about how to treat some individual diseases, or some patients with multiple interacting diseases, remains incomplete and inadequate. Furthermore, managerial knowledge—relating to the application of scientific knowledge to individual patients—is also incomplete. Thus far at least, for many individual patients and patient problems, increased scientific knowledge has not been the same as increased certainty. It has not been a road map to what to do for an individual patient and to improved health system performance.

Health care, of course, is not the only enterprise facing such a tension between visions of certainty and uncertainty. Fields as diverse as space travel, war, and new-product development have faced a similar issue. For instance, in his addendum to the 1986 Rogers Commission Report on the *Challenger* shuttle disaster, physicist Richard Feynman noted that managers and engineers at NASA—like health delivery organizations, a science-driven organization—had fundamentally different perspectives on the uncertainty and risk inherent in shuttle flight; engineers thought that the flights were orders of magnitude more risky than did NASA managers. Feynman argued that "for whatever purpose, be it for internal or external consumption, the management of NASA exaggerates the reliability of its product."[43] A similar clash of perspectives was apparent at NASA during the *Columbia* shuttle disaster seventeen years later, and managers here too chose a set of management tools better suited to a predictable than an uncertain enterprise.[44]

So if two differing, even clashing, perspectives exist among managers and clinicians, how should systems for delivering health care be designed, and how should care be managed? And which sets of tools are most applicable, when and why? What, if any, are the limits of the applicability of managerial tools drawn from other industries? Examples from outside the health care industry, most notably from NASA's two shuttle catastrophes, suggest that the choice of perspective is extremely important, with far-reaching effects. Later chapters will argue that it is indeed possible to design processes, organizations, and systems that manage care in these circumstances, but to do so requires a deep understanding of the fundamental nature of that care. Hence, before such questions can be answered, it would be helpful to understand the exact nature of the process we are trying to manage. What is the nature of health care and the health care process?

3

The Nature of Care

The previous two chapters focused on one of the core elements of systems for delivering health care: the state of the knowledge underpinning medical practice. They discussed the way this knowledge has informed current approaches to the management of systems for delivering health care—in particular, the extent to which these management approaches are based on underlying presumptions of ever-increasing certainty. The next two chapters will look at how patient care is undertaken in the face of uncertainty and consider another element of a system for delivering health care: the care process. Without a deep understanding of the nature of the health care process (that is, the work of care) and its relation to the patient's health problem, it will be hard to design processes, organizations, operating systems, or practitioner roles to efficiently and effectively deliver care.

These chapters will argue that the care process—what is actually done to solve an individual's health problem and create relief—is a problem-solving process that relies on making a probabilistic match between the general body of knowledge about a disease and the individual patient with a health problem. The care process acts on the patient's problem, connecting medical knowledge about the disease as a phenomenon with specific knowledge about the patient. However, the problem-solving process of health care is complex and nuanced. Patient problems, and the knowledge about them, vary, and thus the processes used to solve them also vary. In particular, the nature of the patient's problem—the extent to which it is structured or unstructured—influences the process by which clinicians make the connection between disease knowledge and patient and thus solve it. Even though the practitioner may know a lot about the disease—and in many cases enough is still not known—she or he may not initially know how to solve that patient's problem. Putting the two together may require repeated tests of a match between disease and patient, and thus the care process is essentially an experimental activity.

THE CARE PROCESS

The care process has many outward manifestations. A complex angioplasty performed in a cardiac catheterization laboratory brimming with modern electronics; a clinician's healing touch at the bedside, or periodic observation, or vaccination of a well child during a scheduled checkup; the daily routine of pill taking by a patient at home; and a clinician's counsel or answer to a question, from a patient or a colleague, delivered in a private office, busy hallway, telemedicine consultation, or e-mail message—these are all health care. Such observable activities are associated with some less easily observed (and less frequently grouped under the rubric of health care)—for instance, organizational processes such as information transfer, and cognitive processes such as individual risk assessment and decision making.

These activities of health care appear very different in numerous ways. They are undertaken in different organizations at different points in time by a diverse group of participants using different technologies. They have distinctly different aims (to prevent a future disease; to slow a disease's advance; to cure it; when this is not possible, to palliate its symptoms; and in all cases to reduce the fear of an uncertain future). And they are often approached as separate phenomena, each requiring its own organization and management. But they are all components of the same process.[1] The purpose of this chapter is to examine the process of care in more detail and understand its fundamental nature—that which is constant over time and place and is independent of changes in knowledge, technology, financing, reimbursement, regulatory context, or social mores—with the goal of framing an approach to its management. The way in which managers conceive of and model the health care process—whether they frame it as an uncertain or certain activity—determines the approach they take to designing the operating system responsible for the delivery of health care and the set of tools they use to manage that system.[2]

Chapter 1 described an increasing use of production metaphors to describe the care process. Linear flow diagrams and care paths represent care as an orderly sequence of steps through which the patient is progressed, and assume that the inputs and end points of each step of diagnosis, treatment selection, and treatment execution can be defined and articulated, that each step leads predictably to the next, and that care processes can therefore be designed in advance. And in some situations this is certainly the case. However, as chapter 2 described, for other patients, diagnosis, treatment selection, and treatment execution are less like steps in a production process and more like phases that merge as the uncertainty surrounding the patient's illness and its optimal treatment is progressively reduced. The phase of diagnosis is often only truly complete after the treatment phase is over inasmuch as successful treatment is the ultimate confirmation of the diagnosis; and unsuccessful treatment brings the diagnosis into question and may initiate a new search for the problem's cause. Similarly, even a successful treatment may be fleeting, rendered obsolete by a change in the underlying disease, the patient's life circumstances, or the hypothesized diagnosis.

Thus one of the most important characteristics of the health care process is continual problem solving, characterized by iteration, rework, and repeated modification. Before we consider operations designs or approaches to health care management, it will be important to first examine the problem-solving nature of the health care process.

HEALTH CARE AS PROBLEM SOLVING

Unless a health problem is identified through routine screening, a patient seeks care from a health care provider because he or she perceives a problem: either the presence of symptoms or the absence of potential or previous physical and mental function. Although the point at which a deviation from a feeling of health and well-being becomes a problem, and what the patient does about it, varies from one patient to the next, such a deviation usually initiates a search for a cause and a solution. The patient can adopt one of three approaches: wait and see, self-treat, or seek a provider's assistance.

In all three cases, solving the problem involves the typical steps of defining the problem and the criteria by which a potential solution will be evaluated, generating alternative solutions, testing each solution against these criteria, and selecting the best of these.[3] Even waiting and seeing is a form of problem solving; it is an explicit test of the hypothesis that there is no significant underlying cause for the problem and that it will go away without any specific treatment. Problem solving in health care is no different from that in other contexts, except that in health care these generic problem-solving steps are named. They are the four well-known phases of medical care: diagnosis, treatment selection, treatment execution, and posttreatment monitoring.

For many patients' health problems neither the cause of the problem nor its solution can be known in advance. Only through the care process—and the above four phases—is the problem solved by determining its cause and implementing its treatment. Hence the care process involves hypothesis generation and hypothesis testing, sometimes repeatedly. The diagnosis is a hypothesis of the problem's cause, and this hypothesis is confirmed or denied either when a definitive test verifies the diagnosis or when the treatment for this cause is successful. The relationship between diagnosis and treatment is thus dynamic and reciprocal; the diagnosis implies a treatment and the treatment confirms or disconfirms the diagnosis. Medical problem solving is thus truly a process—not an event—which may be cyclical rather than linear. And the phases of care are discrete steps only inasmuch as logic demands that one necessarily precedes the other.

The obvious activities of health care—the visible procedures and products described earlier—are signs of the underlying problem-solving process of health care: information gathering, clinical testing, decision making, and treatment execution. Each activity contributes to the understanding of the cause of the patient's problem or to the solution of that problem. Each generates or tests hypotheses of cause and appropriate treatment, and thus yields the knowledge necessary to eventually solve the problem.[4] Each reduces the patient's and the clinician's uncertainty about the cause and most effective treatment of the problem and thus takes them closer to realizing an effective and lasting solution.[5]

Although these activities correspond to the same four phases of health problem solving—problem identification and characterization (diagnosis), solution (treatment) planning, solution execution, and postsolution monitoring—how problems are actually solved within these four phases depends on the nature of the specific problem.[6] That is, the problem-solving process unfolds differently in different situations and for different types of problems.

Not only do different patients have different types of health problems (discussed below), but different participants in the health care process view the same problem differently. Although patients identify problems in their health and well-being (such as pain, shortness of breath, or malaise), clinicians also focus on underlying problems of biochemistry and physiology. By characterizing and resolving deviations from biological normality, clinicians solve component problems, with the ultimate goal of solving the patient's overall health problem. Moreover, the problem-solving process is both enduring and international. Ancient medical texts imply something similar thousands of years ago: the comparison of individual patients with written exemplars in order to reach a diagnosis and treatment. Traditional healers in the modern world also use a similar process, but they concentrate on other underlying problems and causes, such as marital or social disharmony, and draw upon different bodies of knowledge.

THE PROCESS OF PROBLEM SOLVING

Few health problems are truly new. Most are well known, and even very recent diseases, such as AIDS or SARS, are well described.[7] Our understanding of individual problems and how to solve them is contained in medical texts and current journals as well as in the heads of experienced clinicians. For any patient, problem solving does not start from scratch, but is based on an existing body of knowledge about diseases and their treatments, and technologies and their uses. Each symptom and laboratory abnormality is associated with a long list of known possible causes (the differential diagnosis). Textbooks and review articles contain case descriptions of the "classic case" that include how to diagnose it, how to differentiate it from other similar problems, which treatments resolve the problem, and how to choose among them. That is, the solution space—occasionally large and continually expanding as medical knowledge increases—is nonetheless reasonably well defined for most problems.

But the textbook knowledge is about the problem, disease, or technology as an independent phenomenon. As described in writing or in conversation among practitioners, this knowledge is unrelated to an individual patient in whom the problem or disease may be present or to the local context in which the technology will be used. Although the problem itself is typically not new, its occurrence in a particular patient typically is. And the manifestation of the problem or disease in that particular patient may deviate slightly, or even significantly, from its classic description in the medical literature; few patients exactly mimic the classic case description or follow the classic course of a disease. Although we can make general statements based on the behavior of populations, we as yet understand illnesses too poorly to be able to precisely predict the course of a disease in any one individual. Hence, although how to solve a problem may be well understood in general, how to solve it in the case of a specific patient with that problem is not known. The goal of the problem-solving process of health care is to solve the problem in the individual patient, and this is achieved by connecting the patient with a disease, and thus with a menu of known treatments from which one can be selected and executed.

The process of care first connects the individual patient with a problem with the general body of knowledge about the disease to create a new entity, the patient with the disease (shown schematically in figure 3-1). Both characteristics of the disease (such as its biology, typical manifestations, and set of known treatments) and characteristics of the patient (such as

FIGURE 3-1

Connecting the patient with the disease

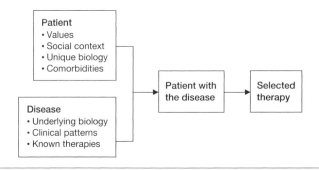

his or her unique biology, behaviors, preferences, and social circumstances) are considered in the explanation of the cause of the patient's problem and the planning of a solution. However, the disease as manifest in a specific patient is different from the disease as an isolated phenomenon. As an isolated phenomenon, the disease is associated with a set of therapies known to cure or modify it. When the disease is manifest within an individual patient, the available treatment options for it may be limited as a consequence of the patient's biology, coexisting diseases and therapies, or the individual's personal preferences. In effect, because the disease is manifest in a patient, the solution space is reduced. Moreover, the solution space is further limited by the poor state of medical evidence discussed in chapter 2.

Typically, to understand a problem's cause and to decide what to do to solve it involves a focused search among the known alternative explanations and known courses of action that compose the solution space (what Gaba calls "pre-complied responses").[8] Tests are used to distinguish among competing explanations for the problem, eventually reducing the list of differential diagnoses (which may be quite long) to a single best explanation of cause.[9] These tests include not only the familiar laboratory and radiological examinations, but also simple focused interrogation and physical examination, and of course the passive test of "wait and see" (in other words, to use the passage of time as a diagnostic test). Diagnosis connects the patient with the disease, and therefore with a (possibly more limited) menu of treatment options from which a treatment can be selected. The treatment, when successful, confirms that the correct match has been made between the patient and the disease.

And as chapter 2 discussed, every phase in the care process, and most activities undertaken during the phases, is associated with significant uncertainty. Uncertainty surrounds the very definition of a disease, the observations of signs and symptoms (and indeed the distinction between normal and abnormal) that give clues to the diagnosis of the disease, the outcomes and meaning of diagnostic tests relating to a sign or symptom, and the outcomes of therapics.[10] Symptoms and signs may be nonspecific; no test is perfectly sensitive, specific, or error free; and generally effective treatments may not be effective in a given individual. And compounding the sources of uncertainty discussed in the previous chapter is the fact that the patient in the office may not be at all like those patients in the trials. For example, women, the elderly, African Americans, and those with multiple coexisting diseases are typically underrepresented in clinical trials.

Health Care as an "Experiment"

Unlike manufacturing processes, health outcomes cannot always be determined by specifying the antecedent process steps. Rather, realizing a health care outcome requires a sequential search of two spaces—possible causes and possible solutions—and an explicit test of a proposed solution. Each step progressively reduces the uncertainty surrounding what is wrong with the patient and what to do about it. To this extent problem solving in health care is somewhat experimental, inasmuch as it involves deliberate structured activities designed to generate information and reduce uncertainty.[11] Identification of the cause of a problem involves serial testing. Implementing a solution is an experiment inasmuch as the outcome of any treatment is not known in advance (and often cannot be). To say that routine health care is experimental is not, however, to imply that unproven treatments are being used on patients without their consent, as in Nazi Germany, or that proven treatments are being withheld from unsuspecting and nonconsenting patients, as was the case during the Tuskegee syphilis experiment. Rather, what are being tested during the process of care are the hypotheses that the particular patient has the disease and is typical of other patients with the disease who have received the same treatment—that is, the fit between the current patient and the body of knowledge about the disease and its treatment.

TEMPLATING AND TESTING

The searches of the cause and solution spaces that characterize problem solving in health care usually involve what von Hippel and Tyre have called *templating*.[12] This is a form of trial-and-error-based problem solving in which a specific patient situation is compared with a known pattern (the template). In health care the templates are the textbook descriptions of the "classic case" of the disease, described above. These illustrate the essential features of a problem and its cause, including the specific symptoms of which the patient is likely to complain, and the way the patient is likely to respond to various tests and therapies (thereby setting the clinician's expectations of what is normal and what is to be considered abnormal). The extent of a match is assessed by comparing either similarities or differences between the template and the particular characteristics of the current patient (i.e., pattern matching). Usually this involves some sort of explicit testing; if the patient has the hypothesized disease, then, when measured, a particular serum indicator will show a specified deviation from normal, or a radiological image will show a characteristic pattern. If the physiological parameter measured does not deviate in the expected way, then the diagnosis or likely response to therapy is called into question. The specific tests chosen are those ones that are most likely to reveal key differences between the patient and the template or most likely to confirm the expected similarities. In this way diagnostic tests and tests of therapy are used to confirm the goodness-of-fit between the patient and the disease. With each test, the fit is improved and uncertainty about the patient's problem is reduced. Each step in the health care process is a turn of the experimental wheel, and uncertainty is reduced through focused search, testing of options, and trial and error. As investigation and treatment proceed, the patient's health problem becomes ever more tractable. A likely cause and therapeutic options are identified, as are the risks associated with each option (probabilities of positive and negative outcomes).

This central activity of medicine—the repeated testing of fit between the current patient and an idealized description of a disease—has a long history. The oldest known medical text, the Edwin Smith papyrus, is thought to date from the second millennium BCE.[13] This text describes the care of forty-eight (predominantly surgical) conditions. Each condition is described in the same stylized way: presenting complaint, examination findings, prognosis, and treatment (prognosis precedes treatment because some conditions are deemed not worth treating—for example, a skull wound that penetrates the cranium). In this respect the text's structure bears striking resemblance to a modern medical textbook. What has changed over the ensuing three millennia is not the practice of medicine—the experimental nature of the problem-solving care process—but the knowledge base about diseases and their characteristic features and behavior with which patients are compared.

The activities of templating in health care are closer to what Garvin calls *probe and learn* than unguided trial and error.[14] In the former, a testing strategy is deliberately planned, and the tests that are chosen are those most likely to distinguish two specific templates or differentiate the current patient from a specified template. Unguided trial and error, in contrast, is less efficient; results are harder to interpret, and each iteration may yield less useful information.[15]

However, no matter how many tests are performed, uncertainty can never be completely eliminated. As Kassirer has noted, because each test has an inherent error rate, "more tests do not necessarily produce more certainty."[16] The purpose of most of the activities in the health care process is to reduce uncertainty enough so as to allow the best therapeutic option to be identified and tried. And how much certainty is "enough certainty" is largely a function of the relative proportions of risk and benefit inherent in the particular therapy and the patient's and the clinician's appetites for uncertainty.[17] When the therapeutic benefit is marginal and the therapy carries a high risk, clinicians naturally seek to be more certain before recommending it. On the other hand, the certainty required when an intervention has low risk and high benefit is commensurately less. For example, mammography is generally considered relatively safe as a screening test. This is because the amount of radiation involved is very low and not thought to meaningfully contribute to the risk of developing breast cancer, and the potential yield (breast cancers found per one thousand mammograms performed) is relatively high for women older than fifty years.[18] Hence all that a clinician really needs to know before recommending this screening intervention is that the woman still has her breasts and is older than fifty. Little additional information about her breast cancer risk is routinely sought, at least currently. The problem-solving process of health care continues until the level of certainty achieved is enough—enough to allow the patient and his or her clinician to make an informed choice about whether or not to accept the therapy.

However, not all medical problems are the same, and therefore neither is all medical problem solving. The templating process described above applies to a particular type of problem: those that are well structured, for which medical knowledge is highly specified and a template actually exists. Not all problems are like this. How the series of iterative tests during the care of an individual patient are actually conducted, however, depends on the nature of the medical problem and the nature of the medical knowledge about that problem.

THE NATURE OF MEDICAL PROBLEMS

Although all health problems require diagnosis, treatment selection, treatment execution, and outcome monitoring, the duration and conduct of each phase varies depending on the nature of the problem being solved. Some health problems are simple, rapidly diagnosed and easily treated, such as a urinary tract infection in a woman with a past history of that disease. These kinds of problems require few or even no iterations or testing. The patient may know the diagnosis and what to do about it the minute she perceives symptoms.[19] Other problems are either completely unheard of or so complex that they simply have never been solved before, so that there is no template that serves to structure the problem or frame an approach to its solution. For instance, physicians in Wisconsin recently successfully treated a case of rabies in an unvaccinated teenager with a never before tried therapy: an induced coma and a cocktail of four antiviral drugs.[20] Not only was it not clear that the patient would survive—rabies has until now been considered universally fatal in unvaccinated patients—but it is still not exactly clear which of the components of the treatment, if any, contributed to the positive outcome. As in other domains, health problems are either structured or unstructured.

Unstructured problems are defined by what they are not: well structured. There is no clear representation of the problem (i.e., template), no process for searching for a solution, no criterion against which a proposed solution can be tested, and no proven sequence of steps that is known to lead to the resolution of the problem.[21] New diseases present clinicians with truly unstructured problems because they represent situations that have never been seen before, and for which neither underlying science nor a body of empirical experience is available to guide decision making and problem solving. In the modern era these are relatively uncommon; examples include AIDS in the early 1980s and SARS in the early twenty-first century. When the first cases of AIDS were observed in 1981, not only was the solution space undefined; it was not even clear what the nature of the problem was. It was guessed that some source of immunocompromise was at the root of the problem, because *pneumocystis carinii* pneumonia, the infection observed in young men that heralded the beginning of the AIDS epidemic, was previously regarded as a disease of the elderly and infirm, and these were groups that were also immunocompromised.

Unstructured problems are solved not by the iterative testing of the fit between the patient and one or more known templates (because these do not exist), but by first creating a set of one or more alternative options and later testing these against some prespecified criteria. This is closer to trial and error than to probe and learn. When medical problems are unstructured, each intervention is truly an excursion into the unknown. The early years of the AIDS epidemic are an example of this. Although it was recognized early that the infections that were the obvious and early manifestation of AIDS had an immunodeficiency at their root, the cause of that immunodeficiency was unclear for several years. Competing theories of cause in the early 1980s included viral infection, recreational drug abuse, a variant of graft-versus-host disease, immune system "fatigue," and divine retribution for homosexuality.[22] As a result, many public health and therapeutic interventions were tried, most without success, and the first prevention recommendations were not released by the CDC until two years into the epidemic. The first effective treatment was approved four years after that.[23]

Many difficult health problems are not completely unstructured, but partially structured. That is, the problem is not completely unknown. Similar or related problems are well known or well understood, and the solution space is at least partially defined. A disease itself may not be a new phenomenon, but the patient group in which it is present is. More often, research undertaken in one patient group has not been generalized to other patient groups. For example, medications tested only in adults with a given disease are often used in children with the same disease. Similarly, doctors often use pharmaceutical treatments off-label—that is, to treat diseases for which these medications have not been formally tested.

Another source of partially structured problems is patients with multiple interacting diseases. As chapter 2 discussed, many patients present with several diseases, and although each may be well described and have a generally agreed treatment strategy, the combination of the diseases may be less common, and the diseases may interact in complex ways such that the recommended care for any one of the individual diseases may not apply in the presence of the others. The problem posed by a particular combination of diseases is less well structured than the problem posed by any one of them. What is right for each of the diseases may not be right, or even known, for the patient with all of them.[24] Consider, for example, a (real) patient with Factor V (Leiden) deficiency and mild Von Willebrand disease concurrently. The former is proclotting, and the latter is associated with increased bleeding. Hematologists are conflicted over whether such a patient should take aspirin, a drug that promotes bleeding.

Still other health problems are highly structured. They are well defined and easily recognized, so that their causes can be rapidly identified by one or few diagnostic tests, and once a cause has been found, the solution is immediately apparent (i.e., both the problem and the solution sets contain only one or a very few elements). The process for solving these kinds of problems can be described by a highly specified protocol such that the majority of the uncertainty about the problem and how to solve it is reduced before the patient even presents to the health care provider. This is possible because most of the work of solving the problem has gone into structuring the problem through the development of diagnostic tests and evidence-based treatment protocols.[25] When problems are highly structured, all patients with the same problem can be managed the same way, and the major focus for the health care delivery organization becomes the execution of the known solution (rather than an iterative process to discover a solution previously untested in this patient). Unlike with unstructured problems, where tests are used to explore a range of possibilities (diagnoses or solutions), tests used in the context of a highly structured problem have the purpose of confirming the problem cause. Typically, highly structured problems are found with diseases that are common and well understood, and when the patient has only one problem or the problem involves only one body system.

Thus the approach to solving a patient's health problem—the care process—depends on how highly structured that problem is, and this in turn is a function of the knowledge about that problem. One way of understanding this connection is to consider the relationship between the stage of knowledge and the nature of a production process that uses this knowledge.

THE STAGE OF KNOWLEDGE IN HEALTH CARE

The extent to which a medical problem is structured—solvable using a proven set of steps—depends on the state of technical knowledge about the cause of that particular problem and how to solve it.[26] The greater the knowledge, the easier it is to make a prediction about outcome and thus describe the approach to problem solution as a discrete set of steps.

Bohn and Jaikumar, writing about production processes, have described eight levels of technical knowledge—the knowledge required to produce a product or service—ranging from complete ignorance to complete understanding.[27] The characteristic that differentiates data (the output from sensors that report the "measured level of some variable"), information (data organized and given structure), and knowledge is the ability to make predictions.[28]

Knowledge in a production process allows the manufacturer to predict that a certain set of process steps will yield a certain product characteristic, and increased knowledge allows better predictions. Bohn and Jaikumar's scale is reproduced in table 3-1. Each successive level represents an increased understanding of the relationship between cause and effect, a better characterization of the relevant variables and their interactions, the way in which individually and together they affect an outcome, and a better understanding of how to measure and manipulate these variables in ways that contribute to increased product quality or reduced cost.

A similar classification can be applied to the process of health problem solving and health care delivery. Increased knowledge about abnormalities of cellular processes and physiological functioning and the design, manufacture, and actions of therapeutic agents ultimately allows increased control over disordered biological processes and thus the cure of disease and the

TABLE 3-1

The stages of knowledge

Stage	Name	Description
1	Ignorance	Phenomenon not recognized or the variable's effects seem random
2	Awareness	Variable known to be influential but can be neither measured nor controlled
3	Measure	Variable can be measured but not controlled
4	Control of the mean	Control of the variable possible but not precise, control of variance around the mean not possible
5	Process capability	Variable can be controlled across its whole range
6	Process characterization	Know how small changes in the variable will affect the result
7	Know why	Fully characterized scientific model of causes and effects, including secondary variables
8	Complete knowledge	Knowledge of all interactions such that problems can be prevented by feed forward control

Source: Reprinted from "Measuring and Managing Technological Knowledge," by R. E. Bohn, MIT *Sloan Management Review* 36, no. 1 (1994): 61–73 by permission of the publisher. Copyright © 1994 by Massachusetts Institute of Technology. All rights reserved.

amelioration of symptoms. Clinicians are less able to treat the patient when essential knowledge relating to disease processes or therapeutic modalities is lacking. Table 3-2 shows how the stages of technical knowledge might be applied to the care of a diabetic patient through the control of blood glucose levels. Increased knowledge in areas such as glucose metabolism and its disorders, the biochemistry of obesity, the chemical structure and functioning of insulin, and the electrical resistivity of blood has allowed tighter control of those factors (blood glucose, serum lipid levels, etc.) that contribute to the development of complications in diabetic patients. Hence the care of diabetic patients, which once presented clinicians with a fairly unstructured problem, can now be prescribed with a set of clinical steps that include specific medication and lifestyle choices and dosing schedules.

Not all medical problems are as highly structured as the control of serum glucose. For example, in the management of coronary artery disease (CAD)

TABLE 3-2

Stages of knowledge in diabetes care

Knowledge stage	Time	Description
1: Ignorance	Classical times to eighteenth century	High mortality from a wasting disease in which the urine is noted to be sweet. No treatment available.
2: Awareness	Early twentieth century	Starvation diet noted to improve life expectancy.
3: Measure (but cannot control variable)	1914	Sugar in the urine measured by ferric chloride (thirty minutes) and then Benedict's test (five minutes).
4: Control of the mean	1921 to mid-twentieth century	Impure insulin controls blood sugar, but treatment effects variable.
5: Control of the variable across its whole range	Mid- to late twentieth century	Pure insulin with daily urine testing and dosing controls blood sugar.
6: Know how small changes in the variable will affect the result	1993	Multiple testing and dosing with combination insulins renders sugar normal throughout the day and reduces complications.
7: Control of secondary variables	1990s	Other risk factors (e.g., diet, exercise, cholesterol) specified and controlled.
8: Complete knowledge	Sometime in the future	Artificial pancreas (either closed-loop device or islet cell transplant) obviates the need for ongoing diabetic care.

risk, the role of serum cholesterol is fairly well understood. Cholesterol is known to be influential (stage 2), can be measured (stage 3), and can be broadly controlled with statins and other cholesterol-lowering agents (stage 4). However, cholesterol levels cannot be fine-tuned (stage 5), and the relationship between other factors such as C-reactive protein and triglyceride levels has not yet been fully characterized (stage 7). This is not to say that cardiac risk factors and problems such as hypercholesterolemia cannot be solved. Rather, the approach to the solution of such problems cannot be completely specified using a single sequence of standard steps. Some experimentation and adjustment is still required.

As both tables imply, there is a relationship between knowledge stage and knowledge codification. The literatures on knowledge management and organizational learning make a deliberate distinction between two types of knowledge: tacit and explicit.[29] The distinction is important because of what it implies about how the knowledge is initially acquired and how it is subsequently transferred (either between clinicians or between the clinician and the patient). Explicit knowledge refers to knowledge that is transmittable in formal, systematic language, whereas tacit knowledge is deeply rooted in action and a specific context.[30] Tacit knowledge is acquired through experience and transmitted through mentorship, while explicit knowledge can be taught in the classroom or communicated as written instructions or algorithms. The knowledge required to ride a bike is often cited as an example of tacit knowledge. Although it is possible to describe how to ride a bike in broad terms, in the final analysis it is only possible to learn to ride one by trying to ride and experiencing the feeling of balancing and falling. Tacit knowledge is typically corporeal—relating to the five senses. For example, although it is technically possible to combine the approximately five hundred known chemicals in a glass of red wine, winemakers rely on sight, taste, and smell. Wine connoisseurs must taste and smell something that remains unmeasured. An expert winemaker who identifies a wine that will be at its best in four years is relying on tacit knowledge, since there is, as yet, no chemical formula or even rule of thumb that would allow a less experienced taster to make this prediction with any degree of accuracy. The winemaker must taste, see, or smell something that tells her how a wine will taste in several years, characteristics of a young wine that cannot be captured in a chemical formulation or a recipe. In a similar fashion, a cardiac surgeon who makes a prognostic statement about a patient based simply on the feel of his or her heart during bypass surgery is also relying on tacit knowledge. Practitioners develop tacit knowledge through practice and experience, not study of texts. The surgeon will have previously felt many hearts, both more and less diseased, and observed the patients' subsequent outcomes.

As a production process becomes better understood, the key variables that determine the quality and cost of a product or service are identified and ultimately controlled. Then the steps required to create the product or service can be specified in advance. In effect, it becomes possible to write a process "recipe" so that a health problem can be solved be applying a proven sequence of steps known to lead to a solution, typically codified as a decision algorithm, clinical protocol, or a care path. This is the case in some aspects of diabetes care. Whereas in the early twentieth century, management of the serum glucose required a good deal of experience, intuition, and trial and error, it now can be completely described by a highly codified set of rules. As the stage of knowledge required to control serum glucose has risen and the knowledge has been codified, the problem of glucose control has become more highly structured.

In summary, when knowledge is higher stage, cause and effect relationships are better characterized, primary and secondary variables are defined and measurable, knowledge is codified, and hence health problems are more highly structured (see table 3-3). Whereas solving poorly structured problems

TABLE 3-3

Knowledge stage and approach to problem solving

Stage of knowledge	1, 2	3, 4, 5	6, 7, 8
Problem type	Unstructured	Semistructured	Highly structured
Problem-solving mode	Unstructured problem solving	Pattern matching	Rules application
Knowledge type	Tacit	← ⎯⎯⎯⎯ →	Explicit
Testing strategy	Hypothesis generation, trial and error, serendipitous observation	Testing, directed probe-and-learn cycles	Verification
Test type	Exploratory	Discriminatory	Confirmatory
Number of iterations	Many	Few	One
Practitioner expertise	Expert	← ⎯⎯⎯⎯ →	Novice
Management focus	Individual patient and problem Efficient experimentation, learning, and solution discovery	← ⎯⎯⎯⎯ →	Class of problems Solution execution

Source: Adapted from R. E. Bohn, "Measuring and Managing Technological Knowledge," *Sloan Management Review* 36, no. 1 (1994): 61–73.

requires an unstructured search and repeated empirical testing and trial-and-error cycles, more highly structured problems can be solved by following a discrete set of predefined steps. In between, problems are solved by testing the applicability (i.e., goodness of fit) of well-established patterns. Moreover, as will be discussed in the next chapter, more highly structured problems can be solved by less expert clinicians who can easily follow the predefined steps laid down in the protocol. Hence the process for solving health problems depends on the stage of knowledge and changes from experimental to prescriptive with higher knowledge stage.

PROBLEM STRUCTURE AND THREE
APPROACHES TO PROBLEM SOLVING

Three different approaches to problem solving in health care reflect the extent to which problems are structured, which in turn depends on the stage of knowledge relating to the problem. Unstructured problems are ones in which the uncertainty is highest and for which medical opinion and practice diverge.[31] Practitioners may not even agree on the diagnosis, let alone on the therapy. Solving poorly structured problems requires reasoning from first principles, repeated empirical testing, and iterative trial-and-error cycles. These cycles aim to open up possibilities and generate diagnostic and treatment hypotheses for later testing, and the tests used are exploratory—aimed to generate the maximum possible information. Although the outcome from any individual trial-and-error cycle may only marginally reduce the uncertainty surrounding the cause of the patient's problem and its treatment, each cycle builds on the learning from the previous ones. The cause of the patient's problem and the best treatment are eventually discovered as uncertainty is progressively reduced.

Solving semistructured problems also requires repeated testing. However, in this situation the tests chosen are not those that generate the most information and new hypotheses, but those that most efficiently distinguish between known members of the sets of possible causes of and possible treatments for the problem. Although the problem and its solution cannot be uniquely specified, they can be described by a finite number of well-recognized patterns (templates) that serve to direct choices of tests. Each probe-and-learn testing cycle is directed rather than open ended, and thus fewer cycles of testing, hypothesis refinement, and retesting are needed to arrive at and deliver a solution to the patient's health problem. Testing in this situation is part of a process of pattern recognition and confirmation.

An exploratory test used during the process of solving an unstructured health problem and a discriminatory test (or "probe") used to differentiate two diagnostic possibilities may be one and the same test, although used with different intent. For example, an admission chest X-ray of a complicated patient is an exploratory test in which the aim is to see whether there is anything abnormal in the chest. It is being used in a very different way from a chest X-ray of an elderly patient who complains of shortness of breath. In this latter case, the X-ray's purpose is to search for the presence or absence of specific factors such as cardiac enlargement or lung hyperinflation. The former finding would be consistent with the hypothesis of congestive heart failure as the cause of the shortness of breath and distinguish it from emphysema, another possible cause of shortness of breath with which the latter finding is more consistent. A therapy can also be used as a probe to differentiate two possible causes of a problem. If the patient with shortness of breath experiences symptomatic improvement with a drug that promotes fluid loss (i.e., a diuretic), then the cause was most likely congestive heart failure.

Historically, all health problems were solved using iterative testing cycles since there were no clear rules governing clinical choices, just a set of loose descriptions and aphorisms. Because disease causation and therapy were poorly understood, most medical care was delivered in what could be termed the *consultative* model of care delivery. The patient with a problem consulted an expert, and together they engaged in a kind of joint empiricism to solve the problem.

However, over the last several decades, the increasing volume and specificity of medical knowledge described in the previous chapters has made a third approach to problem solution possible. When health problems are highly structured diagnosis, medical treatment and health outcome are tightly coupled, and the health care process can be described in a standard protocol. An "on/off" test can confirm the single diagnosis, and this diagnosis implies one best therapy that applies, by and large, to all patients with that particular problem. For these highly structured problems, the clinician's and the health care manager's primary focus is on the reliable execution of the known solution rather than the development de novo of a currently unknown solution. As described in chapter 1, much diabetes care falls into this group. The diagnosis is clinched on the basis of a single blood test, and (in the case of type 1 diabetes) the treatment is insulin, serum glucose moves predictably in response to precise doses of pure (now artificial) insulin, and dose can be governed by an algorithm either expressed as a "sliding scale" or embedded in the software of a glucose monitor. (However, even the care of the patient with diabetes, a disease notable for its high stage of knowledge, cannot be fully automated. The impediments to full process specification and control are those residual secondary variables that remain hard to characterize, measure, and control. Examples of such variables include the determinants of patient behavior [e.g., medication compliance], such as individual psychology and social milieu.)

ITERATIVE AND SEQUENTIAL CARE PROCESSES

In routine practice the care process is operationalized in two broad ways, one that has as its central feature iterative testing and probing (when problems are unstructured or semistructured), and one that features a fairly orderly and well-demarcated sequence of prespecified steps (when problems are highly structured). Four features—with implications for process and operating system design and management—characterize the former operationalization, the iterative care process. First, as the term implies, it is iterative, being composed of multiple cycles of hypothesis proposition and testing. Second, it is recursive, inasmuch as each cycle builds on the former. Each iteration generates new information about the patient—either generating possible explanations of the cause of a problem, or ruling causes in or out, or confirming that a therapy works—and this new information is the starting point for the subsequent cycle.[32]

Third, to some degree, the health care process for unstructured and semistructured problems is customized to the unique needs of the patient and the unique ways in which the health problem and underlying biological abnormality is expressed in him or her. Although the disease may not be unique, the disease in the particular patient is a unique phenomenon. Because each patient presents with his or her own combination of diseases and preferences, the specific tests and therapies chosen, and their sequencing, are unique to the individual patient. Each test has the potential to widen the range of possibilities, thereby requiring further tests that thus make the flow of the patient through the delivery systems unpredictable.[33] Finally, the process is uncertain. The combinations of and interactions among multiple diseases and problems in the same patient, and the inherent imperfection of diagnostic tests discussed above, mean that the cause of a problem and the patient's response to a treatment for it may remain uncertain during much of the health care process. Each cycle of diagnostic tests, procedures, and therapeutic medications results in a gradual reduction of uncertainty.

In contrast, the operationalization of the care process for dealing with highly structured problems tends to be more linear. Because the cause and solution sets have so few members, there are fewer or no feedback loops, and the process unfolds as an orderly sequence of steps. Therefore, the process can be more highly standardized. In this case each patient with exactly the same problem experiences (or should experience) exactly the same set of process steps. The disease is treated as the same in all patients. Such standardization is possible because the care needed by an individual patient is more certain. Most of the uncertainty surrounding the solution to the particular problem has been reduced during the design of the protocol that specifies the patient's care. The solution has been shown to work in any patient, regardless of context.

As already noted, this latter type of care process is a relatively new phenomenon. Only in recent decades has the knowledge stage about medical problems advanced to the point where a problem can be so uniquely characterized, a pathognomonic on/off test can be used to immediately confirm a diagnosis, and a solution can be so highly specified. And, as later chapters will discuss, the advent of this type of health care process has important implications for managers of health care delivery organizations.

In fact the term *health care delivery* is something of a misnomer, inasmuch as it conjures an image of the movement of a well-defined product or service to a specific location. Although it is certainly true that well-defined care processes do exist (in those cases where a single best treatment is known), much health care delivery remains an emergent process of repeated testing and serial reconception.[34] Particularly when health problems are unstructured or semistructured, the care process bears more resemblance to an experimental than a production process. The process is one in which the cause of and solution to the patient's problem is discovered through repeated search.

In summary, the care process in reality involves two very different types of processes: one a customized and unprogrammable search, and the other a highly programmed sequence of known steps. The former, hereafter referred to as the *iterative* care process, has much in common with the new-product development process (where each patient can be thought of as a new "project"), with its repeated hypothesis testing through design-build-test cycles.[35] And the latter, hereafter referred to as the *sequential* care process, is closer to the above notion of "delivery" and has more in common with a manufacturing process in which a well-defined product or service is built to specification. Learning (and, more specifically, learning by doing) is central to the iterative process, whereas the sequential process places less emphasis on active learning (because most of the learning has already happened prior to a patient's arrival) and more on the execution of what is already known.[36]

To make things more complex, the care of the same individual patient may at some times involve an iterative process and at others a sequential process. In patients with a complex disease or set of diseases, for example, the phases of diagnosis, treatment planning, and the first trial of a new treatment may be an iterative process; whereas treatment execution in the same patient, once stabilized, may involve a sequential process. Processes applicable to all patients, independent of their diagnoses, such as a process of infection control or medication reconciliation, are often sequential processes, even though the rest of these patients' care may involve an iterative process. And an iterative care process (for arriving at a solution to a patient's health problem) may make use of tests and therapies for which the execution is highly standardized and the process sequential. For example, the process for performing an MRI or inserting a central line may be highly standard, even though the care process of which this action is a part may be iterative.

The phases of treatment execution and monitoring are often very different from diagnosis and therapy selection, a fact that allows them to be separated operationally. Moreover, elective cases are operationally different from emergent cases. The former are notable for their lower variability, a characteristic that derives in part from the fact that most of the variability has been isolated in the diagnosis and treatment selection phases, which, in the case of much elective surgery, often take place in another setting than the specialty hospital—a fact that allows focused factories to be so efficient.

It would be tempting to equate iterative and sequential processes with the "art and science" of medicine, respectively. However, to liken an iterative care process to art is to misrepresent its essential activities. Discovering solutions to unstructured and semistructured problems through repeated search cycles is the essence of science. Iterative processes are the application of the scientific method to the care of an individual patient. A cause of and solution to the problem is hypothesized for each patient, data then collected (either with a diagnostic test or a trial of therapy) and analyzed, and the hypothesis confirmed or denied. And sequential processes, because they are less hypothesis testing than solution implementation, are less like science than like a production process.

The importance of the distinction between iterative and sequential processes is that they are very different operationally. As chapter 5 will discuss, the operations literature suggests that they be designed and managed differently exactly because they are so different; they make use of different resources, tools, and personnel. Managers in other industries would frame these two processes in very different ways and adopt very different approaches to designing and managing them. However, many diversified, multipurpose health care delivery organizations do not make a clear distinction between these two processes. They tend to apply the same set of management tools to both, and are not deliberately designed to optimize the performance of either process. Recent years have seen examples of a de facto separation of these processes: iterative processes in general hospitals, and sequential in specialized procedure-oriented institutions, such as those that undertake joint replacement only.

But both approaches, either not distinguishing between these two processes managerially or carving off elective procedures into stand-alone institutions, fail to account for two important issues: the comingling of the two processes during a single episode of care of many patients and the important interplay between them. Chapter 5 will describe approaches to designing processes and organizations that accommodate the former issue, but before that, chapter 4 will examine the dynamic relationship between iterative and sequential care processes and the implications of this relationship for the design of care.

4

Care Processes and Knowledge Types

The foregoing description of iterative and sequential care processes has treated them separately. However, they are in fact linked in an important way. Differentiating between unstructured and structured problems, and iterative and sequential care processes, is not only important for understanding the design of care processes and organizations; it is also important because the relationship between these different approaches to problem solving places additional design requirements on delivery organizations. At the heart of this relationship is the dynamic nature of the knowledge that is the substrate of the care process. This chapter will discuss the interplay between the various types of knowledge for care and the different care processes.

The stage of knowledge relating to any given health problem is not fixed. It increases over time through the combined effects of basic science research, clinical research, and clinicians' individual experience. A previously unstructured, ill-defined problem, without a clear single solution or associated best practice, may ultimately become highly structured and well defined. And as the stage of knowledge and the problem's structure increase, both the approach to problem solving and the approach to managing the activities of health care change. A problem that was once solved through an iterative care process is now solved with a sequential one. That is, over time, processes tend to evolve from iterative to sequential, a movement that will continue as long as, for any individual health problem, knowledge continues to develop and knowledge stage increases. Hence, to create effective delivery organizations, health care managers must account for continuing change in medical knowledge.

Moreover, even though increasing medical knowledge helps make health problems more structured, and thus shapes whether the care process will be iterative or sequential, more than just medical knowledge is needed to implement it in practice and deliver effective care efficiently. Individual practitioners' knowledge about the patient as an individual and organizational knowledge about how to conduct the care process are also required in order to apply that medical knowledge successfully to a patient to create relief.

As we shall see in this chapter, all these sets of knowledge change over time. Although medical science is an important source of knowledge about diseases, the day-to-day practice of care is also an important source of knowledge (a theme taken up in chapter 6). The dynamic relationship between the two types of care processes implies other work for the organization: learning.

The evolution of knowledge stage, problem structure, and approach to problem solving is particularly evident for a disease such as diabetes, and the history of this disease provides a good example of the ways in which the stages of knowledge relating to a disease change over time and of the implications that this knowledge change has for the design of care.[1]

EVOLVING KNOWLEDGE AND ITS IMPACT ON THE DESIGN OF CARE: DIABETES REVISITED

The term *diabetes* used by Aretaeus in the second century BCE meant "siphon" and was based on the observation that those afflicted were plagued by excessive thirst, weakness, and frequent urination. And the word *mellitus* comes from the observation that the urine of diabetic patients was sweet (in Latin *mellitus* means "honey sweet"). In fact, early researchers, upon finding sugars in excessive urine, concluded that diabetes was a kidney disorder. Much later, by the close of the nineteenth century, it became evident that the pancreas was the organ affected—because a dog with its pancreas removed developed diabetes—and that a hormone that mediated sugar metabolism was produced in the mass of cells known as the islets of Langerhans. However, oral administration of a pancreas extract did not relieve the disease. Although it was possible to quantify the amount of sugar in the urine in the early twentieth century—first with a laboratory test that took thirty minutes and then with a five-minute test called Benedict's test—control of the sugar was not possible until Banting and Best's famous discovery, in 1921, of insulin. Prior to this, therapy was highly experimental. The goal was to prevent (or, more likely, delay) death in young patients with type 1 diabetes, either through overfeeding (to compensate for lost sugar) or through deliberate starvation (to purge the body of excess sugar). The only treatment that showed any effect was the starvation diet that prolonged the life expectancy in juvenile patients from 1.3 to 2.9 years, and of course morphine to dull the pain.

The discovery of insulin not only confirmed the origin of the disease; it also revolutionized the treatment of diabetes and changed both the goals of treatment and the model of care delivery. Once a virtual death sentence, diabetes now became a treatable disease. The first patient ever treated with insulin, a fourteen-year-old boy, had his health dramatically restored with the drug in 1922. However, this treatment was by no means easy. Not only did patients have to inject themselves four times a day with thick stainless steel needles on glass syringes (including waking themselves up at night for the fourth dose), but problems also remained with both the measurement of sugar and insulin therapy itself. Early measurements of sugar levels were approximate at best. Benedict's test, introduced in 1914, measured the level of sugar in the urine and therefore only reflected the average serum sugar level three to four hours previously. The test's accuracy was further limited because it required that a sample of urine be mixed with the Benedict's solution, and then boiled for five minutes before the color was read and interpreted manually (by comparing the color of the solution with a standard color chart). Furthermore, early insulin preparations were highly impure, so that the therapeutic effect of any single dose was highly variable (a problem compounded by the fact that patients developed reactions to the impurities). For example, the potency of Iletin, Eli Lilly's first mass-marketed insulin, varied by plus or minus 25 percent. Impurities of early insulins were of the order of 50,000 parts per million (ppm).[2] Finally, as the blood sugar level is the result of a complex interaction between diet, exercise level, and insulin dose, patients still had to struggle to balance these factors to maintain good health. The net result was that sugar control was not very precise, and many patients suffered hypoglycemic episodes as a result of insulin overdose, or hyperglycemic complications resulting from undertreatment. Lots of small-scale experiments were required to divine the best balance of a diet and insulin regimen. High levels of impurity prevented the development of a standard dosing regimen. Nonetheless, with increased understanding of the disease and the treatment technologies, the goal of treatment had shifted to the prevention of urinary sugar loss through balancing diet and insulin dose. And because, as a short-acting protein, insulin had to be injected frequently, the patient immediately became an important focus of the design of diabetes care delivery systems. "Wandering" nurses provided support, visiting patients in their homes to teach parents menu planning, food preparation, and how to give injections to children.

Within thirty years, however, insulin purity and measurement technology had improved significantly. Impurities dropped from 50,000 ppm in 1925 to 10,000 ppm in 1950 and 10 ppm in 1980.[3] The first long-acting insulin, protamine insulin, which simplified the treatment regimen, was developed in 1936. And serum glucose estimation by the patient became possible in 1961 with the introduction of home glucose-monitoring kits. (Serum monitoring was available prior to this but was restricted to the doctor's office because of its high cost.) As tighter control of serum, rather than urine, glucose level became feasible, the goals of treatment changed once again. In 1941, Elliott Joslin, the founder of Boston's famous Joslin Diabetes Center, noted that "the object of the treatment of diabetes is to prevent the loss of sugar in the urine."[4] By 1953, he was writing, "The object of the treatment of diabetes is to prevent its complications by avoiding an increase of sugar in the blood with the loss of sugar in the urine."[5]

Since then, advances in both technological and clinical understanding have had a dramatic impact on the treatment and prognosis of diabetes patients. Human recombinant insulin (1981) has rendered impurity a thing of the past, and oral hypoglycemics (1956) increased the treatment options available. Disposable needles (1958), insulin pens (1985), and pumps (mid-1970s) have made self-injection ever easier, thereby further increasing the decentralization of care toward the patient. Dosage can now account for minute-by-minute variations in serum glucose levels because measurement of this variable has become both reliable and simple with the introduction first of dipsticks (1961) and more recently of glucose meters, including one worn as a watch (2001). And diabetes education has become a science of its own; the 1978 edition of the *Joslin Diabetes Manual* stated, "Education is not an addition to treatment, it *is* treatment."[6] All of these improvements in understanding, reflected in both technological advancement and clinical practice changes, have freed diabetic patients from dependence on formal health care delivery structures (hospitals, clinics, and wandering nurses) and allowed the care of their disease to be delivered in their communities and integrated with their own lives. Moreover, there can be no doubt of the positive impact of these improvements on the most important outcome, the incidence of the vascular complications that are the scourge of diabetes, since the publication of the results of a major randomized trial (the Diabetes Control and Complications Trial, DCCT) in 1993, which caused the American Diabetes Association to revise its clinical guidelines.[7]

Today, detailed treatment algorithms are embedded in diagnostic and therapeutic technologies and underlie highly specified clinical process measures. As we have seen, with respect to diabetes care, physicians are judged more by how well they execute the known best-practice treatment strategies than by how skilled they are at inventing unique treatments. Diabetics are empowered by knowledge that is notable for both its richness and the ease with which it is accessed, and they are therefore highly involved in the decisions that govern the day-to-day management of their disease. Physicians are no longer the center of the care delivery process. Care is delivered by diverse teams comprising educators, nurses, dietitians, pharmacists, and even personal trainers. The physician's role has been transformed from sole decision maker to team member. In fact, in the care of an uncomplicated diabetes patient, the physician's role has become more like that of a worker responsible for the faithful execution of a well-developed standard operating procedure than someone responsible for developing a procedure de novo. Moreover, new technologies—closed-loop glucose-monitoring and insulin delivery systems and islet cell transplants—hold the promise of removing members of the caregiving team altogether in the not-too-distant future, perhaps eventually "automating" care.

In effect, with increasing technical and organizational knowledge, the problems of diabetes and its treatment have become more highly structured, and the process of care of the diabetic patient has evolved from an iterative process to a sequential one. Early in the twentieth century, the cause of the disease was unknown, and even when it became known, it was impossible to control the disease because insulin impurities and glucose measurement inaccuracies prevented accurate calibration of the treatment. In fact, some patients who did not respond well to treatment turned out to have a different disease entirely (type 2 diabetes). And thus physicians and nurses had to test their diagnoses and treatments empirically, one patient at a time. With increases in insulin purity (and therefore predictability of response), reliability of delivery, and accuracy of measurement of serum glucose and HbA_{1c}, care became prescribed by a highly specific guideline and managed through the process and decision management techniques described in chapter 1. Furthermore, control over what Bohn and Jaikumar term *secondary variables*— such as cholesterol, blood pressure, and diet—has also improved, meaning, at least for some patients, a normal life expectancy (see chapter 3, tables 3-2 and 3-3).[8]

THREE KNOWLEDGE BASES FOR CARE

The rich history of diabetes treatment is an example of the way in which the knowledge underpinning care is actually several types of knowledge that interact with one another: formal medical scientific and organizational knowledge, and individual experience. The dramatic changes in the process of diabetes care over the last century have depended on developments in all three knowledge bases.

Scientific Knowledge

Clearly, increased scientific understanding of the disease and its treatment technologies has played a critical role in diabetes treatment over the century. Changes in glucose measurement and insulin delivery technologies, insulin formulation, and diet and exercise recommendations have brought about a transformation of both the basic model of diabetes care (who delivers care, where, and how) and the approach to the management of diabetes care (guidelines, compliance rate–based quality measurement, pay-for-performance). Advances in understanding in gross anatomy, histology, and histopathology led to the identification of the cells that secreted the key hormone controlling glucose metabolism. Isolation and purification of the hormone allowed an improved understanding of the pathophysiology of abnormal glucose metabolism. Improvements in both insulin production and medical engineering allowed accurate delivery of a therapy and ultimately control over glucose levels. Clinical research connected disordered glucose control with the well-recognized signs and symptoms of the acute disease, and finally more effective long-term treatment of disordered blood glucose was shown to lead to a reduction in the long-term complications of the disease.

Organizational Knowledge

Evolving organizational knowledge has also played an important role. From the outset, because of the chemical nature of insulin, diabetic patients were more involved in the management of their condition than in almost any other disease. The patient was the only viable candidate for the task of drug delivery. Hence the effectiveness of diabetes treatment has always been highly dependent on patient behavior, not only to the extent that the patient undertook risky behavior (such as eating cakes and lying on the sofa) but also to the extent that he or she followed the testing and dosing schedule correctly. Each patient reacted differently to the treatments of the day—either because of variation in the purity of the insulin being used at the time, or because of individual differences in metabolism, diet, and exercise pattern, or because each patient paid a different amount of attention to measurement and insulin dosing. As diabetic care became more sophisticated, integrating ever more precise acute insulin treatment with education and long-term lifestyle change, teams of caregivers and delivery organizations organized into systems of care—comprising specialized diabetic educators, diabetologists, psychologists, and information system specialists—were needed to provide the totality of care needed by each patient. Prescribing the right insulin dose was not enough. It became necessary to engage patients in their own environments to facilitate and support behavior change and coordinate the activities of many individual physician and nonphysician subspecialists in order to exert complete control over any individual patient's disease. Hence, over time, organizational knowledge about the provision of diabetic services became key to its successful treatment.

Individual Experience

In practice, clinicians of all professions and subspecialties who provide care to diabetic patients draw on a third knowledge base: their own experience. Over the century, it became clear that diabetes was not simply a pancreatic disease but a multisystem disorder with an important social component. Care of the diabetic required an understanding of clinical medicine, individual behavior, and social and organizational behavior. It required knowledge relating to other conditions—such as obesity, cardiovascular and peripheral vascular disease, and renal and ocular disease—and the reconciliation of any conflict that might result when combining recommendations for the treatment of each disease derived from disease-specific research. It also required integration of the knowledge derived from the medical knowledge base with the capabilities, norms, and routines of the organization in which care was being delivered and an understanding of the patient's unique biology, capabilities, social context, and preferences. Over time, as clinicians treat more patients, they internally integrate these various knowledge bases to develop their own stores of experience relating to the management of the diabetic patient. In effect, clinicians develop a third (tacit) knowledge base, their own unique experience base, which they bring to bear on the solution of future problems. This knowledge base is applied not only to the current diabetic patient but to other patients with other problems.

Although the three knowledge bases predominantly reside in different locations (depending in part on whether the knowledge is tacit or explicit)—medical knowledge in texts and journals, organizational knowledge embedded in the culture, norms, and routines of the organization, and experiential knowledge within the individual clinician—they are united at the moment of the clinician–patient interaction. Depending on whether the state of knowledge is such that a patient's problem is highly or poorly structured, the clinician will make more or fewer modifications to the testing strategy and treatment choice for that patient. Over the last century, evolution in all three knowledge bases has been critical to the transformation of diabetes from a disease character- ized by poorly structured problems, highly experimental treatments, and itera- tive care processes to a disease addressed by a highly structured disease management strategy and sequential processes. They have interacted with each other in important ways. At various times in its history, new medical sci- ence has allowed, or forced, new ways of organizing care delivery for diabetic patients: new processes (e.g., standard guidelines and sequential processes of much modern diabetes care), functions (e.g., education and lifestyle change), professions (e.g., wandering nurses), and organizational structures (e.g., care management teams and disease management companies). And these new ways of organizing care delivery have required caregivers to develop new, often managerial, skills.

CHANGES IN THE NATURE OF KNOWLEDGE
FOR HEALTH CARE AND IMPACT ON DESIGN
OF CARE

It is not simply that over time we develop more of the medical and organiza- tional knowledge required to relieve patient suffering, however. With time, the nature of that knowledge changes. Of course, increasing volume of knowl- edge is as striking as it is important. The recent explosion in the volume of medical and social science knowledge has been fueled by investments in basic science and clinical research. Between 1994 and 1999, the National In- stitutes of Health (NIH) budget grew from $10.9 billion to $15.6 billion, and investment in research and development by pharmaceutical companies grew from $13.5 billion to $24 billion.[9] The surge in knowledge, at least as mea- sured by the number of scientific publications, is unlikely to abate in the near future. And, as chapter 1 discussed, the specificity of that knowledge has increased dramatically over recent years.

But other important characteristics of the knowledge have changed in concert with increasing volume and specificity, in ways that facilitate the transition from iterative to sequential care processes for solving health prob- lems. The evolution of surgical wound infection prevention illustrates these other characteristics.

Aseptic surgical technique to prevent surgical wound infections has been practiced since the time of Lister in the mid-nineteenth century, and in more recent times prophylactic antibiotic administration prior to abdominal surgery has been routine practice. Modern practice is to use particular antibiotics that have been tested for this purpose and found to be effective in preventing wound infections. A paper, published in 1992, went even one step further than specifying appropriate antibiotics. It demonstrated the exact timing of drug delivery before surgery that was required for maximal protection against infection.[10] Analogous to the case of diabetes, the knowledge pertaining to the prevention of surgical infection has evolved from general recommendations regarding aseptic technique to highly specific prescriptions for drug choice, drug dosage, and even the exact timing of drug administration. Whereas each caregiver in the nineteenth century would have had his or her own way of cleaning and dressing a wound—developed over time and with experience, and taught by example—modern caregivers follow a single standard protocol.[11]

In a similar fashion, current knowledge about the insulin regimen to control an individual patient's blood sugar level is equally specific. Whereas early knowledge about diabetes was at such a low stage that blood sugar control was initially impossible and then imprecise, it is now at such a high stage that it has been formulated as an algorithm and embedded in home glucometers that recommend an insulin dose based on the past blood sugar determinations.

> *Knowledge content.* The specific content of the knowledge—what we know about—of diabetes treatments and infection control has changed over time. To put it another way, knowledge evolves from "knowledge that" a phenomenon exists (but it cannot be influenced or explained), to "knowledge how" (to influence the phenomenon), to "knowledge why" (an understanding of complex interactions in the causal system that results in the observed phenomenon). Anton van Leeuwenhoek observed microorganisms in the 1670s, Louis Pasteur showed that they caused disease (knowledge that), and Joseph Lister demonstrated that surgical wound infections could be prevented with chemical inhibition with carbolic acid (knowledge how). Yet it was not until the twentieth century that a clear understanding of how infectious agents caused disease was developed (knowledge why).[12]

> *Knowledge form.* In the examples above, the form the knowledge takes has also changed. Initially, both diabetes care and surgical infection prevention depended on the tacit knowledge of the individual

caregiver. Nowadays, that knowledge can be codified as an algorithm, a generalizable rule, or a specific instruction. It has become explicit.

FROM TACIT TO EXPLICIT KNOWLEDGE

The categories of tacit and explicit knowledge are not mutually exclusive, however; they anchor two ends of a spectrum. Between the two extremes of knowledge that might never be represented in symbols and knowledge that is represented as code, is a third form of knowledge: knowledge that is not truly tacit but is as yet "unvoiced," with the potential to ultimately become explicit.[13] This knowledge is unvoiced either because no one has thought to do so, or because the current costs of codifying the knowledge—creating a specialized vocabulary and a set of models—are too great, or because the technical capability to render the knowledge explicit does not yet exist. For example, an individual worker may acquire an ability to assess some physical phenomenon and its meaning through experience, such as the color of molten metal that indicates it is at the "right" temperature, or the softness of a heart that indicates it is adequately oxygenated. The knowledge upon which this assessment is made is usually thought of as tacit; it is corporeal, rooted in that worker's experience, and not easily articulated. However, with enough investment, the physical characteristic in question may ultimately be assessed by technological means, thereby allowing the specification of the exact implications that various values of that characteristic have on the outcome of concern.[14] Thus the relationship between tacit and explicit knowledge (in particular, technical knowledge) is fluid, a fact that is especially important in health care.[15] Some technical knowledge that is explicit today was tacit at some time in the past (see figure 4-1). With clinical experience and bio-medical research some tacit knowledge becomes codified.

FIGURE 4-1

The transition from tacit to explicit knowledge

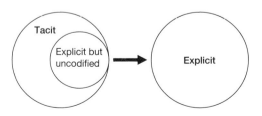

Automated electrocardiogram (EKG) reading provides an example of the transition from lower-stage tacit knowledge informing individual expert judgment to higher-stage explicit knowledge expressed as an algorithm embedded in software. The interpretation of an EKG was initially a task for the specialist cardiologist, who examined each EKG for subtle patterns that were diagnostic of various abnormalities of electrical conduction within the heart. When nonspecialists interpreted EKGs, they were usually sent to a cardiologist to be double-checked. Initial attempts to replace specialists' pattern recognition and expert judgment with automated rules were of limited success, and a significant amount of disagreement between automated systems and cardiologists remained.[16] However, by the 1990s, some of these programs were beginning to perform as well as cardiologists in identifying major cardiac disorders.[17] Today it is uncommon for the cardiologist to disagree with the machine.[18]

In summary, the volume, specificity, content, and form of the knowledge for patient care all change over time. In practical terms, this means that the stage of the knowledge required to solve a particular health problem progressively increases over time. Key variables are identified (for example, serum glucose), and mechanisms to measure and control those variables are developed (for example, urine, then serum glucose measurement, and insulin, respectively). Interacting secondary variables—such as the patient's diet, exercise, and individual psychology—and the organization of services and teams of caregivers are ultimately elucidated, and an understanding of how to modify these variables is developed. Thus advances in adult education and the design and management of health care teams all contribute to increased disease control. And as the stage of knowledge increases, the location of the knowledge changes, eventually moving from the experience base of the skilled artisan to be embedded in an algorithm or a piece of technology. And this in turn means that the care processes that apply this knowledge to individual patient problems are themselves in continual flux. That a particular health problem is solved using an iterative process today does not mean that will be so in the future.

However, although all three knowledge bases are expanding, it is important to recognize that they are doing so neither evenly nor at the same rate. The new knowledge that is added to each knowledge base is sometimes high stage and sometimes low, sometimes explicit and sometimes tacit. The net result is that even the most advanced health care for any patient may remain a mix of iterative and sequential processes.[19] Even if the medical science knowledge base is highly developed, comprising only high-stage knowledge, the organizational knowledge base may be less well developed, and the knowledge here may be lower stage. That is, for any given problem, we may know a great deal about which tests and therapies to use to solve it, but less about how to organize those tests and therapies to ensure that they are accurately delivered to all who need them. And we may know even less about how to coordinate a system of care that reliably acts on the outcomes of these tests and therapies.

All of this adds complexity to the job of a health manager designing care processes and organizations. Not only must managers design processes and organizations that accommodate different kinds of care processes; they must also make these flexible to changes in the underlying knowledge base and thus to the care processes.

THE ORIGIN OF NEW KNOWLEDGE
FOR PRACTICE

Why is the knowledge for care so impermanent? Is it simply because we spend so much on formal medical research, or do other forces drive continual evolution in the knowledge bases? From where does new understanding arise, and how does knowledge actually make a transition in form and content—from tacit to explicit, "knowledge that" to "knowledge why"?

To a large extent, of course, it is the research. In modern times, the vast majority of new knowledge in health care comes from the deliberate research that is driven by rich funding from both the public and the private sectors. Analyses of cross-sectional disease-specific observational databases (for example, a stroke registry) and long-term cohort studies (such as the Framingham Heart Study), and testing of specific hypotheses about a test or therapy through randomized controlled trials (with greater levels of rigor respectively), all contribute to the growth of explicit knowledge.

But it is also clear that formal research is not the only source of new knowledge for care. To begin, the ideas for formal studies such as those above come not only from previous research—each clinical trial or basic science experiment answers some questions but also suggests others—but also from observations made in clinical practice. The tradition of the physician scientist who makes observations in the context of routine care delivery and follows these up with scientific inquiry has a rich history in medicine. For example, while working in the obstetric unit of Vienna General Hospital in the 1840s, Ignaz Semmelweis (1818–1865) made the observation that the mortality rate from puerperal fever (postdelivery infection of the womb) varied dramatically between the hospital's two obstetric wards. In one it was a crushing 29 percent, while in the adjacent ward it was only 3 percent. Semmelweis "judged the only difference between the two was that births in Ward One were handled by medical students and those in Ward Two by midwifery pupils."[20] So, as an experiment, Semmelweis transferred the medical students to Ward Two. The high mortality rate went with them. Then in 1847 his friend Jakob Kolletschka, a professor of forensic medicine, cut himself while conducting an autopsy and died of a disease similar to puerperal fever. Semmelweis wrote that "as we found identical changes in [Kolletschka's] body and those of the childbed women, it can be concluded that Kolletschka died of the same disease."[21] He eventually concluded that the medical students were transferring infection from the autopsy room to the obstetric ward. When he ordered hand washing with chlorinated water, the mortality rate dropped dramatically.

Observation of a phenomenon is the first step in building theory.[22] Early scientists in any field spend most of their time describing and categorizing what they observe, or reporting on anomalies or deviations from what previous theories would have predicted. In analyzing similarities or differences between observations, they then propose associations between the observations and the constructs they purportedly represent. When those associations have not previously been recognized, and there exists no language or model to describe them, the scientists draw analogies, as Semmelweis did between the deaths of his friend and his patients. Converting tacit to explicit knowledge is a process Nonaka and Takeuchi, writing about innovation and new knowledge creation in the production setting, call "externalization."[23] According to these authors, externalization is accomplished through the "sequential use of metaphor, analogy and model." A metaphor allows something that is only understood intuitively to be expressed in terms of something else already understood or more easily expressed. And "once explicit concepts are created, they can then be modeled."

Thus some tacit knowledge (the "unvoiced"), either medical or organizational, derived from individual experience in routine practice can be converted to explicit knowledge though externalization and then deliberate scientific testing and analysis. In this sense, routine practice is both evidence based and evidence creating, as chapter 6 will discuss in more detail. In this way, what was once tacit becomes explicit. The importance of this phenomenon, the conversion of tacit to explicit knowledge, is that it both helps explain the relationship between scientific, organizational, and experiential knowledge, and it explains the dynamic connection between iterative and sequential care processes in health care delivery. As we have seen (in chapter 3), care processes are experimental. However, these experiments are informal and unstructured, and consequently there is substantial caregiver-to-caregiver and patient-to-patient variation in both the "experiments" and their outcomes. This variation offers the observant clinician the opportunity to detect individual anomalous results, or patterns among observations over multiple patients—outcomes that do not fit well with accepted patterns of patient responses to tests and treatments and that serve as a source of ideas for future, more formal, scientific testing. That is, iterative care processes are an important source of hypotheses that, when confirmed though formal testing, can be developed into the protocols that are the core of sequential processes. Over time, iterative processes can beget sequential processes. Routine health care fuels the research enterprise.

In fact, the way in which science is conducted (in any discipline, and certainly in health care) reflects the stage of knowledge and the extent to which that knowledge is tacit or explicit. With low-stage knowledge, most advances depend on observations made in clinical practice rather than the deliberate manipulations of experimental conditions that characterize formal research trials, simply because when knowledge is low stage, key variables cannot be clearly articulated or completely controlled, and therefore rigorous interventional trials are impossible. In the case of infection prevention in the early nineteenth century, a key variable, "dirt," was suspected, but this variable was unmeasured (in fact, it was not measurable at the time) and largely uncontrolled (stage 2 knowledge). Semmelweiss was only able to exercise control over this variable crudely—by swapping caregivers from one ward to the other. And even this experiment did not prove conclusively that an agent being transferred on doctors' hands was the cause of postpartum infection. That would have to wait for the isolation of specific pathogens known to cause postpartum infection and the development of antibiotics with action specific to these pathogens.

There is, in health care, a well-established hierarchy of investigative techniques by which new medical knowledge is developed. Descriptive studies (case reports, case series, and cross-sectional surveys) often give the early clues about a disease's cause or the previously unidentified effects of a therapy and are used primarily for hypothesis generation.[24] Hypotheses are formally tested using some type of analytic study—case control, cohort, or interventional studies—and of these, the randomized controlled trial is considered the gold standard of proof. All of these study designs are at some level comparative. In case reports and case series, that comparison is implicit—the practitioner is comparing the particular patient under observation with the usual or expected pattern.[25] Observant practitioners thus identify cases that are, for some reason, interesting or unusual. (And often it is only the more experienced practitioners who are able to recognize that something unusual has occurred.) For example, a 1961 case report of a forty-year-old pre-menopausal woman with a pulmonary embolism (blood clot in the lung) who had been taking oral contraceptives for five weeks was the first clue that there might be an association between the drug and this otherwise highly unusual occurrence in such a young woman.[26] Similarly, the June 1981 case series describing something very unusual—five young homosexual men with *pneumocystis carinii* pneumonia—raised the possibility of a previously unrecognized disease, AIDS.

More formal analytic studies are based on explicit comparisons and deliberate manipulation of some experimental condition. The experimental method of clinical trials involves assembling groups of patients who either are different in some specified way (case-control trials) or are the same in all known ways and then deliberately rendered different by applying an intervention. When all other variations can be controlled (through either patient selection or statistical adjustment), differences in the outcomes of the experimental and control groups can be attributed to the single factor: the known difference or the deliberate intervention.

This distinction—investigative methodologies in which the basis of comparison is either implicit or explicit—depends on the stage of knowledge. At low stages, new knowledge is generated through serendipity and chance observations that rely on the expertise and judgment of the individual practitioner—the expert's ability to recognize unusual patterns or associations.[27] At higher stages, when variables can be controlled, more formal experimentation becomes possible. Controlled experimentation is only possible when some control can be exerted over the variance—that is, when knowledge is at stage 4 or above. And of course, this distinction connects directly back to the recommendations for practice (guidelines) discussed in chapter 1. Practices supported with evidence from randomized controlled trials (Muir Gray level 1, chapter 2) are explicitly encouraged through the use of such clinical process management tools as guidelines, critical pathways, and financial incentives.

However, not all knowledge inevitably undergoes this transformation—from tacit to explicit, from low stage to high stage. Social knowledge in particular tends to remain tacit because the behaviors and interactions among a group of people are hard to represent in words or symbols, whereas technical knowledge is more likely to become explicit over time.[28] This helps explain why some technical knowledge, even though codified, is hard to implement in practice. Additional tacit knowledge may be needed to not only interpret the code but to implement it.[29] A piece of music is an explicit code, but to interpret it requires the tacit knowledge of the musician. Implementation of the codified knowledge contained in a clinical guideline may involve social and organizational knowledge that remains tacit. This fact may help to explain, at least in part, some of the variation in clinical practice. For example, the evidence supporting hand washing as a method to limit nosocomial infection is very solid. However, if current hand-washing rates are anything to judge by, mobilizing all the members of a delivery organization to studiously wash their hands remains difficult. Hand-washing rates the world over are a cause for concern. Although we know a lot about the importance of hand asepsis and the impact of poor hand hygiene, we know much less about the practicalities of promoting hand hygiene among staff. For example, a group of neonatal clinicians (a team of doctors and nurses participating in a Vermont Oxford Network clinical practice improvement collaborative) rated the evidence supporting various practices intended to encourage hand washing and increase staff compliance with hand-washing guidelines (such as a "climate intervention" that included education and repetition, role modeling, monitoring, and feedback) as a 3 on the Muir Gray scale.[30]

Moreover, this transformation—health problems currently solved using an iterative process eventually become able to be solved with a sequential process—does not necessarily mean that in the long run all health care will tend to be sequential processes. The progression in health care is not an inexorable one toward ever-increasing standardization of decisions and tasks. Quite the contrary. New problems are always arising, and many of these are initially unstructured. Not only are new health problems continuing to arise naturally (for example, AIDS, SARS, and avian flu), but ironically successes of medical care are creating new problems as they are solving older ones. For example, the elderly patient with multiple, interacting chronic diseases is a relatively new phenomenon, and to some extent represents our success at treating diseases such as coronary artery disease, hypertension, and diabetes. Success in the field of cancer therapy is creating a new class of patients, the "cancer survivor," with its own set of new problems.[31] Moreover, issues that in previous generations might have been thought of as social phenomena or stages of life, such as obesity and menopause, are now considered potential health problems. And as new health problems arise, the stage of knowledge about them is initially low, and their care processes tend toward being iterative.

In summary, the knowledge bases underpinning medical care each contain knowledge that ranges from lower to higher stages. For any particular health problem, the stage of knowledge determines not only where the knowledge is to be found and how it can be expressed but also the strategies available for increasing the knowledge pertaining to that problem. Further, observations and implicit comparisons by expert practitioners in the course of their daily work generate hypotheses that can ultimately be tested by more rigorous scientific methods and explicit comparison, so that over time the body of medical science from which medical practice derives its common standards of care is updated. Knowledge stage evolves with accrued experience and explicit experimentation. What was low stage knowledge becomes higher stage.

Thus medical practice itself has the potential to be the engine of its own improvement. And day-to-day practice is one of the forces that drive this evolution. Iterative and sequential processes are related to each other inasmuch as iterative processes can generate sequential processes. When each episode of care for each patient is a set of small experiments—a turn of the scientific method—it has the potential to generate new knowledge. When the patient's care is undertaken with an iterative process, each probe and each trial of therapy results in an observation of how much the hypothesized cause and solution fit the patient. They are also a test of how good the explanation of cause is, how effective the treatment of the problem is, and how capable the delivery organization is at executing the solution to the patient's health problem. That is, as well as solving the patient's problem, little by little care processes advance our understanding of the class of problems of which this particular patient is an example. Templating tests not only the product but also the template. And in so doing, each patient potentially contributes to the accretion of understanding that raises the stage of knowledge pertaining to that problem and its solution. In this way, iterative processes can be a source of the new knowledge required to specify sequential processes, and sequential processes can be a source of new knowledge about themselves (when they are appropriate and when not) and the organization that implements them.

THE IMPACT OF KNOWLEDGE EVOLUTION:
APPROACHES TO PROBLEM SOLVING

An increase in the stage of knowledge toward greater specificity occasions a change in the way individual clinicians solve a particular problem and how the care process is operationalized. As, over time, problems become more highly structured, the way clinicians approach their solution moves from unstructured trial and error, to guided probe and learn, and finally to the simple application of codified rules and algorithms (see figure 4-2). In effect, a hierarchy analogous to that applying to investigative methods in the advance of medical science also applies to the approach to solving an individual patient's health problem. When the stage of knowledge is higher, decision making is more analytical than intuitive, and searches of the solution space are more focused.[32] At the highest stages of knowledge, a problem is solved by the application of a highly specified rule. With increasing knowledge stage, problems that were once solved through unstructured problem solving and trial and error become solvable through templating and pattern recognition, and ultimately rules application.[33]

This phenomenon is not unique to health care. The same observation has been made in manufacturing industries; during the twentieth century—starting with Frederick Taylor and Henry Ford, and the subdivision and articulation of specific tasks—production knowledge was increasingly codified, such that this knowledge became a property of the production system, not the individual worker. Studying the steel, semiconductor, and mechanical (fabrication) industries, Balconi found that tacit knowledge for production has become largely obsolete.[34] Workers, who were once essential for solving complex problems in production, have become operators of machinery that has production knowledge embedded in its software. And as in other industries, although the progression from unstructured problem solving to

FIGURE 4-2

Evolving approach to health problem solving

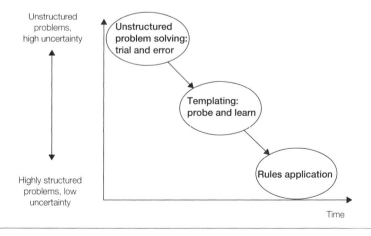

templating to rules application is a continual process, the level of knowledge for solving a particular problem changes erratically and inconsistently. It may stagnate, awaiting a new discovery or chance observation to initiate the jump from one level to the next. And thus the approach to solving a problem may remain unchanged for years. The progression represented in figure 4-2 is less gradual development than a punctuated equilibrium.

The importance of the evolution represented in figure 4-2 (and the fact that the approach to solving different problems differs) lies in what it implies for how operations are organized—what kind of workers are required and which tasks they are assigned. The shift from iterative to sequential care processes has implications for the design and control of clinical care processes, the scope of clinician practice (which type of clinician ought to be attending to which type of problem), the use of technology, the timing of care delivery, and the site in which care is delivered—put more simply, when, how, where, and by whom care is delivered. Once again, the history of diabetes treatment provides an example of the impact of increasing knowledge stage and approach to problem solving on the organization of health care services.

THE DIMENSIONS OF DESIGN: WHEN, WHERE, HOW, AND BY WHOM?

Managers designing care processes and organizations have only a limited set of design decisions available to them. They can choose their approach to managerial control from the limited set of tools described in chapter 1. And, more broadly, they can determine when and where care is delivered, how care is delivered, and by whom. The theory described above—the stage and evolution of knowledge, process, and decision—shapes the design options available for patient care, designs that will be discussed in chapters 5 and 6.

When

The primary focus of diabetic care early in the twentieth century was the acute disease and its manifestations: frequent urination and drinking, wasting, and diabetic coma. Later, as this acute disease was brought under control, focus shifted to the management of longer-term complications: peripheral vascular disease, kidney failure, and cardiac and ocular disease. Still later, focus shifted again to the management of other, secondary risk factors—for example, raised cholesterol and blood pressure. The current focus of research is on the cure of the disease, through either transplant or gene therapy. With improved understanding of the relationship between obesity and diabetes, and with an epidemic of obesity taking center stage, focus has also shifted to the prevention of the disease itself through management of its risk factors. Thus, over time, the focus of diabetes management has moved proximally in the chain below:

Disease risk factors → Acute disease → Complications
of acute disease

With increasing knowledge, the point in a disease's progression at which it is possible to intervene shifts, typically moving proximally in the above sequence. Of course, this progression occurs unevenly in medical practice; in some diseases the primary focus is on prevention, and in others it is still on symptom control. (Table 4-1 gives examples of the way uneven development of knowledge is reflected in the point at which we commonly intervene in a disease.)

The importance of the timing of intervention is its implication for the design of care processes and organizations (to be discussed in chapter 5). Different skill sets, care processes, and delivery organization designs are appropriate for primary prevention and symptom control.

TABLE 4-1

Variation in a disease's point of intervention

	Diabetes	Cervical cancer	Rheumatoid arthritis	Schizophrenia
Symptom control	Morphine	Palliative care	Pain control (nonsteroidal anti-inflammatory drugs)	Serotonergic agonists
Disease modification	Insulin	Cauterization of carcinoma in situ	First generation: gold, methotrexate Second generation: anti-TNF	
Cure	Pancreas replacement	Total abdominal hysterectomy		
Primary prevention	Obesity reduction	Human papillomavirus vaccination		

How

With increasing knowledge stage, patients' health problems are solved by applying highly specified known solutions through sequential care processes embedded in care maps and critical pathways. Decisions that must be made at various points in the care process are also highly specified, often guided by decision support technologies that specify all the components of a decision. This decision specification may take the form of a computer algorithm or be embedded in an on/off diagnostic test (of the form "if the result is A, do B; if the result is X, do Y"). Process management aims to maximize reproducibility, reliability, and efficiency and minimize variation, not to support innovation and experimentation. And with higher-stage knowledge, physicians' performance can be judged by outsiders who examine adherence to specified (evidence-based) care processes.[35] In fact, diabetes is one of the few diseases for which the relationship between process and outcome is sufficiently well understood to allow performance measurement of this kind and the use of performance measurement for these purposes. In the absence of such an evidence base, this approach to medical management is infeasible.[36]

Where and by Whom

When a patient's care uses a sequential rather than an iterative process, it can often be undertaken by less expensively trained clinicians in less specialized settings and controlled with the use of process measurement. For example, the site of diabetes care has shifted from the hospital to the outpatient clinic and finally to the patient's home (and even to his or her gym). Such a progression is typical of chronic diseases, for which the majority of care revolves not around those acute debilitating episodes of worsened disease, often carried out in an acute care hospital, but around the day-to-day activities of disease management in the patient's own home environment.

A change in the site of care is often associated with a change in the health care "worker." When knowledge is codified, it can be made widely available and accessible to less expensively trained or less experienced workers, including patients themselves. Problems can be solved by such workers following preset rules.[37] When this happens, the locus of control over an individual patient's medical care moves outward, from the core clinical professions to allied health professions, and from the practitioner to the patient. That is, with increasing knowledge and codification, decision rights devolve from physicians to technicians and patients. The situation is reversed with iterative care processes. Here caregivers are typically more expensive, and care requires the application of the tacit knowledge of experienced practitioners who are often located in centralized specialist facilities and practices.

To some extent, however, the structure of a health problem is in the eye of the beholder. What for one clinician is a poorly structured problem is for another more highly structured. Where less experienced clinicians see no discernable pattern or set of actions that might lead to the problem's solution, and thus make slow and labored decisions, seasoned experts see clearly recognizable patterns and make instantaneous and intuitive decisions. By definition, unstructured problems are ill defined, and no template exists to aid in their solution; characterizing the problem (diagnosis) and testing a solution (therapy) both require some amount of experimentation. But experienced problem solvers do not necessarily start from scratch. Although occasionally the problem solver must reason entirely from first principles (as in the first cases of AIDS), in many situations the experienced clinician has melded many variables and data points into sophisticated patterns that serve as a starting point for problem solution activities, such that the problem is not entirely new or unfamiliar to him or her.

In effect, with experience, clinicians develop their own personal set of templates and tacit rules (heuristics). Thus expert clinicians tend to make decisions rapidly and intuitively. But where the expert sees a more structured problem, the novice sees less structure; the novice laboriously applies the explicit rules he or she learned during training.[38] Hence in any given care delivery system, where and by whom care is provided are not simply determined by the stage of knowledge as an absolute; they are also influenced by the local availability of expertise.

THE DYNAMIC NATURE OF CARE

This chapter has described the way in which the knowledge used in the care process may change over time, from poorly specified and tacit to highly specified and explicit. As knowledge evolves, so does the approach practitioners can take to solving individual patients' health problems—from unstructured trial and error to more structured and directed probe and learn, and ultimately to the application of codified rules. The fundamental nature of health care as a set of problem-solving activities does not change, but the way in which these activities can be carried out does change. That is, the evolution of knowledge drives an evolution in the process of problem solving.

This evolution is ongoing. New, less well-structured problems are always arising as the burden of disease continually shifts with the advent of new diseases or new problems in old diseases. Although the universe of health problems contains problems that are unstructured, semistructured, and highly structured, any individual problem may become more structured. This transition in a problem is driven in part by learning from previous instances of the same problem. We learn how to deal with a problem through multiple episodes of dealing with individual patients with that problem. In this way, day-to-day care is the engine of its own transformation.

That caregivers daily face a set of problems requiring different approaches to their solution, and that the approach taken to solving an individual problem changes over time, has immediate implications for the design and management of health care organizations and systems. Not only are the processes for solving unstructured and structured problems different, requiring different management approaches, but the problems that are the objects of these processes change. Improving knowledge about individual health problems changes where, how, and by whom these problems can be solved—making possible the development of new health care delivery models, products, services, organizations, and businesses for the treatment of any disease—and changes the tools managers can use to exercise control over those enterprises. And the dynamic relationship between iterative and sequential care processes (the former a source of ideas for the latter) means that at its heart, day-to-day health care is a learning activity. The next chapters will examine the implications of multiple approaches to problem solving and the relationship between them for the design, management, and improvement of health care processes and organizations.

SUMMARY

The goal of the first section of this book was to develop an understanding of the fundamental nature of health care by examining the knowledge upon which patient care is based and the way this knowledge is expressed through the processes of patient care. The purpose of such a prolonged discussion, of course, is to better inform our thinking about the design and management of health care delivery organizations.

In particular, chapters 3 and 4 argued that the process by which patient health problems are solved is by its nature experimental and that its operationalization is a function of the problem being solved—unstructured problems requiring an iterative process, and structured problems a sequential one. The extent to which a health problem is structured itself depends on the stage of the underlying knowledge, where lower-stage knowledge is associated with less well-structured problems, and higher stage with more structured.

In the second section, the focus shifts to the implications of these considerations for the design of care. The central element of this discussion is the third component of a system for delivering health care: the organization. The next two chapters will outline the internal arrangements of the care delivery organization in which the different kinds of care processes take place, and show how these are shaped by the care processes themselves.

The importance of distinguishing different care processes lies in the impact that they have on the design of care delivery organizations—units, practices, or hospitals. Iterative and sequential care processes require support by very different sets of organizational structures and internal policies. Chapters 5 and 6 will discuss how care delivery organizations, either diversified or focused, should be designed to account for the two types of care processes, the dynamic relationship between them, and the changes in these processes over time.

5

Managing Care
The Design of Operating Systems

C hapter 1 described an evolution in management currently under way in the health care industry: from managing the institutions in which care takes place to managing the care itself. It argued that the outcomes of care, both positive and negative, have become the output and responsibility of the delivery organization, which is itself evolving from the context of care delivery into a "care production facility" whose primary "product" is patient relief (the cure of disease and the relief of suffering). In spite of this gradual shift in organizational focus, many current proposals for improving the efficiency and quality of care—for example, insurance plans with increased patient financial accountability, competition based on quality, and various forms of physician financial incentive—are silent on the organizational arrangements and new processes by which care should be delivered in order to realize the better clinical outcomes they promise: safe, timely, efficient, reliable, and appropriate care. Where reform proposals do address systems for delivering care, they predominantly focus on structure (e.g., integrated delivery systems), not operations.

How, then, should the complex and nuanced problem-solving care process, in its different manifestations, be managed? Is it simply a matter of motivating physicians and hospitals to try harder and do a better job (through financial or nonfinancial incentives) or telling physicians what to do (using such tools as guidelines or utilization management)? This chapter will discuss an approach to managing care—the tools available, the ways in which multiple tools are integrated, and the organizational structures and culture required to generate better clinical performance. The chapter begins with the operational importance of a distinction between iterative and sequential care processes.

THE ASSOCIATION BETWEEN PRODUCT, PROCESS, AND ORGANIZATION

The importance of differentiating two distinct processes for health problem solving lies in the different approach to their design and management, an issue that is well understood outside of health care. Writing in 1979, Hayes and Wheelwright argued that not only do products go through a life cycle—from prototype, to low-volume runs of products with variable features, to high volumes with standard features—but so too do the processes used to manufacture them.[1] Prototypes are made one at a time in a job shop, multiple related products in a product line are produced using batch processes, and long runs of highly standardized products are produced on an assembly line. Early in the product life cycle, manufacturing processes are fluid but not very efficient, capable of creating the many unique parts that a prototype might require and responding to the myriad of engineering changes that result as product developers refine their designs. The production facility is characterized by general-purpose machinery and a broadly skilled workforce. Later on, when a product and its components become highly standardized, and the product is produced in high volume, production processes tend to become much more rigid and often capital intensive (requiring specialized machinery uniquely configured for one component or product) but highly efficient. As the product evolves and matures, then, the process used to manufacture it changes. That is, there is a tight connection between the nature of the product and the type of process used to manufacture it. Much the same is true for services; the nature of the process by which a service is delivered depends on the nature of the service.[2]

Moreover, production processes do not exist in isolation from their organizational contexts. Researchers have observed that not only is there a relationship between the product and the process used to produce it, but this correlation extends to the organization in which the production process sits. The architecture of the product—the product's components and the way they relate to and interact with one another—is reflected in the architecture of the production process and the firm itself. An effective organization's subunits (departments), formal reporting relationships, and informal communication channels all coalesce around its conception of the components of its products and the relationships between them. For example, firms making cars that have drive trains, chassis, and brakes usually have drive train, chassis, and brakes departments, and these departments relate to each other in well-understood ways. This relationship is so tight, in fact, that when the architecture of the product changes, the firm may fail because it is unable to create the new product using the old process and organizational architecture.[3]

The relevance of these insights into production and service industries outside of health care is that the two problem-solving processes of care, iterative and sequential, described in the preceding chapters are so different that, as with other service processes, they may require different organizations to deliver them. At a minimum, they need different operating systems.

THE CONCEPT OF AN OPERATING SYSTEM

Chapter 3 described care as a problem-solving process. In production terms, the care process can be defined as that set of tasks and decisions that takes the "input" of a sick patient (plus some other resources, such as capital, labor, and raw materials) and converts these into a value-added "output"—namely, a patient whose health has improved. How this transformation actually happens depends on the "input" itself—whether the sick patient's problem is unstructured or structured. However, neither the iterative and sequential care processes nor the knowledge upon which they are based is free standing. They sit within a system comprising many other structures and business processes that allow them to function. Such processes include how necessary supplies and information are delivered to the physician and patient, the way that an operating room or a radiology suite is made available, and how long-term improvements in performance are conceived of and operationalized. The structures include the physical environment in which care is delivered, the workforce assembled to do the work of care, and the departmental structures used to organize staff and activities. The term *operating system* describes the configuration of all the resources and activities that come together to create a service or product.

The components of a health care operating system—the care process, the physical plant in which care is delivered, the technology and human resources used, the strategic decisions and managerial policies governing the disposition of these resources, the definition of the nature of the health care service being provided and the patient segment being served, the design and sequencing of key tasks, and the positive incentives and negative boundary conditions that shape workers' behavior—all act together to both facilitate and constrain the process by which a patient's health problem is solved. Thus an operating system represents a set of design choices (and inherent trade-offs) about what care to deliver and how to deliver it—choices that are, of course, constrained at any given time by such factors as the current state of scientific knowledge;

FIGURE 5-1

Components of an operating system

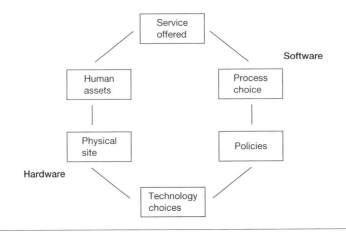

the availability of key resources, such as technology, staff, or capital; and the local regulatory environment. The design choices that define a health care operating system fall into six broad categories (see figure 5-1). The first three of these are the "software" of a care delivery organization—its design and policies—and the second three are the "hardware."

COMPONENTS OF AN OPERATING
SYSTEM: SOFTWARE

The software encompasses the range of services offered, the type of care process for delivering those services, and management policies that control and define delivery.

Scope of Services

The first group of choices pertains to the particular business the care delivery organization is (or is not) in—that is, which care the delivery organization will provide, to which patients, and what care it will not provide. Some service delivery organizations eschew particular service lines, such as mental health services, obstetrics, or pediatrics. Others specifically offer services for a particular gender (women's hospitals), age group (children's hospitals), or disease or body system (cancer centers, breast centers). Still other organizations configure themselves around a particular severity of illness rather than a specific organ system or disease. In-store clinics for example, currently experiencing rapid growth in the United States, offer care for extremely low-severity illnesses such as skin rashes and "red-eye."[4] Finally, organizations must decide which services should go together—an obvious example being the collocation of invasive cardiological and cardiac surgical services—and which should not go together but be "outsourced." For instance, originally a research laboratory and clinic, Boston's Dana-Farber Cancer Institute responded to a high-profile inpatient death due to a medication error by outsourcing inpatient care to a neighboring hospital, calculating that inpatient care was not its primary focus. Such decisions, which are essential for defining the organization's range of operations, also have the potential to be controversial. For example, one of the issues at stake during the recent controversy regarding for-profit specialty surgical hospitals in the United States was whether these hospitals, which have been accused of deliberately not providing services to complex or emergency cases, should be reimbursed in the same way as a full-service hospital (the so-called whole hospital exemption).[5] Conversely, other organizations have been criticized for providing too wide a range of services—for example, in-store clinics.[6]

Tied to the question of which services to offer is a set of choices about how "much" to offer and therefore how much spare capacity to build. Large not-for-profit urban hospitals may run near 100 percent capacity utilization (the percentage of the available capacity that is actually used), while private and for-profit hospitals tend to keep much more spare capacity so that an admitting physician—who is these institutions' primary customer—will never have to wait for an available bed. An associated set of design decisions relates to how that capacity is allocated (scheduled)—for example, by assigned block time or first come, first served.

Process Type

A second set of choices relates to the detailed way in which the chosen services will be delivered. For instance, a particular patient's care may be highly customized (a unique sequence of individually chosen tests and therapies designed in the moment for that patient and that patient alone) or highly standardized (delivered uniformly to all patients with the same or similar clinical problem). Delivery organizations differ in the extent to which they standardize or customize clinical processes—even with respect to the care of patients with the same medical problem. For many health care delivery organizations around the world, the care an individual patient receives is determined by the decisions clinical staff make on the day, and there is little attempt to plan patient care ahead of time. The focus is instead on ensuring that key resources, such as operating rooms or scanner slots, have enough capacity to meet spikes in demand (the "asset-focused" approach; see table 1-3, chapter 1). Other organizations make some attempt at standardizing care, either by creating detailed clinical pathways specifying testing and treatment types, frequencies, and sequence for a given diagnosis, or by standardizing individual components of care, such as the medication delivery process or central line placement.

The degree to which an organization standardizes care has implications for the way work is organized—the physical layout, flows of patients, information, materials, and the assignment and sequencing of tasks. In effect, organizations in which care is more customized look more like job shops, while those in which care is more standardized resemble service production lines.

Management Policies

A third set of choices surrounds the way in which resources are allocated and the care process and the behavior of staff undertaking it will be controlled and improved. These management policies comprise everything from physician incentive and pay-for-performance systems, financial and clinical performance measurement metrics, the centralization or decentralization of management authority, scheduling algorithms, and risk management practices, to departmental structure, staff and teams' role definitions, and the allocation of decision rights. It is through the definition and enactment of these policies that managers measure, control, and promote performance. These policies also define the organization's approach to improvement, either through basic science and clinical research or through some process improvement strategy embodied in such management philosophies as Total Quality Management, Six Sigma, or the Toyota Production System.

COMPONENTS OF AN OPERATING SYSTEM: HARDWARE

The software described above determines the functioning of the hardware—the physical plant and the specialized medical technologies and human resources it houses.

Human Resources

The key design choices in human resources include which individuals to hire (what specialized skill sets), what mix of staff to hire, how and how much to further train them, and how to group them into teams. Organizations vary dramatically in these choices—in the extent to which they rely on, and structure their services around, nurses, nurse-practitioners, physician assistants, junior medical staff, specialist consultants, and family members; and in the investments they make in training (some going so far as to develop their own schools for nursing and allied health professions or academies for quality improvement). These choices interact with those above to help create and maintain a particular culture within the care delivery organization.

Technology

A second set of hardware choices centers on technology and technology acquisition. This includes the amount and configuration of information technology and the activities—such as medication delivery—that it helps automate, as well as a range of large and small testing technologies ranging from scanners to bedside testing kits.

Physical Site

Finally, there are a number of choices around the physical site. Broadly, these choices fall into two groups: the location and the physical configuration of services. The former relate to where care will be delivered—in doctor's offices, in malls, in community clinics, in specialist facilities, at home, or in large diversified hospitals—and the latter to the way any individual location is laid out. Pavilion hospitals of the nineteenth and early twentieth centuries, for example, were constructed with a highly decentralized layout intended to promote airflow among the wards in order to facilitate the removal of the toxic miasma. Modern twentieth-century designs have been focused on the delivery organization's centralized expensive assets, such as operating rooms, radiological equipment, and intensive care units. More recent designs have been more "patient friendly," configured to improve the patient's experience of care.[7]

THREE KEY DESIGN ISSUES FOR
AN OPERATING SYSTEM

Importantly, the myriad choices outlined above are not independent of one another. Quite the contrary—some choices determine others and they often require difficult trade-offs. It is hard to pay surgeons on procedure volume when operating room space is extremely limited. Furthermore, managers are rarely unconstrained in these design choices. Although medical knowledge is global—the science informing care is equally available and relevant to all—the operating systems that bring that knowledge to bear upon individual patients' problems are local. They depend on the resources available locally and the regulations that determine how those resources may be deployed. Even more importantly, an operating system cannot do everything equally well. Although it is possible for an organization to meet the needs of two different sets of customers, it is hard to "perform both tasks equally well, or as well as two different organizations could that each focused its attention on the needs of a specific type of . . . customer."[8]

Successful operating systems share three important design features, discussed below. Because many operating systems in health care delivery organizations were not deliberately designed—instead they simply accreted over time—many do not exhibit these features, and require redesign if their performance is to be improved. The three key design features of effective operating systems are internal and external alignment, and a capability for dynamic change. Each implies a set of design choices for managers. One choice, for example, might be to standardize all care and business processes.[9] This choice implies many others—for example, what to standardize and how to configure all the other elements of the operating system to support this specific process choice.

Internal Alignment

Many of the managers' choices in putting together an operating system tend to go together naturally. For example, a physician pay-for-performance incentive system—in which physicians receive a bonus for meeting previously specified productivity or quality targets—requires a measurement system that reliably collects the measures upon which physicians are to be paid. If these measures are clinical outcomes—such as mortality, survival or cure rates, or quality-of-life scores—then the measurement system must collect not only the basic outcomes but all the clinical data required to appropriately risk adjust them. Moreover, the physician must have enough volume of the relevant patient type for the measurements to be reliable.[10] Similarly, the range of services provided by an in-store clinic must be consistent with the activities permitted for nurse-practitioners (who typically staff these services), the testing and therapeutic technology that can be maintained and delivered in a small kiosk, and scientific evidence upon which the highly standardized care protocols they employ are based.

When choices on one dimension do not fit with those on other dimensions, the operating system risks being unworkable. Extending in-store clinics' menus to include services for which well-accepted evidence-based guidelines do not already exist would completely change the nature of the patient–provider interaction (it could require more than ten minutes) and the training required of the professional staffing the kiosk (requiring a doctor). Both changes would destroy the clinics' basic value proposition to patients—fast and convenient care—and their revenue model. In other words, all the components of an operating system described above (the scope of services, process type, management policies, human resources, technologies, and physical site) must be aligned with and supportive of one another.

The need for internal alignment in an operating system increases the challenges of managing care. Even if the clinical problem is one that is well understood and for which the clinical strategy is well characterized (the certainty that is so alluring; see chapter 1), managing care is not simply a matter of writing and promulgating an evidence-based clinical protocol. It requires the construction of an operating system in which all the components—measures, incentives, technology, auxiliary providers, and so on—fit together well. Even though the effectiveness of hand washing in infection control is incontrovertible, hand-washing rates continue to fall well short of 100 percent. The knowledge alone does not suffice. Without the appropriate positive incentives and negative sanctions, group norms, conveniently placed cleaning fluid dispensers, and patient and provider training, adequate levels of compliance are unlikely.

External Alignment

Of course, an operating system in which all the components are well aligned internally may still not meet patients' needs. The operating system as a whole needs to be aligned with its goal (see figure 5-2). Usually, this is the patient segment it is intended to serve, and the value it intends to bring to that patient group. The lean, low-tech, highly standardized care provided by in-store clinics—which are well configured to meet the needs of patients with isolated episodes of acute, simple, and predominantly self-limiting health problems—is completely inappropriate for patients with complex, chronic, or multiple problems, even though the in-store clinic's operating system is well aligned internally. In short, there must be a match between the value that an operating system is configured to deliver and the needs and desires of the patients it serves.

Sometimes an operating system is configured to meet a goal that is less than the high-level goal of patient relief but is a key component of the care

FIGURE 5-2

Internal and external alignment

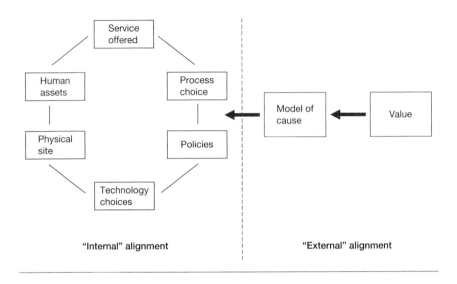

process. An operating system could be configured to specifically support only one particular phase of care, such as diagnosis. The breast cancer clinic at University of California, San Francisco Medical Center (UCSF), for example, offers its patients a same-day diagnosis and treatment-planning service. Over a four-hour period, colocated breast surgeons, radiologists, nurses, and pathologists come together to resolve (diagnose) suspicious findings from breast cancer screening. Their goal is to reach a diagnosis by determining that a biopsy is not necessary or by performing a biopsy. Patients are then triaged back to screening, to the surgeon for discussion of treatment options in the case of a cancer, or to prevention options, as appropriate.[11] This operating system is completely different from one configured to efficiently execute treatment such as elective knee replacement. It makes use of a staffing pattern (multiple specialists) and a process (joint case conferences) aimed at supporting an iterative care process that is as efficient as possible. In effect, the operating system for diagnosis (which often supports an iterative process) is not the same as that for treatment execution (frequently a sequential process).

The connection between an operating system and the specific goal or patient value it is designed to support is the hypothesis about what causes that goal or value. To match the value to the customer with the design of the operating system requires an understanding of the way in which the performance of a particular operating system creates that value, and the way in which the interactions among the operating system's various components contribute to that performance (the "model of cause" in figure 5-2). Without a sophisticated understanding of exactly those specific actions that cause patient relief, and the ways in which they must be carried out, it will be difficult to design an effective operating system for care.

In the case of UCSF's breast cancer clinic, the goal is an accurate and rapid diagnosis, and the selection of a treatment plan that is consistent with the individual woman's values and preferences; and the clinic's operating system is designed to meet that goal. In the case of acute coronary artery blockage, the goal is short "door-to-lysis" time, and emergency room operating systems are designed accordingly. It is this model of cause that is the practical connection between evidence-based medicine and operations management. The model of cause informs the operating system design that is ultimately responsible for executing it.

Of course, all this presumes that managers have a clear idea of the value they aim to bring to the patients served by their organization, a prerequisite for designing an operating system to deliver that value. An operating system can be designed to emphasize different priorities—for example, low cost, rapid response, customer service, high conformance quality, high performance quality, innovativeness, or convenience. Since no operating system can deliver all of these kinds of value, hard choices and trade-offs are inevitable. These trade-offs influence the choices in the six operating system components.

Dynamic Responsiveness

Finally, operating systems need to be dynamic. That is, they have to be capable of changing to respond to changes in their environments. In the short term, such changes might include the advent of new technology that allows something formally done in an inpatient setting to be delivered to outpatients, changes in the availability of a certain clinical professional that forces a change in staff mix, or changes in regulation. In the longer term, of course, these changes are driven by the phenomenon of evolving knowledge, and evolving technology based on that knowledge, described in the previous chapter. Chapter 6 will describe the design of operating systems that are not only flexible to such changes but designed specifically to both foment and exploit them.

AN EXAMPLE OF ALIGNMENT: ISTITUTO CLINICO HUMANITAS

Istituto Clinico Humanitas (ICH), located in the town of Rozzano about 5 kilometers south of central Milan, Italy, provides a good example of internal alignment.[12] ICH was originally constructed as a 378-bed private for-profit hospital on a greenfield site and opened in 1996. When opened it was predominately a surgical hospital. Although it was located in one of Milan's most rapidly growing areas, ICH did not offer a full range of services; it was initially without pediatric, obstetric, mental health, or infectious disease services and had only a small emergency room. Its top ten admission diagnoses (by volume) were all interventional procedures.[13] However, these procedures were all delivered with the utmost efficiency. In spite of the fact that the majority of its patients were covered by Italy's national health system (and therefore ICH was paid the same rates as a public not-for-profit hospital), the hospital turned a profit from clinical operations after only eighteen months.

The hospital was initially staffed by senior physicians, recruited from Milan's prestigious academic hospitals, who not only contributed to the young hospital's prestige but brought patient volume when they shifted to ICH. These physicians were paid a salary made up of an 80 percent fixed component and a 20 percent variable component. The variable component combined measures made at the unit level (such as the unit's overall profitability) with those at the individual doctor level (e.g., patient volume and time to completion of the medical record—required for reimbursement). In order to help physicians participate in ensuring the institution's financial performance, ICH trained physicians in cost accounting and regularly presented details of the institution's financial performance at meetings of clinicians. A second incentive was applied at the unit level; a transfer price was assessed on the unit for every bed-day used, so that physicians had an incentive both to use a bed and an operating room slot they had booked and to facilitate patient discharge from the postoperative bed.

In an attempt to ensure that surgeons were not prevented from operating by the lack of a postoperative bed, the hospital had multispecialty recovery wards—located in a ward block that was designed such that the walking distance from the medical services block, or the other wards, was minimized. Patients were routed in real time to open beds by an "operations planner" making reference to a bed availability report updated daily (but available in real time in the hospital information system). So as to ensure a nursing workforce comfortable with the challenges of managing patients from several different clinical specialties on the same ward, ICH established its own nursing school in 2000. And finally, physicians were encouraged to be available to support nursing staff and their colleagues by being offered use of the hospital's outpatient facility for their private practices—so that they did not leave the hospital to see their private patients.

The hospital distinguished itself by purchasing the latest technology, typically ahead of surrounding hospitals. The emergency room had its own dedicated radiology department and CT scanner. Rapid turnaround of diagnostic results was important at ICH. For example, echocardiograms were performed by specialist cardiologists, not technicians, who dictated their report as they performed the examination, so that reports were provided with minimal delay.

ICH's operating system—staff, training, special roles, physician and departmental incentives, location and physical design, management information system, technology choices and utilization—was set up to optimize financial performance, predominantly determined by admission rate and length of stay. By locating in a rapidly growing and underserved part of Milan, creating an attractive facility with the latest technology, hiring highly regarded senior doctors, and locating their private practices on the campus, ICH managed the admission rate. Patient throughput was enhanced by the incentives, the operations planner role, the multispecialty wards, and the specially trained nursing staff. Finally, restrictions on the range of services offered minimized the patient variability that would reduce the predictability of patient flow through the institution. In effect, all the elements of the operating system supported each other (internally aligned), and together as a system, they supported the value that ICH offered its patients: easy access to affordable, high-quality surgical care (externally aligned). Note that internal alignment such as this can be achieved not only at the level of an entire hospital, as at ICH, but equally to a small unit (e.g., Duke's congestive heart failure [CHF] clinic, discussed later) or an entrepreneurial business (e.g., in-store clinics).

However, when ICH significantly expanded its emergency room in 2003, it was suddenly faced with a misalignment between its operating system and a new patient population: complex elderly medical patients. A local shortage of long-stay beds made these patients harder to place, resulting in a dramatic increase in length of stay, blockage of elective beds, and making it harder for physicians to meet their units' performance targets. Nursing staff, predominantly trained in postoperative care, were not well prepared to care for these patients, with their myriad social needs. And the hospital's systems for managing bookings and patient throughput were not capable of expediting these patients' discharge. Although still internally aligned, ICH's operating system was no longer externally aligned.[14]

OPERATING SYSTEMS FOR ITERATIVE
AND SEQUENTIAL CARE

As ICH's experience suggests, different services and processes require different operating systems. The design of an operating system to provide resources to doctors, who provide care, is very different from that which provides care. Moreover, among operating systems designed to provide care, the configuration of an operating system for patient problems that are addressed by a sequential process, when care is orderly and reasonably predictable, is different from that required when care is provided with an iterative process, when care is unpredictable and variable. The health care delivery organization's basic design (for example, the extent of centralization or decentralization), its culture and norms, the type and mix of staff, the extent of standardization of clinical practices and decisions, the types of measures used to assess performance, and the financial and nonfinancial incentives, all differ for sequential and iterative care processes. Table 5-1 outlines some of these differences in their operating systems.

As table 5-1 makes clear, the operating systems for sequential and iterative care are very different from one another. Their basic goals differ: the

TABLE 5-1

Operating systems for sequential and iterative care

	Sequential care	Iterative care
ORGANIZATIONAL MISSION		
Value proposition	Efficient delivery of a problem solution	Evaluation and management of complex, difficult, and multiple problems
BELIEFS AND APPROACH		
Basic philosophy	Ideal exists	Ideal unknown
Approach to uncertainty	Reduced before care commences	Reduced during care
Strategy	Manage toward ideal	Discover ideal
SCOPE OF SERVICES		
Scope of services	Narrow	Diversified
Capacity utilization	Higher	Lower

TABLE 5-1 (CONTINUED)

	Sequential care	Iterative care
PROCESS TYPES		
Type of process	Sequential	Iterative
Degree of standardization	Higher	Lower
Production model	"Assembly line"	"Job shop"
MANAGEMENT POLICIES		
Organizational design	Centralized	Decentralized
Span of management control	Wide	Narrow
Physician performance measures and incentives	Process based	Outcome based
Approach to improvement	Drive out variation	Exploit variation for learning
HUMAN RESOURCES		
Idealized employee	Conformer, rule follower	Problem solver, experimenter
Motivation	Doing a repeated task well	Trying new things to see what will happen
TECHNOLOGY		
Type of technology	Specialized	General purpose
PHYSICAL SITE		
Degree of collocation	Decentralized	Centralized

reliable delivery of a well-characterized solution to a well-understood problem in the former, and the de novo characterization of the problem and development of a solution in the latter. These different goals lead to a different framing of the enterprise and its task: manage toward a well-known ideal versus discover an uncertain ideal.[15] Patient variability is less in those situations where a problem is solved through a sequential process, since all patients are largely treated in the same way because most of the uncertainty surrounding their health problem has been reduced before they enter the care delivery organization—their care is defined by the evidence-based protocol. With lower patient variability and greater process standardization, the operating system can sustain higher capacity utilization; less capacity in diagnostic testing and treatment needs to kept in reserve to deal with the unexpected. Other characteristics of the two operating systems flow from these basic differences. Tasks and decisions in sequential processes tend to be highly standardized and specified (with criteria sets and if-then statements), and thus these processes lend themselves to monitoring with process measures (rates of compliance with the specified process) and performance incentives being tied to process measures. The kinds of staff recruited to work in such organizations are often those who prefer a predictable working life. Technologies tend to be configured for a highly specific task. And so on.

Of course, the two operating systems outlined in table 5-1 are archetypes. With the occasional notable exception (see below), few pure forms of either exist in practice. Most U.S. care delivery organizations are diversified, organized around a general-purpose operating system, and not specifically optimized to execute either iterative or sequential care processes. Although they are structured largely as job shops and treat most patients as unique cases requiring customized care, they also deliver some highly standardized care (or try to). In fact, many delivery organizations' operating systems are not really systems, inasmuch as their components do not work well together in any organized way. They have not been specifically designed to deliver any particular type of care. They often have not been deliberately designed at all. Instead, they have accreted, over time, the aggregation of past capital budget allocations and technology purchases, building campaigns, and contract negotiations with payers and organized groups of nurses and doctors.

Moreover, many community hospitals are challenged to create a coherent operating system for care because they don't have direct control over some of the important elements of an operating system. Few options exist for aligning the interests of the hospital and the physicians (see chapter 7). Commonly, community hospitals in the United States contract with physicians and physician groups in order to secure patient volume and thus may not be in a position to deliberately develop a workforce that matches other elements of their operating system. Outside the United States, where hospital physicians are often salaried employees, professional politics may limit the development of well-aligned operating systems. Academic medical centers, in which physicians are salaried employees, are only now experimenting with reimbursement models that make physician incentives consistent with the rest of the operating system. Few organizations make a substantial commitment to staff training in the way Istituto Clinico Humanitas does. They typically measure financial variables but rarely tie these to clinical measures. Those clinical variables that are part of routine clinical performance measurement tend to be ones required by outside assessment organizations such as the Joint Commission on Accreditation of Healthcare Organizations (JCAHO; now called The Joint Commission). And scope-of-practice regulations influence which professionals can undertake which tasks.

Those delivery organizations with well-aligned operating systems are often those that reduce operational variability by providing care to meet the needs of special groups of patients—specialist inpatient and ambulatory surgery centers, laser eye surgery centers, wellness centers, chronic disease management programs, in-store clinics, and of course, Canada's famous Shouldice hernia hospital. Unlike diversified delivery organizations, each has its own operating system, designed specifically to provide care for a relatively homogeneous (and highly selected) group of patients and patient needs—many times by for-profit businesses seeking efficiency and productivity. These organizations have effectively segregated their patient populations—sequential care separated from iterative—thus avoiding the problem ICH faced in applying an operating system configured for one group of patients and patient needs to another very different group. This enables them to create an operating system for each. Notably, many of these organizations have chosen to focus on patient populations with less inherent variability, configured an operating system that supports a purely sequential process, and avoided the population requiring an iterative care process.

The archetypal operating systems described above anchor two ends of a spectrum—from less complex, more highly structured to more complex and less highly structured patient problems (see table 5-2). But modern health care systems provide care for many different types of health problems, each of which may be delivered by a different professional, who undertakes different work, in a different setting, sometimes governed by a standardized protocol and sometimes not, and each may be reimbursed differently. In effect, each different type of patient care requires its own operating system. Over the last two decades, new business models (e.g., disease management, in-store clinics) and professionals (e.g., case managers, hospitalists, care coordinators) have emerged to meet the needs of a particular patient group with a particular health problem using a specifically configured operating system. Each has picked off some element of care previously provided by a diversified organization.[16]

Table 5-2 shows five different classes of clinical work and their associated operating system.[17] Screening and prevention and the management of isolated self-limited conditions are perhaps the most highly standardized of clinical activities, followed closely by the management of chronic, stable single conditions such as asthma and diabetes. These are closest to the sequential end of the spectrum. Patients with multiple chronic diseases that potentially interact, and therefore require individualized adjustment or complete override of the recommendations of commonly recognized guidelines, and patients with complex, emergent, and poorly characterized conditions are closer to the iterative end.

TABLE 5-2

Common operating systems

	SEQUENTIAL ⟵				⟶ ITERATIVE
	Screening and prevention	**Simple, single, self-limited condition**	**Single, highly protocolized disease**	**Multiple, highly protocolized diseases**	**Complex, poorly protocolized diseases**
Example	Measles vaccination	Recurrent urinary tract infection (UTI) in otherwise well woman	Asthma, diabetes, some cancers, well-characterized procedures (e.g., total hip joint replace-ment, or THJR)	Common clusters of chronic conditions	Complex cancers
Predomi-nant work of care	Disease finding, social out-reach and education	Confirmation of patient self-diagnosis and provision of treatment	Reliable delivery of highly specified process	Adjustment of interacting protocols	De novo creation of unique clinical management strategy
Operating system example	Centralized screening program	In-store clinic, pharmacy-based primary care[a]	Disease management, disease-focused specialist hospitals	Primary care, inpatient hospitalist care	Asset-focused "job shop," academic medical center

Note: Although it is outside the scope of this book, it could be argued that the care delivered by each of these distinct operating systems could and should be reimbursed differently—for example, screening through bulk funding; single, highly protocolized diseases by capitation; and complex, poorly protocolized conditions through fee-for-service.

a. In-store clinics in the United States are typically kiosks located within a drugstore that provide a fixed menu of services. In the United Kingdom, an alternative model centers on pharmacists providing a wider (and less well-specified) range of primary care services.

One feature that many of the new business models in table 5-2 share is the ability to separate off the particular patient group for which their operating system is configured. In-store clinics, for example, only provide care for patients requiring a sequential process and refer all other patients to a local emergency room or a primary care practitioner. The criteria for these referrals are embedded in the highly structured protocols that are at the heart of the clinics' operating system. For organizations such as these that are able to separate different types of care, the fact that sequential and iterative care processes require such very different operating systems does not present much difficulty. In-store clinics do not have to design and run an operating system for iterative care processes. Similarly, specialist surgical hospitals that focus on one or a limited range of procedures can configure the operating system around a sequential process, especially if they do not have an emergency room. However, for health care delivery organizations that serve the needs of a diverse patient population, such a strategy is simply not feasible. They must manage sequential and iterative processes at the same time, at least within the same organization and often within the same building. If they are to exploit the benefits of fitting an operating system to the needs of a particular patient group, they must address the challenge posed by the coexistence of multiple operating systems for multiple patient populations.[18]

MANAGING SEQUENTIAL AND ITERATIVE CARE PROCESSES CONCURRENTLY

Several factors force organizations to provide both sequential and iterative care. Of course, any institution responsible for meeting the needs of a diverse population with a wide range of medical problems—some tending to the sequential end of the spectrum in table 5-2, and some to the iterative end—is in this position; this includes, for example, those institutions that are the sole provider in an area or those that have been assigned accountability for a defined region. Such organizations include critical access hospitals in the United States and many district hospitals or regional health authorities in countries with a national health system.[19]

Beyond the diversity of needs within a large population of patients, the requirement to provide both sequential and iterative care also may apply to the same patient. As figure 5-3 represents, uncertainty surrounding care—what care to provide and how to provide it—is not uniformly distributed throughout an individual patient's care process. It is likely to be highest during the diagnostic phase, shown at the left of figure 5-3, and less during treatment execution, when the patient's condition is under control and stable and his or her health, hopefully, returned. In those conditions for which multiple potential treatments are available, and in those cases where patient preferences play an important role in treatment selection, uncertainty is once again increased while treatments are being evaluated and one selected.

For any patient for whom figure 5-3 is a representation of the time distribution of the uncertainty surrounding his or her care, the early portion of

FIGURE 5-3

The distribution of uncertainty throughout a patient's care

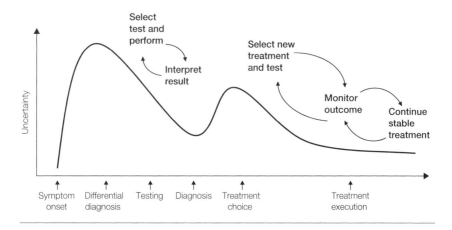

care—diagnosis and treatment selection—tends toward an iterative process, and the latter tends toward a sequential one.[20] And while test selection and interpretation are often not protocolized, test execution—for example the actual placement of a central line—may be. Improvements in performance can be realized by specifying exactly *how* a test (e.g., central line placement) or therapy should be carried out, even though it may be more difficult to exactly specify *when* such a test or therapy should be used.[21] Thus within the episode of care of any complicated patient are components that more closely resemble iterative care and others more akin to sequential care. And the delivery organization must be competent at both. Of course, those organizations mentioned above, with internally well-aligned operating systems, have often chosen to focus on the right-hand side of the uncertainty distribution in figure 5-3. Examples of such organizations include laser eye surgery centers or elective surgical hospitals, which treat conditions for which the diagnostic and treatment selection uncertainty is relatively easy to resolve, or has already been resolved inasmuch as diagnosis and treatment selection have been completed before the patient is admitted for a procedure.

Finally, the same patient may present the need for a different care process at different points in time, either because the single patient suffers from multiple conditions simultaneously, some requiring an iterative process and some a sequential process—the cancer patient who needs an elective hip replacement, for instance—or because the stable patient has precipitously developed a serious complication. For all these reasons, health care delivery organizations that have not so restricted their range of services that they only provide highly standardized care to homogeneous patient populations must be able to support both iterative and sequential care processes.

In practice, two dominant strategies exist for managing these two types of care process concurrently—separating and integrating—each with its own advantages, disadvantages, and unique challenges.

SEPARATING SEQUENTIAL AND ITERATIVE CARE PROCESSES: THE HOSPITAL WITHIN A HOSPITAL

The "separating" strategy involves sorting a heterogeneous population into multiple, more homogeneous subpopulations; but instead of rejecting those patients who are not a good fit for the organization's operating system—an accusation leveled at for-profit specialist surgical hospitals and a design feature central to the operation of in-store clinics—the organization runs multiple separate operating systems, each specifically configured to meet the needs of a particular subpopulation.[22] In its simplest form, this means one operating system for patients whose care can be highly standardized (a sequential process) and one for those requiring customized care (an iterative process), sometimes termed a *hospital within a hospital* (or *plant within a plant* in the operations literature).[23]

The rationale for this operational design dates to the work of Skinner on operational focus. Skinner noted that "simplicity, repetition, experience, and homogeneity of tasks breed competence."[24] Separating unique sets of linked tasks, and thereby limiting the number of organizational routines, allows the "work force and management to become effective and experienced in the task required for success." Operational focus can be achieved either by focusing the entire organization on a limited set of products or services (for example, disease- or body system–specific specialist surgical hospitals) or by focusing one unit within an organization on a limited range of activities (the hospital within a hospital).

Although not completely uncontroversial, the evidence for the performance benefit of operational focus is quite compelling.[25] For example, McLaughlin et al. found that freestanding outpatient surgery centers performed better than hospital-based outpatient surgery services on a range of measures.[26] Similarly, Huckman and Zinner found higher performance in clinical trials, in terms of both the output and productivity, conducted in dedicated clinical trial centers, compared with traditional (unfocused) hospital patient care units. The challenge in such research is to differentiate the benefits of focus from the effects of increased volume (which allows investments in specific processes and technologies), increased learning (from repetition), and risk selection (of patients into a focused delivery setting). However, even after accounting for the effects of these three and other possible causes of improved performance, the benefits of reducing the number and scope of tasks persist.

Case Example: Congestive Heart Failure Care at Duke

Duke University Medical Center's congestive heart failure service is an example of the plant-within-a-plant approach.[27] Duke's CHF service essentially ran two production lines, one for patients whose clinical course was unfolding predictably and one for unstable patients or those requiring specialized care (represented schematically in figure 5-4). The former was run by nurse-practitioners (NPs), and the latter by cardiologists. Patients could enter the service either during an inpatient admission for CHF or by being referred from primary practice. On admission, each patient was jointly evaluated by a cardiologist and a nurse-practitioner and then assigned to one line or the other.

FIGURE 5-4

Separating iterative and sequential processes

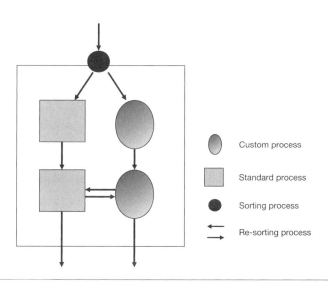

○ Custom process

▢ Standard process

● Sorting process

⟵ Re-sorting process

Duke's operations design comprised four key components:

1. *Standardized clinical process.* This sequential process centered on a detailed and highly standardized clinical management protocol—jointly developed by the service's cardiologists and nurse-practitioners—that guided the work of the nurse-practitioners. This was a protocol, not a guideline (see "The Central Role of the Guideline in Managing Care," chapter 1); for example, it contained detailed instructions on drug and dose choices, relevant clinical measures that were to be tracked, the levels these measures were expected to attain, and decision rules for managing deviations in the clinical measures.

2. *Customized clinical process.* This process was the more familiar iterative process of diagnostic evaluation and treatment testing. Cardiologists worked up and treated each patient individually for diseases such as conduction abnormalities and interventions such as AICD (automatic implantable cardioverter-defibrillator) placement.

3. *Sorting process.* The sorting process occurred on entry to the CHF service and was undertaken by the cardiologist and the NP at the intake visit. An important purpose of this joint meeting was to determine "to which production line was the patient best suited." As both the cardiologist and the NP had been involved in the development of the protocols used by NPs to guide patient management in the standard line, they both had a very clear idea of the care each patient would be getting and were therefore well able to judge whether the standard line would be appropriate for the patient. This was such an important decision that it was left to the most highly trained (and expensive) team.

4. *Re-sorting process.* To guard against the possibility of error in the sorting process, and to accommodate unexpected changes in a patient's condition during care or unexpected response to therapy, it is essential to be able to shift patients back and forth from one line to the other.[28] Duke's design accomplished this in several ways: (1) the NP's protocol contained embedded criteria for referral out to the cardiologists; (2) the NP and the cardiologist jointly reviewed each patient on the NP track every fourth patient visit regardless of the patient's progress; and (3) the service's culture was highly supportive of nurses informally referring patients out of the standard pathway (speaking up).[29]

The advantages of such a design are that it accommodates all patients and does not necessitate that those patients for whom the operating system is not well configured be referred to another provider organization. It is flexible to the changing needs of individual patients, and it has the potential to free up specialist time (inasmuch as the cardiologists at Duke do not need to see the stable patients quite so frequently). However, this operations design demands not only a substantial investment in setup—developing and testing the protocols and performance measures—but an underlying organizational culture of collaboration and teamwork across disciplines that, at least in some organizations, have in the past viewed themselves as competitors. This is especially important when managing the interface between the two lines, particularly when they make demands on the same resources (see below). Moreover, Duke's design does not cover the entire spectrum of uncertainty represented in figure 5-3. The NPs' work largely begins after the diagnosis of congestive heart failure has been made and esoteric causes of this condition, that might warrant cardiologist evaluation and treatment, have been ruled out. That is, the patient's care before entering the clinic has been undertaken through an iterative process.

In this design the ability to re-sort is pivotal. It guards against potential damage caused by a mismatch between the patient (and his or her needs) and the operating system in which the patient's care is delivered. Equally importantly, a "re-sort" is a key piece of information for performance improvement. Rather than simply being an annoyance (or "failure"), as it is often thought of, a re-sort is in fact the result of an explicit test of the operating system and its ability to meet a particular patient's needs. Failure to capture and learn from re-sorts risks limiting the performance improvement potential of a hospital-within-a-hospital design. The importance of, and approach to, capturing such information systematically is further discussed in chapter 6.

MANAGING THE INTERFACE BETWEEN
ITERATIVE AND SEQUENTIAL CARE PROCESSES

Although limiting the range of clinical activities by focusing, and meeting the needs of a heterogeneous population by delivering care in a hospital within a hospital, can improve performance, realization of the potential benefits of this operations design rests on successfully addressing two significant management challenges, both linked to the relationship between the hospital within a hospital and the rest of the hospital. The first pertains to shared resources. Istituto Clinico Humanitas provides an example of some of the possible problems.

When ICH expanded its emergency room, its operating system was no longer appropriately configured to manage an entirely new group of patients (i.e., it was not externally aligned). The hospital responded by creating a hospital within a hospital (an ER hospital)—three new wards dedicated to patients admitted through the ER—with the aim of creating a different operating system for emergency patients and keeping them separate from the operating system focused on elective surgical patients. Hence the new wards were physically separate from the elective hospital in an adjacent building, staffed independently (their own physician and nursing staff), and had their own dedicated resources (for example, a separate radiology suite). However, complete separation was not feasible. It was not economically viable to replicate a full-service hospital within these three wards. ER patients occasionally, and unpredictably, demanded some highly specialized services that were only available in the elective hospital—in particular, inpatient consultations from specialists who were committed full-time to the elective services. Because the physician incentive structure remained unchanged—physicians' variable compensation attached to measures of unit productivity and profitability— there was no financial incentive for specialists to provide more than the occasional voluntary courtesy consultation to patients in the ER hospital. Moreover, on those occasions when ER patients did spill over into the elective hospital—either because the ER hospital was full or because a consulting specialist preferred to transfer the patient to his or her own area—as expected, they tended to reduce the productivity in the elective hospital.

Competing demands on shared resources can extend beyond specialist consultations. An academic hospital in Pennsylvania boasts a highly efficient orthopedic service that largely focuses on delivering standardized care to elective arthroplasty patients. This is a highly productive and profitable practice that functions like a hospital within a hospital with its own operating system: its own preadmission testing area and dedicated anesthetic and operating rooms, standardized preoperative and operative processes, team configuration, and finances. However, because the practice is so successful, and busy, it places substantial demands on a multitude of shared resources such as space, other preadmission testing services, operating room staff, central sterile supply services, trainees, and investment capital. The institution's inability to resolve the competing demands of this focused practice and the rest of the orthopedic service has led to open conflict among the surgeons, and between the surgeons and the hospital administration.

The second management challenge relates to the interface between the custom and standard "production lines." Both the Pennsylvania hospital and

ICH are trying to keep their two systems as separate as possible, and their problems stem in part from an inevitable, and irreducible, commingling of patients and services. In Duke's model, however, the interface between the clinic within a clinic and the rest of the institution is intentionally porous. Patients are supposed to move back and forth between the two lines with ease as their clinical condition demands. Indeed, this is part of the value of Duke's operations design. Because standard and custom care are in reality ends of a spectrum (see table 5-2, earlier), with many patients and their problems falling somewhere in between, the ability to flexibly move patients from one production line and operating system to the other and back again is an essential component of Duke's design.

However, transfer between operating systems does not necessarily occur naturally; ensuring that it is triggered precisely and occurs seamlessly requires specific effort. Operating systems for standard and custom work not only differ in the design of their processes and the allocation of tasks, but they also are associated with very different organizational cultures—to such an extent that switching between them can be difficult.

The loss of the space shuttle *Columbia* is a tragic example of how difficult it can be for an organization to rapidly switch operating modes.[30] After so many years of successful launches, NASA had almost come to treat space flight as routine. Staff framed their enterprise in production terms, rather than as a research and development program, as had been the predominant frame in the early years of the Mercury, Gemini, and Apollo programs.[31] Indeed, as far back as 1972 President Nixon referred to the shuttle program as "routinizing" space travel, and in 1982 President Reagan announced that the "fully operational" shuttles would "provide routine access to space."[32] The operational frame led NASA to become preoccupied with schedules and deadlines, and, after reports of a foam strike, to analyze requests for satellite imagery of possible damage to the shuttle vehicle in terms of their possible impact on the turnaround time for the next launch.[33] Of course, conformance to specifications and attention to routines and schedules is entirely appropriate in production settings (and for predictable sequential processes). However, the days that followed the first detection of the foam strike were not routine. When responding to an ambiguous threat—a signal that may or may not portend a bad outcome—an alternative approach is called for.[34] Managers must amplify the threat, treat it as a real threat, and initiate a response—even though the threat may later turn out to be a false alarm—that draws upon previously developed expertise in rapid problem solving under conditions of both uncertainty and time pressure. When under threat, the organization will have to

rely on problem-solving techniques that employ small sample sizes, simula-
tions, back-of-the-envelope calculations and "thought" experiments—not the
approach to data collection and analysis usual during routine production
work, especially in a science-driven organization.

Of course, to be effective, this alternative approach to problem solving
has to be initiated. The *Columbia* shuttle disaster demonstrates how difficult
it is to make the transition from one mind-set to another. Had NASA been
able to initiate a response to the threat posed by the foam strike—by rapidly
diagnosing the threat and searching for an effective solution—as it had been
in the case of the Apollo 13 crisis, the outcome might have been different.[35]
But, in the case of the *Columbia*, the search for a diagnosis and a solution
was not even initiated. Like all organizations facing an ambiguous threat,
NASA downplayed the threat posed by the grainy film of yet another foam
strike. Individual cognitive biases (especially the confirmation bias that
blinds people to potentially disconfirming observations), failures of team
design and functioning (that made it difficult for individuals to speak up),
fragmented organizational structures (with rigid communication channels),
and the data-driven culture of a scientific organization (with its high burden
of proof) all conspired to decrease the likelihood that the ambiguous threat
would be treated as a true threat. An organization's natural response to an
ambiguous threat is to downplay the threat and wait and see, in effect using
the passage of time as the primary diagnostic search strategy.[36]

Clinicians and health care delivery organizations are prone to the same
trap. Threats to patient well-being are often ambiguous, and the clinical status quo seductive. Initiating an alternative response to solving the patient's
problem, by escalating it to the level of an emergency and changing care from
sequential to iterative care, is often delayed far too long. For example, an
observational study of ninety-one consecutive adult patients with noncardiac
diagnoses transferred to the ICU found that 62 percent were transferred
more than four hours after objective clinical criteria identified a problem
warranting an escalation in the site of care—a transfer from one operating
system (the ward) to another (the ICU). This delay was associated with a significant increase in morbidity and mortality.[37] Sachs's detailed analysis of a
recent fetal death in a thirty-eight-year-old low-risk woman admitted for
elective delivery describes similar phenomena to the *Columbia* case at the
root of a failure to escalate.[38] Although the multiple successive signs of
the worsening condition of the mother and fetus (rising maternal blood pressure, falling fetal heart rate) were clear, the threat that they represented to
mother and child were not fully appreciated by several clinicians who came

in contact with the patient. And once they were appreciated, the resident in question did not seek additional help, even though senior obstetricians were at hand and departmental policy instructed the chief resident to call the director in cases such as this.[39] Thus at several points throughout the night, in spite of signs that the labor was going badly, it was allowed to continue, without the development of a contingency plan or clear criteria for action—the same wait-and-see orientation to action that characterized NASA's response to the foam strike video.

The practical difficulty of shifting from one problem-solving mode to another is important because the porosity of the interface between standard and custom care depends on the ability to identify and respond to sometimes vague signals (and ambiguous threats) that the patient needs care delivered in an alternative operating system. The success of Duke's approach to separating standard and custom care depends on the organization's capability to identify and respond to ambiguous threats—that is, staff and management's skill at identifying and responding to these kinds of threats. It is not enough to simply design two processes, task sets, and operating systems. The interface between them needs to be actively managed so as to avoid the risk that patients will languish in one site of care long after another has become more appropriate. And this means creating a culture and management style appropriate to the care of the particular class of patients as well as the other elements of the operating system.

In practice, there are several mechanisms for triggering the transfer of a patient from one specialized operating system to another.[40] Duke's CHF clinic employs three of these: explicit criteria that indicate when the patient should be transferred to another operating system (at Duke these are embedded into the nurse-practitioner managed protocols), a group process (in Duke's case, a regular meeting of the physician and the nurse-practitioner to determine whether the patient is still appropriately placed), and a culture that supports speaking up about current or impending anomalies or problems. Of course, the process of transferring the care of the patient from one production line to another at Duke is made easier because (unlike NASA) the clinic is small and the colocated staff members have had time to develop a relationship and an implicit understanding of each other's roles. Larger organizations tend to rely on formal triggers. For example, in two hospitals affiliated with the University of Melbourne, Australia, that have deployed medical emergency teams (also called rapid response teams), a call to the team is initiated when one of several explicit criteria, posted on the wall in each ward, is met. These criteria include not only clinical measures, such as a heart rate less than 40 or greater than 130 beats per minute, but also the more general "staff member is worried about the patient."[41]

In conclusion, addressing the need to provide custom and standardized care—iterative and sequential processes—concurrently by segmenting them is not simply a matter of implementing a protocol or care pathway in a general services unit. To be effective, this strategy requires creating two complete operating systems— with all the hardware and software components discussed above—and actively managing the interface between them.

INTEGRATING SEQUENTIAL AND ITERATIVE CARE PROCESSES

An alternative strategy to segmenting a heterogeneous population and running different operating systems for those patients requiring sequential care and those needing an iterative care process is to integrate custom and standard elements of care in the same operating system and thus use the same operating system for the entire episode of care. This option—which is facilitated by modern information technology—in effect means inserting islands of standardization into an otherwise customized care process.[42] Boston's Beth Israel Deaconess Medical Center (BIDMC) provides an example of this approach.[43]

Case Example: Information Systems at Beth Israel Deaconess Medical Center

The Beth Israel Deaconess Medical Center is a 585-bed medical center with a long history of clinical computing dating back to the early 1960s. Since its experiments with patients interacting with computers and the early development of a unified patient database, the BIDMC has been using information systems to both support the work of health care and manage the care itself—largely developing information systems and applications in-house rather than purchasing them from outside vendors.[44] Like many institutions, the BIDMC has been using computerized prescription order entry as a way of increasing both the reliability and the safety of medication delivery (for example, through the avoidance of transcription errors and inappropriate doses). But the BIDMC has also developed several other custom applications—all of which draw data from its central database and present these data in different ways for different applications—to manage various aspects of clinical care and support different parts of a patient's course of care in the institution. These applications fall into four broad categories:

1. *Workflow support.* This is a set of tools intended to make it easier and more convenient for the physician and nursing staff to execute their daily tasks. Foremost among these is an emergency department (ED) dashboard that operates much like an airport arrivals and departures board. The status of each patient in the ED—where the patient is; which tests, therapies, or resources (e.g., an inpatient bed) have been ordered; the progress of those interventions (sent, awaiting results, results in, patient awaiting transfer, etc.)—is displayed and updated in real time. These data help the clinical staff expedite the care of patients in the ED and ensure that no patient is left waiting for an evaluation or transfer. The physician order entry (POE) system provides each physician with similar information relating to the status of orders the physician has written—for example, whether tests ordered have been collected or processed or the results are ready, and whether ordered drugs have been approved.

   An analogous set of applications in the online medical record (OMR) assists physicians in their work by organizing information (displaying the daily schedule and associated reminders, keeping "to do" lists, reporting test results, highlighting abnormal results) and making it easy to execute those physician tasks that commonly follow the receipt of a new piece of information, such as sending a letter to a patient, referring a patient to another physician, or reminding the physician to revisit an issue in the future. Tests or therapies that are normally ordered together are displayed together, and the POE system includes information about an order's status (ordered, collected, results ready). In the ED, POE, and OMR applications, the goal is to ease the work of medical practice by providing information about the work to be done and the status of the work in progress.

2. *Information provision.* A second set of applications provides the physician with information about individual patients and the diseases from which they are suffering, thus ensuring that the physician has all the necessary information available to her when she is making a clinical decision.[45] These tools draw in information traditionally not available to physicians during the course of their working days. Not only are patient's medical data and the usual test

results and relevant ranges displayed in the OMR, but the POE system also displays insurance status and cost data. Additionally, the POE system provides a link to relevant review articles pertaining to the management of the disease for which the physician is ordering a therapy (linked to the patient's problem list), and e-mails (or pages) an alert to the physician when an abnormal result is posted.

3. *Decision support.* A third set of applications manipulates the raw information provided to physicians. These decision support tools make suggestions and provide specific advice. As in most clinical IT systems, the BIDMC's POE system undertakes background checks of drug dose choices and makes drug–drug and drug–patient inter-action checks. And while the design of the OMR aims to manage the work of test ordering, it also provides evidence-based criteria for the use of certain high-cost or high-risk tests and calculators that help the physician determine whether the specific patient meets the criteria for the test.

4. *Decision control.* Finally, some of the applications not only support physicians' decision making by manipulating key pieces of information; they also actively limit physicians' choices of tests and therapies and occasionally mandate certain decisions. Thus while the POE system provides a variety of drug alerts, the majority of which can be overridden, it also blocks some orders— for example, when the patient has a strict contraindication recorded or when the dose ordered is above a previously specified high-dose limit. These blocks can only be overridden by making direct application to a senior clinician, such as a chief of service. Short of disallowing specific clinical actions, the system further controls decision making by restricting physicians' menu of choices. Through a contract with a private company and one of the institu-tion's major payers, the system checks each high-cost radiology test order against a rule set to estimate the most cost-effective test for the specific patient and indication. When a physician orders a test on a patient insured by the payer, the order is imported into the company's rules engine, and the physician is presented with a rank-ordered list of the most affordable, most appropriate, and safest tests. A test ordered from this list is automatically authorized by the payer.

Several features of this group of four sets of applications are notable. First, the sequence from workflow support to information provision, to decision support, to decision control represents an increasing level of management control over the details of patient care. Going up this "scale," the function of each set of applications depends on increasing amounts of standardization and specification of the decisions and tasks of clinical care to be effective. Moreover, physician discretion, in what tests and therapies can be ordered, is progressively (if subtly) reduced. Workflow support and information provision applications make it easier for doctors to do what they have done previously (albeit with less convenience sometimes—physicians often find it takes longer to complete a task on a computer than on paper), but impose no or minimal constraint on physician decision making and behavior.[46] Decision support tools use the timely delivery of scientific knowledge—through an algorithm—to the moment that a physician is making a choice or mobilizing a resource to influence, but again not to constrain, a clinical decision. But the tools of decision control—high-dose limits, mandatory procedures, and strict formularies—constrain clinical staff by explicitly specifying which behaviors and decisions are acceptable, and authorizing them.

Second, these tools are not applied equally throughout a patient's inpatient stay. Because the information system allows the BIDMC detailed and real-time access to the process of care, it can use the applications in different ways and at different points in the care process to manage care (see figure 5-5). Those applications that depend on high levels of standardization of decisions and tasks are preferentially used in the phases of care when the uncertainty is less—the execution of test choices and treatment decisions. Information provision and decision support applications are used to influence test and treatment selection decisions, when uncertainty is higher and no single best choice can be specified ex ante and imposed routinely. And workflow support applications, which impose no specific clinical choices, are applied throughout the patient's stay. As the uncertainty surrounding the care of any individual patient reduces over the duration of an episode of care, managerial tools predicated on higher levels of standardization and specification become more applicable (i.e., to the right in figure 5-5). Many of the elements of the BIDMC's information system are not unique to this institution: order entry, drug allergy and interaction checking, and so on. What is notable here, however, is the way in which, as a group, they have been deployed to differentially manage each of the diverse aspects of the care process.[47]

The BIDMC's carefully designed suite of information system applications has allowed it to manage the custom and standard elements of care, not

FIGURE 5-5

Using information systems to manage care at the BIDMC

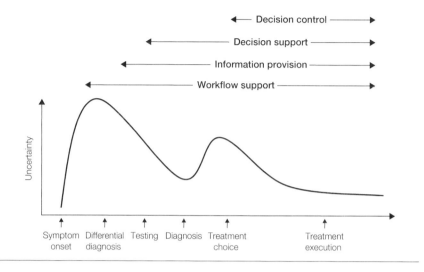

by separating them and assigning them to two different operating systems, as did Duke, but by employing a single operating system capable of managing care according to whether it needs to be customized or can be standardized. Such a system has several advantages. It allows appropriate levels of standardization to be delivered to all patients—targeted at those points in the care where standardization is possible and appropriate. For example, even though the choice of therapy in a given patient circumstance may not be able to be standardized, the way in which a therapy, once chosen, is delivered may be. This means that no patient's care is truly "customized." Even patients in the Duke model, who would be receiving customized care in one of the two production lines, are also subject to standardization where possible. Furthermore, whereas in the hospital-within-a-hospital model, sorting occurs after diagnosis, the BIDMC model also facilitates management of the diagnostic phase of care. The nurse-practitioner pathway at Duke begins once the nature of the patient problem has been determined (and in many cases after the iterative care process is over). The BIDMC system is highly flexible inasmuch as it does not depend on knowing the nature of the patient's problem in advance. And the care of small groups of patients, for which it may be hard to justify creating a hospital within a hospital, can nonetheless be managed.

Although such an approach is highly flexible, with the advantage of accommodating the care of any and all patients within the same operating system, it is not without its own problems. First, because it relies so heavily on an advanced information system, it is potentially very expensive. Boston's Beth Israel hospital has a long and storied history of clinical computing and over the years has developed a significant capability in information system design and implementation. Few organizations have longevity of experience with clinical IT as has the BIDMC or Utah's Intermountain Healthcare.

Second, this approach can feel very intrusive for physicians who may view it as a threat to their clinical autonomy. Implementing such a system is a substantial change management challenge, which the BIDMC has addressed in part by developing many of its key applications in-house, working closely with practicing physicians and designing applications to fit with local physician expectations and patterns of practice. Those institutions that develop an IT system to facilitate care management through the strategic acquisition of vendor systems have to undertake a significant program of communication with and education of frontline practitioners if outright physician revolt, as occurred at Cedars-Sinai Medical Center in 2003, is to be avoided.[48] This task is particularly demanding with a voluntary medical staff.

Two factors influence the success of an integrating approach. The first is the impact of the system on physician workflow. As already noted, the BIDMC information system is carefully designed to facilitate physician work and to fit into familiar routines of clinical practice. The insertion of standard processes into the day-to-day flow of care is triggered precisely and occurs seamlessly so as not to interfere with physician workflow. Computerized physician order entry systems have the potential to increase physician work—many practitioners still find that scribbling a prescription by hand remains quicker and easier than entering an order into a computerized system. Being forced to scroll through screen after screen in order to execute a task that was previously simple infuriates physicians, particularly in an era in which they perceive so many more demands on their time. To address this issue, successful managers devote considerable energy to minimizing the impact of the information system on workflow, by creating intuitive interfaces that physicians find easy to navigate, reducing unnecessary steps, and automating some steps that physicians used to have to undertake by hand (such as visit coding or composing standard letters). Such interfaces place all the tools a physician is likely to need in the same place exactly at that point in the workflow when they are likely to be needed.

The second important design issue relates to the rules that are embedded in an information system.[49] At their most fundamental level, clinical IT systems function by either stopping a physician from doing something, automating something that a physician would otherwise do, or suggesting a particular clinical choice or action.[50] All of these actions derive from an underlying set of rules; such rule sets define what is considered a drug–drug interaction, when and how an appropriate alert will be sent, the parameters of dosage limits and the way in which a dose is to be modified to account for other drugs or medical conditions, and the clinical circumstances under which a test should be ordered. Often such rules are opaque to physicians using a system, either because they are simply inaccessible within the information system, or because they are proprietary to a vendor. Physicians' lack of confidence in the rules engine underlying an information system significantly limits a system's ability to effectively insert standardized processes into the flow of care. At the BIDMC this issue has been addressed by vesting oversight of the embedded rules with the relevant department, and making it clear—in real time as a physician is using the system—specifically who should be called to discuss any limits being placed on him or her.[51]

Thus, even though its operating system design does not create a standardized patient pathway (in advance of a patient needing care, as at Duke), the BIDMC's approach does not remove the need to plan care carefully in advance. Each embedded decision rule, criteria set, and standard order set needs to be planned and validated by the clinical staff to whom it will eventually be applied. Indeed, this has been one of the BIDMC's strengths; because its applications have been developed in-house, the IT group has been able to test each application on the staff who will actually be using it.

CONCLUSION: DESIGNING OPERATING SYSTEMS

This chapter has proposed a broad approach to the design of the operating systems that support care processes that attempts to account for differing processes of care ranging on a spectrum from iterative to sequential. Central to this approach is the creation of an integrated, organization-level operating system for care delivery—comprising a defined scope of services; specific human, technological, and physical resources; a process design and organizational culture; and a set of managerial policies—that defines, supports, and manages the work of medical care (the sequence and timing of tasks and decisions most likely to create positive patient outcomes). On their own, individual components of this operating system—for example, a set of technological resources or clinical instructions, or a payment system—are likely insufficient to generate reliably high quality and efficient care.

In many organizations, such systems have not been deliberately designed to meet the needs of the population of patients the organization serves. This chapter has described two essential design considerations for care delivery systems. The first is fit: a care delivery organization designed such that its components align with, and support, each other and such that the care system as a whole aligns with the patients' needs. And the second is flexibility: an operating system simultaneously capable of flexibly meeting the needs of different groups of patients and the different needs of an individual patient.[52] To manage care is not simply to provide or restrict access to a set of technological resources, or to create a set of instructions for clinicians, or to modify a task-based physician reimbursement system. More and more, it is to design, create, manage, and update complex systems of care delivery—comprising multiple internally and externally aligned operating systems—one organization at a time.

In spite of this being a substantial managerial task in itself, it is not the end of the design challenge. An important subtext to the discussion of fit and flexibility is misfit: misalignment between the individual patient and the care process or operating system. This chapter discussed an approach to coping with such misalignments. The next will discuss an approach to exploiting and learning from them.

6

Evidence-Creating Medicine
Designing for Learning

Designing and managing well-aligned care delivery operating systems addresses only part of the modern health care manager's challenge and fails to address a key problem: the knowledge required to treat patients—both scientific and organizational—is both incomplete and in continual flux. Not only does deliberate and structured scientific inquiry generate new knowledge with the potential to reshape medical practice at a dizzying rate, but the experimental nature of routine medical practice—more noticeable when the stage of knowledge is lower and care processes are iterative—is itself a fertile source of new approaches to curing disease and relieving suffering.

Although the vast majority of these day-to-day experiments yield no more than a solution to the individual patient's health problem, uniquely configured to that patient and his or her context,[1] occasionally they generate broader and more generalizable insights into a disease, a treatment, or a way of organizing health care services (see chapter 4). Each patient interaction has the potential to generate new knowledge about what works and what does not. Increasing process specification and the elucidation of second-order variables (see table 3-1, chapter 3) often arises from practice.

Unfortunately, such knowledge from practice usually remains tacit, appropriated only by the individual practitioner (and sometimes the patient) who makes the original observation. The practitioner translates this new medical knowledge into his or her own professional expertise, and new organizational knowledge into an ability to "work the system." In neither case is the knowledge captured and disseminated in any systematic way. In fact, a study by Tucker and Edmondson found that fully 93 percent of all problems identified and solved by nurses during their daily work were not elevated to a level in the organization where a more generalized solution could be found, tested, and implemented.[2] The new learning by the individual was lost to the group.

This chapter discusses the design of care delivery organizations that generate, capture, disseminate, and implement new knowledge derived not from the medical literature but from patient care—evidence created from medical practice itself. It will address four related concepts: (1) learning about the patient and about the disease that arises from routine care, (2) the central roles of anomalies or variations from what is expected in this learning, (3) the creation of innovations based on this learning, and (4) the design of organizations that systematically capture the learning. It will argue that the act of routine care has the potential to create and capture new evidence about what to do to solve a particular problem and how to do it—new evidence upon which future practice can be based. In effect, routine care is not only evidence based but evidence creating.

INNOVATION FROM PRACTICE

Medicine has had a long tradition of innovation and insight gained from routine medical practice. The history of medicine is replete with serendipitous observations. The elucidation of mechanisms of disease and therapies through science is a relatively new phenomenon. For centuries empirical therapy was the mainstay of medicine—tea from cinchona bark used to treat fever in Africa (which was usually caused by malaria) and foxglove used to treat heart failure; later, these were found to contain the drugs quinine and digitalis, respectively. Even in modern times, long after the establishment of scientific medicine, observation of practice has been an important source of medical innovation.

The sedative thalidomide is a particularly good example of an important medical insight deriving not from explicit and formal experimentation but from observations made in practice. Thalidomide was synthesized in Germany in 1953 and tested in humans between 1954 and 1957; it was first marketed there in 1957 under the trade name Contergan.[3] As was common in Europe at the time, drug "testing" involved introduction into clinical practice and surveillance by physicians, who reported on adverse outcomes they observed.[4]

Suspicions about thalidomide's teratogenic potential arose fairly quickly, especially in Germany, where, as the result of a successful marketing campaign, the drug was widely used. Contergan was initially used as a sedative for the first two to three years; then pregnant women started taking it as an antiemetic. By the early 1960s, some seven hundred thousand German patients (including pregnant women and children) were on the drug. Its use in children earned it the nickname "West Germany's babysitter." Early suspicions about the drug were raised, not by formal testing in an observational or controlled study, but by practitioners who were using the drug in routine practice and were noting that babies with congenital malformations were being born at much higher rates than were expected. As the Australian obstetrician William McBride noted in a letter to the *Lancet* in December 1961, "Congenital malformations are present in approximately 1.5 percent of babies. In recent months I have observed that the incidence of multiple severe abnormalities in babies delivered of women who were given the drug thalidomide ("Distaval") during pregnancy, as an anti-emetic or as a sedative, to be almost 20 percent."[5] The congenital abnormality associated with thalidomide was very distinctive; the condition phocomelia was characterized by foreshortening of the limbs (so-called seal limbs). The first cases of an adverse reaction with the drug—peripheral neuritis—were published in a German journal in 1959, and two cases of phocomelia were presented at a conference in 1960. And over the next year, Widukind Lenz, a German pediatrician alarmed by the sudden rise in birth defects, started specifically asking mothers whether they had taken the drug; he collected thirty-nine cases, which he reported in a conference talk in 1961, ultimately publishing a report in the *Lancet* in January 1962.

Since then, thalidomide has been rehabilitated as an anticancer agent and is currently an important treatment for multiple myeloma.[6] Interestingly, its potential for anti-inflammatory and anticancer activity was first suggested by the empirical observations of another physician who was using it as a sedative. In 1965 the Israeli dermatologist Jacob Sheskin reported on six cases in which thalidomide, initially prescribed as a sedative, had been associated with the reduction of both the symptoms (muscle and joint pains) and signs (skin rashes) of leprosy. In the first case (1963), the abdominal pains of which the patient had been complaining decreased overnight after the initiation of oral thalidomide. But the drug also had a dramatic effect on the patient's characteristic leprotic skin lesions. Within the subsequent forty-eight hours, the lesions had changed from bright red to brownish, and in three days they had disappeared altogether.[7]

However, the derivation of important insights and innovations from practice is not simply a quaint feature of the history of medicine, made redundant by the advent of modern science. Even though formal medical research, manifest as "evidence-based medicine," has come to dominate thinking about the relationship between science and medical practice, important insights continue to arise from daily practice. For example, the dangerous side effect of the diet drug combination of fenfluramine and phentermine ("fen-phen"), heart valve damage, was identified in routine clinical practice. Although serotonin-like drugs had been previously associated with valvular heart disease, anorectic (appetite-suppressing) drugs had not. The first case was observed in May 1996 by a cardiologist at the Mayo Clinic. The patient underwent a mitral valve repair, and "intra-operatively the valve was noted to have a glistening white appearance, suggesting ergotamine-induced valvular injury . . . but the patient had no history of ergotamine ingestion."[8] The same patient was evaluated for tricuspid disease in July that year, and echocardio-graphic findings were found to be "similar to those seen in those patients with carcinoid or ergotamine-induced valve disease." At this time a twenty-five-month history of fen-phen use was elicited from the patient. A second case, with similar findings, was evaluated at the Mayo in January 1997. That same month a physician from North Dakota contacted the Mayo Clinic to inquire whether there was a known association between this drug combina-tion and valve disease, as he had identified twelve patients with unusual valvular morphology and a history of fen-phen use. And in April 1997 yet an-other Mayo Clinic cardiologist, "unaware of the previous cases," contacted a colleague at the Mayo to inquire about an association between fen-phen use and valve disease. In total, twenty-four cases were identified, all "during the course of routine evaluation for various clinical problems." The authors fur-ther noted that "no attempt was made to identify patients by reviewing data bases, conducting cross-index searches of patient files, or soliciting reports of suspected cases from clinical practices."[9] The twenty-four cases were published in the *New England Journal of Medicine* in August 1997, and that September, the FDA withdrew both drugs.

Serendipity often has an important role in such discoveries during the course of routine medical practice. They often arise when a clinician, trying to solve one problem, makes a chance observation about another (as in the case when thalidomide used as a sedative was noted to affect the course of the un-derlying disease) or when a clinician, expecting one pattern, observes another (as in the fen-phen case, when valve changes characteristic of ergotamine-induced damage were observed in the absence of exposure to this drug).

And because each physician–patient interaction is in part an experi-ment, and thousands of clinicians are treating millions of patients each day, there is ample opportunity for chance observations of patterns that are out of the ordinary in some way. Hence such insights are quite common. DeMonaco et al. recently studied the role of "user innovation" in clinical practice in more detail.[10] These authors tracked twenty-nine new chemical entities approved by the FDA in 1998, looking in the medical literature (Micromedex Healthcare Series, a commercial drug information service) and patent applications for new uses of these drugs for indications that were not included in the original FDA application. Over the subsequent five years, 143 "possibly effective or effective" new uses for these twenty-nine drugs were reported, of which 86 (60 percent) were the result of "field discovery."[11] Field discoveries were defined as those new drug uses that were identified by clinicians in the care of their patients.[12]

However, although serendipity is often a feature of anecdotes of new discoveries from practice, DeMonaco et al.'s study suggests instead that directed and deliberate search plays an even more important role. The "experiments" of routine patient care are not random. The clinicians in DeMonaco et al.'s study applied their deep understanding of the pharmacology of the drug to their understanding of the disease process for the disease they were treating, in order to come up with a novel solution to that patient's health problem (as reported by 59 percent of the field discoverers who responded to the authors' survey). They were actively looking for an effective clinical strategy for the patients they were treating in their practices.

OPERATIONAL INNOVATIONS AT INTERMOUNTAIN HEALTHCARE

Not all insights from practice relate to new understandings about the nature of a disease, new treatments, or new indications for existing drugs. Frequently, they simply relate to better ways of doing things—more effective ways of organizing systems and processes of care. That is, they are insights not about what to do, but about how to do it, or how to do it more effectively, reliably, efficiently, or safely. They inform not the content of the clinical "best practice" but the execution of that best practice, and contribute to the organizational knowledge base.[13]

The intensive care unit (ICU) at Intermountain Healthcare's LDS Hospital provides an example of operational innovations arising from practice. LDS's ICU has been at the forefront of the computerization of patient care for many years. For instance, it was the site of an important study comparing standardized ventilator management with extra-corporeal CO_2 removal ($ECCO_2R$) in the treatment of adult respiratory distress syndrome (ARDS), in which the standardized ventilator management was provided using a detailed computerized protocol to manage the ventilator settings.[14] Over the last five years, the ICU has been perfecting insulin treatment of critically ill patients.[15]

These LDS ICU efforts were based on an influential 2001 *New England Journal of Medicine* paper showing that very tight control of serum glucose levels in ICU patients reduced all-cause mortality in a surgical ICU.[16] In response, the ICU staff at LDS rewrote their existing protocol to aim for a serum glucose range of 110 to 120 mg per deciliter. Such a target increased the risk of dangerous hypoglycemic episodes (dangerous because they are associated with a risk of brain damage). And this is exactly what the clinical staff observed: routine blood testing of patients on the protocol identified instances of hypoglycemia. At issue was the fact that patients differed in their sensitivities to insulin. The same insulin dose in two different patients might cause very different reductions in blood sugar level. Thus, in 2001 a Fellow working in the unit developed a set of equations—that permitted the protocol to be computerized—in which changing a constant allowed the protocol to accommodate different insulin sensitivities. Now the protocol could be customized to the individual patient's insulin sensitivity, something that could be detected after the first test dose. The new protocol was implemented, one patient at a time. Each time a low glucose level was detected, staff reviewed the patient and the clinical circumstances surrounding the unanticipated hypoglycemic event and modified the protocol—over forty times in the first week.

As experience with the computerized protocol grew, other patterns emerged. Some patients, in spite of being managed with a protocol that was customized to their specific insulin sensitivity, unexpectedly continued to suffer hypoglycemic episodes. Staff noticed these were more likely in patients with liver failure. In contrast to the previous issue, in which the protocol itself was not sophisticated enough to guide individual clinical decisions about insulin doses, this issue related to an entire patient subpopulation. In response, the ICU team created a separate version of the insulin protocol for liver failure patients, calibrated to a higher target glucose dose.[17] Another modification was made later, once again in response to a pattern that emerged after accumulated experience with the computerized protocol. Patients' insulin sensitivities tended to increase after several days in the ICU, and thus the protocols and their use were modified to account for this fluctuation.

This pattern of work—protocol design, implementation, and modification— is common in the LDS ICU. It dates from the ARDS ventilator protocols in the early 1990s. What is being learned from experience is not the underlying clinical medicine informing physicians' judgments, but how to systematically apply that clinical knowledge. The value of tight insulin control was well known since the DCCT trial in 1993.[18] Individual variation in insulin sensitivity, the role of the liver in glucose metabolism, and the impact of serum cortisol levels—high in the first two to three days of an ICU stay—on insulin sensitivity were also well known. What was less well known were the design principles for, and the management approach to, an operating system that reliably executed on this knowledge, such that all patients benefited from its rigorous application.[19]

Not all such innovations occur at the bedside, as in the LDS ICU. In another example from Intermountain Healthcare, primary care physicians applied a detailed protocol for the management of patients with community-acquired pneumonia. The protocol drew heavily on the pneumonia patient outcomes research trial (PORT), which defined three severity levels for pneumonia. A separate patient pathway was defined for each severity level: mild pneumonia treated as an outpatient, moderate as an inpatient, and severe cases admitted to the respiratory intensive care unit. Routine surveillance of aggregated outcome data by Intermountain's Institute for Health Care Delivery Research, however, identified a group of patients, classified as "moderate" by the severity criteria, who were nonetheless being effectively treated as outpatients. Further analysis revealed that these patients were all being treated by one physician group practice. Although the PORT criteria had identified these patients as having moderate severity pneumonia—thus warranting hospital admission—the treating physicians had established a routine for delivering daily intravenous antibiotics to these patients while they remained outpatients. Ultimately, Intermountain modified the severity criteria used throughout the system, in effect raising the bar for inpatient admission and moving more pneumonia care to supervised community settings, thus applying the strategy developed by this one practice more widely.[20] Similarly to the ICU example, the insights from routine practice related to the way a "best practice" could be implemented, rather than to the practice itself. Of course, in both of these examples, the line between implementation of a clinical practice and the practice itself is not so bright. Rigorous implementation and evaluation of a protocol revealed ways in which the protocol itself (that is, the medical recommendation embedded in the protocol) was deficient and needed modification.

Thus two important—and related—effects emerge from the accumulation of medical and operational insights from practice. The first is an improvement in the implementation of medical practices such that more patients who would benefit from being cared for in a particular way actually

FIGURE 6-1

The effect of learning on the clinical process

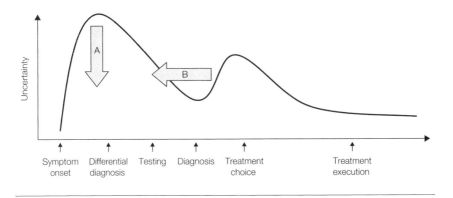

receive that care. This results from iterative improvements in the processes and operating systems that execute known best practices. But the second net effect is to help push medical care for any particular health problem up the stages of knowledge (see table 3-1, chapter 3), the result of improvements in the medical best practice being executed. Over time, primary variables that influence an outcome are validated, and as they are stabilized in the care process, secondary variables emerge. Aggregating the experience from multiple episodes of unstructured problem solving helps reveal patterns that guide future clinical decisions. Likewise, rigorous implementation of pattern-based clinical decisions—that is, structured execution combined with outcome measurement and analysis—allows the refinement of rules (see figure 4-2, chapter 4). And thus the protocols themselves become more highly refined and hence more effective as tools for the management of care. Figure 6-1 represents the net effect of learning in health care; over time uncertainty in any given situation is reduced. As shown by arrow A, the peak uncertainty associated with diagnosis and treatment selection is lowered. The time and number of iterations required to solve any individual's health problem is also reduced (as indicated by arrow B). Care for any particular patient problem migrates from iterative to sequential.

Of course, all this presumes that insights of the variety described above are actually captured in such a way that they can be applied to more than just the individual clinician's or group's patients.

CAPTURING INNOVATIONS IN PRACTICE:
THE ROLE OF SIGNAL STRENGTH

Capturing insights such as these depends first on noticing them. The examples described above display a range of mechanisms of capture. Although they have in common the fact that they all originated from the observation of something unexpected or truly anomalous during the day-to-day practice of medicine, they differ in a crucial way. The signals in the various examples are of different strengths. In the case of thalidomide or an episode of hypoglycemia, the signal is very strong. One clinician checking one insulin-treated ICU patient will note a single episode of low blood glucose. In the case of thalidomide, not only was the malformation (phocomelia) striking, unusual, unique, and characteristic, but it was also (as McBride noted, above) very frequent. Moreover, it was the result of one drug taken at a very specific time in the pregnancy. That is, the connection between cause and effect was very tight. The same was true for Sheskin treating leprosy in Israel; the striking clinical effect occurred the very next day after the drug was initiated. Signs and symptoms returned four days after the drug was ceased (case four), and resolved when the drug was recommenced (drug rechallenge). In all these cases, it was possible for a single physician, observing one or very few cases, to detect an anomaly or discern a pattern.

The same is not true in situations where the signal of aberrance is weaker. In the case of the fen-phen drug combination, while individual doctors were suspicious of a connection between the drugs and the heart valve abnormalities, it was not until several physicians combined their cases that a distinct pattern emerged. As Connolly and her colleagues noted in their *New England Journal of Medicine* paper, "As increasing numbers of patients were identified with similar clinical features, a perceived association between these features and previous or current use of fenfluramine-phentermine evolved. The serendipitous connection between these individual cases was identified as a result of communication among several physicians beginning in May 1996."[21] Signals that are still weaker—for example, excess cardiac mortality in a population already at risk for cardiac events, as in the case of Vioxx, or a small group of pneumonia patients treated in an alternative location by one practice—are usually only identified through systematic analyses of large databases.

The importance of this distinction is that, as outlined in table 6-1, different-strength signals are discovered and captured using different mechanisms. Analyses of large databases are needed to identify weak signals that

TABLE 6-1

Variation in signal strength

Signal strength	Mode of observation	Example	Mechanism of capture
Very high	Insight gained from single or very few observations by one physician	Thalidomide Insulin dosing	Individual observer
Medium	Observed over many cases (by one physician, or aggregated over many physicians)	Fen-phen	Team process Control chart
Low	Observed only through statistical analysis of a large sample	Vioxx Outpatient pneumonia treatment	Statistical analysis of large database Controlled trial

can only be observed when many individual cases are combined. Group processes that allow clinicians to compare and combine their individual experiences, and control charts that identify signals among noise, are used when the signals are moderately strong. And individual observations by single clinicians can suffice for very strong signals in which the connection between cause and effect is very tight.

The ease with which a signal may be observed is governed not only by the strength of the signal itself but also by the background against which the signal occurs. Some anomalies are not recognizable because they are buried in background variation; or because what is to be expected in a clinical process is not specified, and therefore the unexpected cannot be spotted. The central tool of statistical process control, the control chart, is designed to aid identification of relevant signals among lots of noise. Other signals are recognizable (inasmuch as the signal is distinct from the background noise), but they are not observed because the relevant data are not available to those who might recognize the signal. For example, readmission rate has been used as a measure of quality—in particular, to ensure that patients managed on a clinical pathway are not discharged too early. However, patients readmitted after surgery may go to a hospital other than the one at which the original surgery was performed. Thus, a spike in readmission rate after the implementation of a new clinical pathway recommending early discharge might not be observed unless readmissions for all the hospitals in a region are pooled, thus limiting readmission rate as a signal of premature discharge.[22] Finally, as the *Columbia* shuttle disaster demonstrated (see chapter 5), that an anomaly is recognizable and observed does not mean that it will be appropriately reacted to. The Tucker and Edmondson study found that an anomaly may be recognizable and observed, but not surfaced or elevated to a level in the organization where it may be subjected to testing and be learned from by more than the observer, and where it may thus occasion longer-lasting change.

In summary, deriving insight from practice requires observing and making meaning of anomalous observations—something that may not occur without specific managerial interventions aimed at both making the signals more obvious and elevating observed signals to a level in the organization where they can be used to produce meaningful clinical or operational change. And the specific managerial intervention chosen will depend on the strength of the signal of aberrance. Interventions that help make signals easier to observe include (1) process standardization, which in effect makes clear what is to be expected, such that the unexpected will be all the more obvious; (2) control charts, which identify meaningful variation among insignificant variation; and (3) group processes (for example, team meetings), which allow multiple observers to pool their data. In Duke's CHF clinic (see chapter 5), each patient transfer from one operating system to another is a potential signal (a "re-sort"). Because the pathways are so well defined, a transfer is a clear indicator of something unexpected having happened. Organizational processes and culture (see below) can promote the surfacing of individual observations or insights so that they may be subject to further analysis.

THE RISKS OF LEARNING FROM PRACTICE

In the examples above, the individual observations have all led to important clinical or operational insights and improvements. But this is, of course, not always the case. Many anecdotal observations are frankly wrong. For example, in a study of forty-seven published anecdotal case reports of suspected adverse drug reactions, nineteen were not validated at the time the adverse reaction was observed (for example, by rechallenge with the drug), and of these "only seven were subsequently verified."[23] That is, of the nineteen adverse drug reaction reports not immediately verified, "at worst . . . about two-thirds of such anecdotes are false alarms."[24] Alternatively, thirty-five of the forty-seven reports were validated, but this nonetheless represents a true positive rate of 74 percent at best. Some anecdotal observations can be taken to be no more than that: observations. Those where the signal is strong and cause-effect relationship tight—in the case of adverse drug reactions, this would mean an immediate drug reaction such as circulatory collapse or a local reaction at the site of administration, or testing through rechallenge— have the potential to immediately generate new knowledge. But when the signal or the connection between cause and effect is weak, the anecdotal report cannot be (without further investigation, analysis, and validation) the primary source of new knowledge applied to all future patients. Such observations do have value—inasmuch as they can generate new hypotheses or initiate further, formal research—but without further testing, they also have the potential to be dangerous.[25]

A particularly salient (and chilling) example of this problem is the case of autologous bone marrow transplant (ABMT) as a treatment for metastatic carcinoma of the breast.[26] Initially used as a treatment for primary marrow tumors, in the late 1970s ABMT had become a "rescue" treatment after "supralethal chemotherapy or radiation for solid tumors."[27] By the mid-1980s advocates argued for using ABMT to treat advanced breast cancer on the grounds that higher chemotherapy doses would kill more cancer cells (and harvesting and retransplanting the patient's own bone marrow would allow higher chemotherapy doses to be used), although others argued that a dose-response relationship was theoretical. Of the seventy-two articles relating to the therapy reviewed in 1992, all were unrandomized, and only ten met the simple criteria of peer review or an outcome (survival or response) or had more than ten patients in the study. This review found no benefit of ABMT over conventional therapy. Finally, four randomized trials published in 1999 came to the same conclusion, and ABMT was abandoned as a treatment for advanced breast cancer. For over a decade thousands of "desperately ill women had sought bone marrow transplantation as their best chance for survival" on the basis of hope, clinical plausibility, inadequate skepticism, and the absence of randomization.[28]

There are many challenges to learning from anecdotal observations or small samples. Not surprisingly, interpretation of the meaning of an observation is open to many cognitive biases. Most important of these is the confirmation bias: the tendency to treat initial hypotheses as facts, favor confirmatory data, and deliberately not seek disconfirmatory data. Clinicians are likely to ascribe importance to observations that are consistent with their preexisting mental models and to discount those that are not. Observers are also prone to superstitious learning, which occurs when cause and effect relationships are misspecified.[29] This is more likely in situations in which outcomes are insensitive to actions taken. The observer notes an outcome that is temporally related to an action, infers a causal relationship between them, and goes on to repeat that action, even in the absence of a true cause-effect relationship. As Levitt and March note, "In an organization that is invariantly successful routines that are followed are associated with success and are reinforced; other routines are inhibited."[30]

Thus, making observations in practice is a necessary, but not sufficient, condition for increasing medical and operational knowledge. Although practicing physicians may not be able to rely on the evidence base alone to guide their judgments (for all the reasons discussed in chapter 2), neither can they rely solely on individual observations.[31] These observations have to be integrated with one another, and individually and together reconciled with the preexisting knowledge set and previous observations, and then formally tested in some way before the insights from practice can safely be applied to the care of other patients. To do all this requires a larger system for knowledge management.

PREVAILING MODEL OF INNOVATION
GENERATION AND DISSEMINATION

Of course, national health care delivery systems the world over all contain a powerful system for undertaking the task of knowledge management—for generating new knowledge and applying it to individual physicians' clinical decisions. This system directs the flow of knowledge from medical science into practice, and its goal is to ensure that ever-changing medical science is made available to each practitioner so that it can be incorporated into their daily practice. It relies upon a set of loosely coupled industry-level structures and processes (see figure 6-2).

New knowledge is primarily created through basic science research and clinical experience, and refined by randomized controlled trials (RCTs). RCTs act to prevent superstitious learning. However, multiple RCTs may yield conflicting results and implications, especially early trials with smaller study populations. Thus, evidence-based medicine (EBM) has been developed as a process to reconcile and integrate clinical evidence into clear, unequivocal recommendations (guidelines) for practicing physicians (usually employing meta-analysis), often called *best practices*.[32] Recommended practices are communicated to practitioners during their professional schooling and through required continuing medical and nursing education (CME, CNE); and newly updated physicians and nurses are presumed to modify

FIGURE 6-2

The flow of knowledge in medicine

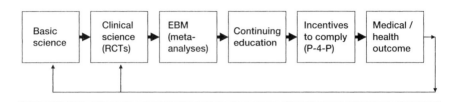

their patient management practices, because it is the right thing to do or, more recently for physicians, in response to a pay-for-performance (P-4-P) scheme. Other mechanisms for ensuring that practitioners are financially and clinically accountable for implementing best practices include capitation and other risk-sharing arrangements between insurers and health care providers, performance monitoring and reporting (sometimes called *physician profiling*), and medicolegal and professional sanctions.

This system has been widely critiqued in recent years. The overarching concern is that it simply does not work particularly well. There is a significant gap between knowledge and practice.[33] Not only is new knowledge not reliably moved into practice, making its adoption uneven, but the process is achingly slow. One estimate puts the time lag between the publication of a best practice and its adoption into routine care at seventeen years.[34] Many of the system's components have also been questioned. Common continuing education strategies such as conferences "have little direct impact on improving professional practice"; pay-for-performance has tended to reward current high performers rather than promote improvement in less well-performing physicians; and the quality of meta-analyses, one key analytic method underlying evidence-based medicine, varies.[35]

However, even if this industry-level system for knowledge management were completely reliable and wholly effective, its design does not specifically support a two-way flow of knowledge—from practice to research as well as from research into practice. It is based on a model of learning in health care in which knowledge flow is linear, unidirectional, and individual.[36] Moreover, it treats the knowledge for practice as a property of the individual practitioner and the industry but not the care delivery organization. Historically, individual delivery organizations have had a limited role in knowledge management in health care. Insights from practice were captured as "experience" by individual practitioners and formally analyzed by externally funded research. Medical research, funded by the National Institutes of Health and private industry, advances the frontier of medical science, and research undertaken at schools of public health, business schools, and such organizations as the Institute for Healthcare Improvement advances understanding of systems of care and care delivery organizations. Managers of delivery organizations tend to focus instead on hiring experienced and well-trained clinicians and ensuring that they remain up to date.

Yet if care is to be managed (and organizations held accountable for that care), then the knowledge for care must become an organizational, as well as an individual, property. Hence the question arises, how can an organization systematically capture the insights that arise from routine practice and more effectively learn from its own experience? And how can it achieve this when the original signals upon which these insights are based vary in their strength?

SYSTEMATICALLY CAPTURING INNOVATION AND LEARNING—INTERMOUNTAIN HEALTHCARE

Utah's Intermountain Healthcare is an example of an operating system designed to not only manage care, as were the operating systems discussed in chapter 5, but also optimize local learning.[37] Any learning system in health care must address the two issues discussed above: lost learning (local learning not captured so that it may be applied globally) and erroneous learning (learning the wrong thing). Intermountain's operating system comprises hardware (departments, individual role definitions, team structures, and information technology) and software (processes, measures, and incentives) that address these two issues. These components all work together to generate, capture, refine and validate, disseminate, and utilize new knowledge about both what to do to solve a health problem and how to do it.[38] These components can be grouped into three subsystems.

The first of these is a *system for defining standard clinical processes*. Intermountain has a large, sophisticated, and refined system for defining standardized clinical processes, termed *clinical process models* (CPMs). At the heart of this system is a set of permanent teams (see figure 6-3). Intermountain has divided its clinical activities into ten clinical programs (or "families of care") by grouping related patient types and clinical work: cardiovascular, neuromusculoskeletal, surgical specialties, women and newborns, intensive (hospital-based) medicine, intensive pediatrics, intensive behavioral, oncology,

FIGURE 6-3

Intermountain team structure

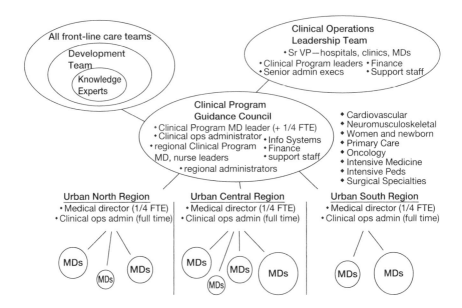

Source: Intermountain Healthcare. Used with permission.

Note: Each of the eight clinical programs represented here has a guidance council made up of a nurse and a physician representative from each of the three regions shown, plus representatives from administrative departments such as IT and finance. Each guidance council gets input from one or more development teams made up of content experts in a particular clinical area. All eight guidance councils report to the clinical operations leadership team.

preventive and health maintenance, and primary care. Each clinical program oversees a number of CPMs: the high-volume, high-cost, and high-impact care processes of that specialty or group of specialties. Some CPMs are centered on a disease or group of diseases, and others on an activity. Thus, for example, the cardiovascular program has CPMs for ischemic heart disease, congestive heart failure, hypertension, and cardiovascular surgery.

Each clinical program is overseen by a guidance council comprising clinical leaders and representatives from administration, such as information systems and finance. However, the detail of each CPM is created by a development team (DT) comprising domain experts for that medical condition. The development team's primary role is to create a standardized, evidence-based, care management strategy (protocol) for that condition. To complete this task, the team includes knowledge experts (usually specialist physicians) from throughout the Intermountain system. The DT does not simply design the protocol for its patient group. It is also responsible for developing a set of performance measures (service, cost, and clinical outcome measures), a set of workflow support tools (such as criteria sets and standard order sets), and a set of educational materials for health professionals and patients. Beyond creating the protocol and its supporting documents, DTs work with the information systems department to design modifications to the electronic medical record, default screens, pull-down menus, and data capture mechanisms that all support the CPM. In effect, the development team develops not just the protocol, but many of the elements of the operating system by which the protocol is implemented. While designing the protocol and its supports, the DTs seek the input of frontline physicians treating the kinds of patients whose care is its subject. Further, the team reports to the clinical program's guidance council, which includes clinical representatives (physicians and nurses) from Intermountain's various geographic regions. These representatives' role is to evaluate the practicality and feasibility of the DT's design for the CPM. In this way, the development of a guideline is not a theoretical exercise; the CPM is intended to be a practical clinical work management tool, and to that end, it is heavily vetted by those groups that will use it.

The second component is a *system for implementing standard clinical processes*. Modifications to the electronic record—such as default screens, letters prepopulated with default text, reminders, criteria sets, and other decision support systems—all make it easier for clinicians to put the protocol into practice. These workflow management tools that "make it easy to do it right" and the allied physician and patient education materials and sessions are important components of the system for implementing protocols.[39] However, although they are necessary, they are not sufficient for ensuring that the protocols are actually implemented. They are augmented by an incentive system that encourages the use of the standard processes—modest incentives based on quality and financial performance (assessed at the physician group level). The measures used in the incentive system are exactly those defined by the DTs in the CPM. Interestingly, the organization's nonclinically trained administrators are also subject to an incentive compensation system that includes some of the same CPM-based clinical performance measures. And of course, underlying any incentive system is a measurement system capable of routinely collecting the data upon which the incentives are based, thus providing detail on the extent to which the protocols that have been developed with such care are being followed.

Taken alone, these two subsystems would simply be a highly competent operating system for managing care—defining standard clinical pathways and ensuring their implementation—not a system for capturing learning from practice. However, a third set of organizational structures and processes represent a *system for managing learning*. In developing protocols, the DTs rely on not only the published literature and the experience of their expert members. They also make reference to variance data from Intermountain itself. Moreover, their work is not over when the CPM is complete. The DTs continue to monitor aggregate data of process variations that result when the protocol is used by working practitioners, the overall outcomes of the care delivered, and the impact of these variations. In addition, they receive feedback—what changes were made and why—from individual clinicians who have found it necessary to override the care recommended by the protocol because it did not suit the needs of that particular patient. No protocol is followed all the time—override rates vary between 5 percent and 15 percent across all the CPMs currently in place—nor is it expected to be.[40] All these data sources become inputs into the next iteration of the protocol at the center of a CPM. That is, all protocols are temporary artifacts. They are updated to reflect both global experience, through continual monitoring of the medical literature, and local experience, captured by monitoring aggregate measures of system performance and individual instances of protocol override. The latter are more than incidence reports of actual or near-adverse events; they can be any instance in which the recommended care did not meet the patient's needs.

Intermountain has two resources that are central to its learning system. First, its information system both provides data for incentive systems and allows evaluation of the impact of the care processes being encouraged by these incentives on patient outcomes. It was just this careful monitoring of processes and outcomes—the comparison of the patient's severity score with his or her ultimate disposition—that allowed the identification of a viable alternative setting for pneumonia therapy. Intermountain routinely collects the kind of highly detailed clinical data that is becoming the industry norm for quality reporting—such as the percentage of diabetic patients with low-density lipoprotein levels less than 100. And Intermountain can quickly search its own databases to test hypotheses, such as the impact of intraoperative and immediately postoperative blood sugar levels on mortality following open heart surgery, or the impact on duration of labor and probability of ICU admission of elective induction of women with a low Bishop score. In this way, the CPMs facilitate local research. The second resource is the Institute for Health Care Delivery Research (IHCDR). This unit's role is to provide the data and analyses needed by the development teams and guidance councils. Not surprisingly, of the institute's nineteen staff, eleven are statisticians. Their analyses helped identify an alternative strategy for managing patients with community-acquired pneumonia.

These three subsystems, each with its own structures and processes, interact with and reinforce each other. In effect, Intermountain's organizational design represents an operating system for learning (see table 6-2). Standard clinical processes are developed, implemented, and overridden in practice. The reasons for, and the impact of, these overrides are evaluated in

TABLE 6-2

Intermountain Healthcare as an operating system for learning

	Software			Hardware		
	Services offered	Processes	Policies and procedures	Physical site	Human resources	Technology
Develop and implement standard practices	Diversified provider	Highly standardized care processes organized around families of care	Predominance of process and compliance metrics[a] Pay-for-performance based on clinical and financial metrics Clinical incentives for nonclinical managers	Dispersed clinics, practices, and hospitals	Employed physician leadership Team structure: clinical program guidance councils and development teams Physician (and patient) training	Computerized physician practices Electronic medical record–based default screens, pull-down menus, and "hot text" Pushed reminders
Detect and analyze variances and update standard practices		Process measures and overrides	Analysis of override and variance data (IHCDR) Culture supporting override		IHCDR strength in biostatistics Development teams	Automated data capture

a. Of the 204 measures in use by the clinical programs in 2008, 60 monitored the utilization of tests, procedures, rooms, and bed-days, and 90 monitored compliance with defined clinical guidelines (Intermountain internal data, August 2008). Note that these measures are an explicit expression of Intermountain's model of cause that links its operating system with the value it intends to create for patients (see chapter 5).

a search for better standard processes. The standard processes are modified accordingly, and this process—standardize, implement, override, modify—starts all over again. In this way, this high-level structure represents a continuous loop and a never-ending routine of activities that generate learning.

SUMMARY: THE PHYSIOLOGY OF A LEARNING SYSTEM

Intermountain's is a system designed to support a linked set of activities and tools that together capture learning from routine practice (see figure 6-4). These activities and tools, which together make up a group of capabilities, are at the heart of any learning system and support knowledge capture and creation and knowledge transfer. The first of these are activities and tools that foster signal detection, with the aim of maximizing the rate of potential hypotheses and innovative insights arising from the day-to-day clinical practice. In the Toyota Production System, the andon cord is one such tool. By pulling the andon cord (a rope running above the workstation), an assembly line worker is signaling an anomaly and initiating a response. In order to aid

FIGURE 6-4

The physiology of a learning system

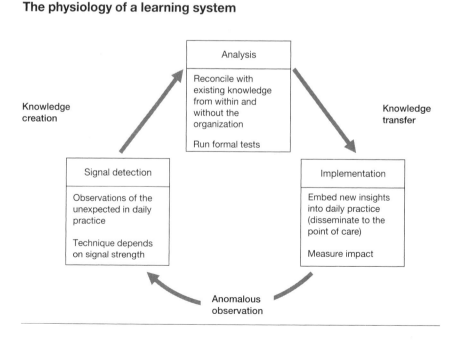

signal detection, Toyota standardizes activities to the greatest extent possible so unexpected events will be all that more obvious to the worker. In Duke's CHF clinic, each time a patient is referred out from the nurse-practitioner-managed delivery process (standardized protocol) into the cardiologist-managed iterative care process, it is a potential signal that the sequential care process is not fully meeting the needs of that patient (a "re-sort"). Moreover, articulating clear expectations of a process's performance—through defined process and outcome metrics and targets—also aids in the detection of unexpected events. The control chart in statistical process control serves the same purpose, but in contrast to the andon cord, the control chart helps identify signals that are either too weak, or embedded in too much noise, to be observed by an individual worker. In the health care delivery setting, potentially very important signals vary in their strength, and thus multiple activities and tools are needed (see table 6-1). So Intermountain employs a range of activities and tools to aid in signal detection: protocol overrides, which are encouraged, by individual practitioners; team discussions at the guidance council and development team meetings; routine monitoring of performance data (using control charts); and focused queries of large databases by staff of the Institute for Health Care Delivery Research.

The second set of activities and tools are analytic. They help make meaning of those signals that are identified, and guard against superstitious learning. In industrial production settings, thousands of andon cord pulls or employee suggestions for improvement are either implemented immediately (because they have strong face validity) or subjected to rapid cycle testing and then implemented. However, in health care, because signals from complex biological systems (and complex organizations) are often ambiguous and open to flawed interpretation, and the costs of failure are so high, rigorous formal testing and high levels of confidence are required.[41] At the simplest level, these analytic activities compare what has been observed with what is known in order to validate the signal itself and determine whether indeed something truly unusual has occurred. That is, they reconcile the signal with existing local and general knowledge. But in order to protect against erroneous interpretation of single observations—particularly in circumstances of high patient risk—the analytic tools must also include deliberate testing, through either rapid cycle experimentation or formal epidemiological study (either observational or randomized studies). In this way, care processes are distinct from business processes. Large-scale analyses of anomalous observations and randomized trials of new business processes are not usually required. Often face validity is high, and small-scale rapid cycle tests are sufficient.

At Intermountain Healthcare, development team members evaluate new ideas and compare them with their own experience and with the published literature. DT members also run grant-funded clinical trials to test some hypotheses, and the Institute for Health Care Delivery Research also supports formal studies into some hypotheses. For example, when a critical care physician had the hunch that delayed transfer to the ICU was responsible for increased morbidity, he, and the institute, ran a study that confirmed the importance of early transfer and resulted in the innovation of rapid response teams.[42]

The third set of activities and tools support implementation of the new knowledge into routine practice. After all, creating new organizational and clinical knowledge is only of benefit if it positively influences the care of the current and subsequent patients. Protocols and the myriad of associated support tools—measurement sets, standard order sets, patient and physician education materials, workflow plans and value maps, pull-down menus and hot text, decision support tools, and so on—help ensure that new knowledge is reflected in practice. In effect, making sure that now that we know what to do, we do what we know. At Intermountain (as at Toyota) standardization of work is a vitally important component of executing on new knowledge. But standardization in this context is not used as a mechanism of control of physician behavior as much as it is as a tool for future learning. Standardizing, where possible, the activities and decisions of care helps make future anomalies both easier to detect and easier to interpret. New knowledge implemented into practice fosters future knowledge development through the observation of the next anomaly. In this way, standardization aids learning because it makes routine care stable and the "experiments" of routine care therefore reproducible and testable.

Together, these three interrelated sets of activities and tools constitute a closed-loop learning system (see figure 6-4). What is important here are not the specific tools employed by Intermountain Healthcare (or Toyota), but the integrated set of capabilities—for signal detection, analysis, and knowledge implementation—that these represent. Different care delivery organizations may use different tools and activities that achieve the same goals. They may use different approaches for surfacing signals and analyzing them, rely more or less on information technology, and take different approaches to influencing physician behavior in order to bring newly developed knowledge back into clinical practice. But they can achieve the same goal—systematically capturing and using the new knowledge generated through routine operations—as Intermountain.

CONDITIONS FOSTERING INNOVATION
AND LEARNING FROM PRACTICE

The tools and activities and the linkages between them represented in figure 6-4 are by themselves insufficient to speed the rate of learning, however. Several other conditions must be present before this closed-loop system can function optimally. Importantly, clinical staff must frame routine care as a learning activity, rather than a "production activity."[43] Some health care delivery organizations do frame new technology or best-practice adoption initiatives as a learning activity. Organizations that frame their new technology adoption efforts this way tend to be more successful adopters.[44] They also tend to be selective in which aspects of technology adoption they view through a learning frame. A study of the adoption of a technology for minimally invasive cardiac surgery found that—consistent with their different missions—academic medical centers tended to focus on the scientific aspects of the new technology and learn more about the applicability of the technique to different procedures and patient populations (learning "why"), whereas community medical centers adopting the same technology tended to focus on the organizational aspects of the new technology and learn more about how to use it more efficiently (learning "how").[45]

However, few delivery organizations treat routine care as a learning activity and seek both organizational and clinical insights from it. Instead, as in the case of NASA, they tend to frame their enterprises in production terms: the "delivery" of care services. And their primary focus is on reducing variation, not learning from it. Academic medical centers' tripartite mission—clinical care, teaching, and research—often serves to separate (and isolate) the activities of learning from those of routine practice. The importance of a learning frame for routine care is that it fosters rigor in experimental methods. It recognizes that routine care is in fact experimental, and sets in place good experimental technique. Standardization of practice is more acceptable (because it limits the number of dimensions that are varying at any one time), feedback is routinely sought, the feedback loop is shortened as much as possible, the method of signal detection matches the expected strength of potential signals, and current clinical practices are treated as "trials." For example, one group of cardiac surgeons in New York made a practice of seeing as many of their valve replacement patients as possible two to five years after the procedure, and as a result made numerous modifications to their procedures and technology choices.[46]

The cultural context in which the activities and tools of a learning system are embedded is also important. Detecting signals depends on workers speaking up about what they are observing, both positive and negative observations. If workers are unwilling to speak up, learning opportunities will be lost. A psychologically safe environment is one in which people believe "that one will not be punished or humiliated for speaking up with ideas, questions, concerns, or mistakes."[47] When individuals learn on their own, the risk is private. Because the knowledge is separable—developing new knowledge doesn't depend on the actions of others—individuals can learn by trial and error alone. And no one need see their mistakes. Developing new knowledge in a group or organizational setting, on the other hand, poses significant social risk. If you make an error, all your colleagues will know about it. Therefore, although individual learning is automatic and unpreventable—imagine trying to stop a young child from learning—group and organizational learning doesn't occur without the deliberate creation of a climate that facilitates it. Organizations that deliberately create a climate of psychological safety (for example, Children's Hospital and Clinics of Minnesota)—often through simple leader behaviors such as inviting input and admitting fallibility—find an increase in the rate of reporting of near- or actual adverse events, and therefore more opportunities to learn.[48]

Finally, the selection of tools to aid in learning must match the nature of the lessons being learned. Learning in health care has two connotations: learning to use what is already known (often called *new knowledge transfer* or *best-practice transfer*) and learning what was previously unknown. These two are often commingled. For example, surgeons learning to use a new minimally invasive cardiac surgery technology learned how to use the technology (efficiency), what kind of procedures it could be used for, and for what kind of patients was it particularly suited (breadth of use).[49] Some of this was known to the surgical community (for example, that a multiple-graft coronary artery bypass graft procedure was feasible through a minimally invasive approach), and some was yet to be worked out (for example, how a team could most effectively work together to reduce the duration of the procedure). When knowledge is codified (and high stage), as in the former example of graft number, it can be transferred relatively easily through lectures, conference calls, and written materials. When knowledge is tacit (low stage), it cannot be so easily transferred—"proximity and interpersonal interaction are necessary for its transmission"—and this is particularly so for the social knowledge required for members of a team to work well together in team-based practice.[50] That is, tacit knowledge is often best transferred through human contact—for example, mentorship, apprenticeship, or team problem-solving sessions and rehearsals.[51] The tools for best-practice transfer are different from those for new knowledge creation.[52]

CONCLUSION: DESIGNING FOR LEARNING

In summary, the learning system in figure 6-4 seeks to exploit the natural experiments occurring during routine care. When the less highly structured experiments of an iterative care process result in a positive patient outcome—as in the case of thalidomide and leprosy—an effective learning system can speed the identification and evaluation of a new insight and the development of a standard protocol and a sequential process. And when the more highly structured experiments of a sequential process fail—and require clinician override—it identifies where the standardized protocol is insufficient or the operating system supporting the care process is failing. In both of these circumstances, learning may have occurred anyway. But the structured approach to capturing new knowledge from practice—comprising the deliberate design of structures and processes and the selection of appropriate tools—of which Intermountain's learning system is one example, has the potential to increase our rate of learning, structure unstructured problems, determine what problems are best suited to an iterative or a sequential care process, and ensure that what we are learning is accurate, valid, and useful. As organizations become increasingly accountable for the outcomes of health care—the cure of disease and the relief of suffering—the scientific and organizational knowledge needed to deliver care becomes an organizational (as well as an individual) asset; and therefore a deliberate approach to creating and deploying new clinical and operational knowledge becomes increasingly important. In effect, this means explicitly treating medicine as evidence creating as well as evidence based.

7

New Roles, Responsibilities, and Relationships

The final element of a system for delivering health care is the practitioner. Earlier chapters have described how dramatic increases in the volume and specificity of medical knowledge and altered approaches to problem solving have affected the design of care processes and health care delivery organizations. These factors have also affected the traditional roles of health care practitioners. Both designs for delivering health care (doing what we know; see chapter 5) and designs for learning from routine care (knowing what to do; see chapter 6) require new roles and responsibilities for practitioners. Furthermore, independent of these design requirements, broader societal changes—such as the rise of the Internet, and the active informed consumer, and the impact of economic forces on service availability—are changing the role of the patient in ways that must be accommodated by future operating systems.

An obvious change is in the number and scope of "practitioners." In the past, as it relates to the care process, practitioners were primarily nurses and doctors. Now the term *practitioner* encompasses a wide range of other people, including other professionals—for example, nurse-practitioners, diabetic nurse-educators, pharmacists in new roles—and even the patient. Not only has the number of medical subspecialties increased significantly over the last century (from 14 Accreditation Council for Graduate Medical Education [ACGME]–accredited subspecialties in 1927 to 103 in 2000), but the number of nonmedical care practitioners has also increased.[1] Patients too have, to a certain extent, become "practitioners" in their own health care. Discharged earlier than in previous generations, patients are given instructions for their own wound care or the phototherapy for their infant with mild physiological jaundice; and family members shoulder much of the burden of end-of-life care.[2] And new organizations—for example, disease management companies and in-store clinics—contribute to health care. In effect, the definitions of *practitioner* and *care delivery organization* have expanded as their numbers and diversity have increased.

This chapter examines the new roles of patients and practitioners, both required by and to be accommodated in operating system designs, and the impact of these on the wider market for health care services. We begin with one role group significantly affected—called to take on new roles for themselves and relate to delivery organizations in new ways: physicians.

NEW ROLES FOR THE DOCTOR

Perhaps the most dramatic impact of the evolution in knowledge and in delivery organizations described previously is not on the work of the manager but on the role of the doctor. The introduction argued that the medical outcome of an individual patient's care, once primarily a function of the judgment and skill of the patient's doctor, has now become also a function of the delivery organization's performance. Poorly functioning clinical and business processes contribute to adverse drug events, and better clinical outcomes result from more effective and reliable processes.[3] Moreover, an individual physician's performance is influenced by the organizational context in which he or she is operating. In examining the performance of surgeons who operated at more than one hospital, Huckman and Pisano found that the "quality of a surgeon's performance at a given hospital improves significantly with increases in his or her recent procedure volume at that hospital but does not significantly improve with increases in his or her volume at other hospitals."[4] Put bluntly, poor organizations can undo the work of the best physicians, and great organizations can make up for mediocre ones. How an institution's operating systems are designed and managed matters for the outcomes of health care. The doctor is no longer independent of the organization in which she or he practices, regardless of whether or not she or he is an employee.

Herein is the source of the physician's changing role. To reliably realize a positive patient outcome—for which both physicians and organizations are increasingly being held accountable—it is no longer adequate for an individual physician to only make sound clinical judgments, enshrine them in medical orders, and leave the execution of those orders to someone else. Without some level of involvement in the design or management of that operating system that helps capture the information needed to make sound judgments, supports decision making, and executes many of his or her decisions, a doctor may not realize his or her goals of practice. Yet active and effective participation in the operating systems outlined in chapters 5 and 6 implies several new roles for which most doctors are not prepared. In spite of the fact that most doctors work in small teams—the ratio of physician to nonphysician caregivers increased from 1-to-3 at the beginning of the twentieth century to 1-to-16 at the beginning of the twenty-first—medical schools not only continue to select students trained in organic chemistry and physics, but few teach the basics of leadership, teamwork, operations management, or organizational behavior.[5]

The question thus arises, what does the doctor have to be good at doing when working in conjunction with organizations that cure patients' diseases and relieve their suffering (i.e., that manage care)? Practicing physicians will likely be required to have one or more of at least three distinct roles in addition to their primary clinical role, irrespective of whether they are in formal management positions. All demand both managerial as well as medical expertise.[6]

The first is the role of designer or "system architect." In this role the doctor must evaluate the current operating system, determine whether its existing design is well aligned with the kind of care it supports, and participate in creating a better operating system design to support that particular type of care. Arguably, only a doctor can do this. This role requires an understanding of clinical practice—evaluating the stage of knowledge for a given disease and determining whether the medical evidence supports a sequential process for solving clinical problems or whether an iterative process is better suited—as well as an understanding of the principles of operating system design discussed in chapter 5. Moreover, as managers look to other industries (e.g., airlines, the military, car manufacture) for metaphors and tools, such as crew resource management and the Toyota Production System, they need clinical input to determine to which patient care processes such tools are most appropriate.

The second role is managerial. Physicians have an important role in helping oversee those operating systems that provide patient care without the doctor's immediate and direct involvement—for example, the sequential care process in Duke's congestive heart failure clinic (see chapter 5). Such work is not easy and does not necessarily come naturally to doctors. The managerial requirements for service firms as they grow and mature differ at each stage in their life cycle.[7] Small firms don't need extensive management control systems—much can be accomplished by simply walking around—but larger firms need a suite of complex control systems adapted to many different functions within the firm.[8] For practicing clinicians, the transition from individual agent (in effect, a firm with only one "employee") to manager of others can be particularly challenging. As an individual agent, the clinician has complete control of the key value-creating steps in the care process; she or he ensures and monitors quality and efficiency by performing these steps herself or himself. The predominant skill set required is clinical. When, however, care is delivered by a larger team and operating system, an additional skill set is necessary. Managers ensure quality and efficiency by motivating and monitoring others, by designing processes and allocating tasks and accountabilities, and by ensuring that the resources those others use in the performance of their daily work are optimally configured. This implies competence in leadership and managerial oversight as well as specific skills not necessarily taught in medical school, such as that of interpreting managerial reports (it is for this reason that Istituto Clinico Humanitas trains its physicians in cost accounting; see chapter 5).

Finally, physicians have another distinct role in fostering organizational learning. Insights and innovations coming from routine practice have to be deliberately captured if they are to inform and improve the care of subsequent patients. As chapter 6 discussed, this requires structures, processes, tools, and a climate conducive to experimentation and learning and tolerant of failure—all of which need physician input to create and maintain. In a study of the adoption of the technology for minimally invasive cardiac surgery, surgeons played a pivotal role in establishing teams that were capable of rapid learning by framing the technology adoption as a learning task, creating a process for structured experimentation, and encouraging other team members to experiment by publicly admitting their own fallibility during trial-and-error tests of the new technology.[9] In effect, physicians help create a learning environment both for routine care (iterative care processes are by their nature learning processes) and for performance improvement. They do this by helping identify and evaluate anomalous observations in routine care, establishing a culture within their teams that supports speaking up; and by establishing processes and structures that support learning.

In none of these three new roles will the doctor necessarily act alone. The roles of other health professionals are also changing. In particular, nurses have a key role in operating system design, day-to-day performance management, and short- and long-term improvement. Quantum improvements in outcome, such as reduced hospital-acquired infections, require the coordinated action of all members of a caregiving team.[10]

IMPEDIMENTS TO NEW PHYSICIAN ROLES

Although the changing nature of medical knowledge and clinical care processes implies new roles for physicians, there are several impediments to the "doctor as designer and manager" model.

Preparation

As already noted, physicians are not explicitly trained for any of these new roles in medical school. Although several professional societies provide a range of postgraduate courses addressing management topics, they are typically brief. And the opportunity cost for a full-time practitioner to complete a longer postgraduate degree—such as those offered by schools of policy, business, or public health—is substantial. Moreover, practitioner training and socialization can specifically work against doctors in these new roles. Medical schools and the medicolegal system continue to emphasize individual action and individual responsibility, an emphasis that hinders doctors' taking a system perspective.[11] In fact, the very characteristics that were once considered hallmarks of a "good doctor"—for example, an encyclopedic knowledge, the ability to improvise, and a "take control" personality—may prevent the doctor from being a good team member. Doctors often presume that in any team it will be they who are the team leaders. In return for their years of training and delayed remuneration, salaried physicians have come to expect a working environment of autonomy, job security, and also deference (the implicit psychological compact)—expectations not necessarily consistent with a highly functioning team of interdependent members, each an expert in their own right.[12]

Attitudes

While some physicians are naturally inclined to a managerial role, for many, anything beyond a clinical role holds little interest. For instance, one survey of physician attitudes toward care management practices, such as guidelines, found that physicians preferred not to be directly involved in the development of screening guidelines, preferring that managers (including those clinically trained) take responsibility for this. What the practitioners did want was control over their day-to-day implementation and customization.[13] Moreover, the three new roles suggested above, all requiring leadership, are in addition to being a member of a care delivery team comprising members of other specialties and other clinical professions. Care is rarely provided by one physician. Moving seamlessly between the roles of system architect and team member requires significant interpersonal skill.

Further, there is a question of mind-set. Physicians, particularly nonsurgeons, have long made a living by selling their advice in fifteen-minute aliquots to patients who have sought them out. Substantial physician involvement in both the *ex ante* design and the day-to-day management of systems that deliver health care—be they at the smaller scale of the practitioner's office or the larger scale of a diversified hospital—will depend on physicians coming to see the organizations in which they work as the effecter mechanisms of their own clinical judgment and decision making, and to appreciate the extent to which good clinical outcomes depend on organizational performance.

Time

Physicians, particularly those in private practice whose time is already pressured—increasingly filled with the paperwork associated with patient care—have little capacity for the longer-range planning and new service development that characterize successful service providers in other service industries. By and large, fee-for-service doctors are not reimbursed for service design and improvement work.[14] Thus, recruiting physicians to the new roles described earlier will require that they be meaningfully reimbursed for such work so as to allow them to free up their time. Intermountain Health care, in contrast, buys a portion of the time of all the physicians involved in the design and management of its care management and learning systems (see chapter 6). Many other organizations argue that they do not have adequate resources for this, and many physician practices have not been either willing or able to make investments in the infrastructure—such as personnel and information technology—necessary to manage care.[15]

PHYSICIAN ORGANIZATION ALIGNMENT

Finally, a chasm often separates physicians and managers. The world over, these groups tend to have conflicting goals—or at least presume that their goals are in conflict. Efficiency and clinical outcome are often perceived to stand in opposition to each other. As a result, physicians and managers may view each other with mistrust and struggle to develop a shared mission and set of joint goals, that is, exactly the kind of unified perspective on which a well-aligned operating system depends.

Industry Structure

The institutional structure of the U.S. health care industry—in which physicians and physician groups are often organizationally and financially separate from health care delivery organizations—increases the work physicians and managers must do to develop improved operating systems. Physicians vary in their commitment to the delivery systems in which they treat their patients, and this variation relates to their willingness to employ "evidence-based care management practices" such as guidelines.[16] In many community settings, physician investors in diagnostic or surgical centers and the hospitals in which these same physicians practice are in direct competition.

Thus, in recent years, organized delivery systems have sought to increase physician–system alignment, often through high-level structural arrangements, such as physician–hospital organizations and related contracting activities and governing board membership. The aim of such arrangements is to create a set of shared goals, but their success has been mixed, in part because the two groups' goals do not completely overlap.[17] A series of studies by Shortell and colleagues found that detailed involvement with physicians' practices—through the provision of "value added" services, such as compensation incentives (salary or stipend), information systems, and practice management support—was much more important than such structural arrangements in creating the greater physician–system alignment.[18] That is, the alignment between physicians and health care delivery organizations necessary to create and run effective systems for delivering health care comes from involving physicians more deeply in exactly that activity. To this end, Seattle's Virginia Mason Medical Center (VMMC) has emphasized deep physician involvement in the Toyota Production System–based care process and unit structure redesign activities. Physician involvement in the creation of their own working environment and the care processes in which they participate has been deemed pivotal to VMMC's efforts to increase quality, safety, and efficiency. Hence, although changes in the nature of knowledge, care processes, and operating system designs imply new roles for practicing physicians, physicians are unlikely to take on these new roles if they do not feel aligned with, and committed to, the care delivery organization. And such alignment will not come about without detailed work by that organization and likely, at least in the United States, some measure of economic integration and financial incentive.[19]

Notably, medical practitioners are not the only profession to have faced such a transition—from individual and autonomous professional to a wider involvement in operating system design and management, and a power base somewhat diluted in the wider organization. The transition from "art" (connoting tacit knowledge, craftsmanship, and the creation of unique goods and services) to "science" (associated with reliability, predictability, consistency, speed, and volume) characterizes the history of many industries, from gun manufacture to airline travel and banking.[20] A central element in these transitions has been an increase in process control—what was once produced individually by hand is now created en masse by computer-controlled machines.[21] This change in manufacturing process has been accompanied by a change in the role of the "artist." Once central to the creation of the product, professionals now design and oversee processes and manage exceptions—new roles requiring no less expertise. Pilots, for example, once responsible for flying the plane by hand-manipulating the controls, now oversee the "automated cockpit."[22] In many industries, the demand by regulators and consumers for increased reliability, safety, and efficiency—coupled with increased technological capability and increased stage-of-production knowledge—was a key driver of this transition. Exactly the same forces are currently at work in the health care industry, and it is therefore possible that health care professionals will not be exempt from such a transition in roles and responsibilities.

NEW ROLES FOR THE PATIENT

One constituent whose role is already changing dramatically is the patient, not through deliberate design of new roles to match operating systems' requirements, but as the result of new resources and economic conditions. Recent management and policy thinking regarding the involvement of the patient in health care delivery systems has changed from viewing the patient as a recipient of medical care and a beneficiary of an insurance product, to recognizing that the patient is an active participant in care. Patients have always made important choices with significant financial implications. In the United States, they have long chosen an insurance plan from the menu of plans their employers made available, and a doctor from the plan's network. More recently, they have chosen therapies—in particular, between branded and generic medications in a tiered drug plan. Patients enrolled in high-deductible health plans coupled with health savings accounts now choose whether to spend discretionary health dollars on tests and therapies. And of course, all over the world, the choice to comply with the recommended therapy, and actually take the medications prescribed, has always been the patient's.

Now new resources, such as the Internet, and forces such as cost containment both allow patients to demand, and oblige patients to take, an even greater role in their own care. In so doing, patients are changing health care's traditional power relationships. They are better informed (albeit sometimes erroneously) and more involved in making these important decisions.

In recent years, policy makers have come to view the choices patients make as a market force that, when harnessed, could force performance improvement in plans, physicians, and delivery organizations. This view has been reflected in both public report cards (for example, those published by the Pennsylvania Health Care Cost Containment Council and the New York Cardiac Surgery Reporting System; see chapter 1) and tiered benefit insurance designs (for example, that pioneered by Minnesota's Buyers Health Care Action Group [BHCAG]).[23] For such a market to work effectively, however, patients need more and better information. With the growth of report cards, researchers recognized a need to support patients as they make these choices, as it became clear that patients initially found such reports confusing and hard to use (see chapter 1).[24] Hence a science of patient education and decision support has evolved that addresses such questions as how to provide information to, and create decision aids for, patients to best aid them as they make choices. For example, researchers at Dartmouth Medical School and Massachusetts General Hospital developed an interactive "Shared Decision Making" program to address the most difficult decisions patients have to make: among competing therapies of equal effectiveness. These programs combined outcome and risk data with interviews with real patients who explained the decisions that they made. In this way, patients were able to develop "vicarious experience" that helped them both understand the science and clarify their own values and preferences.

Although these innovations in information delivery have improved patients' ability to make decisions they have always made—thereby making them more effective participants in their own health care—they have not necessarily changed the fundamental way in which patients are involved in their own care, allowed patients to make different classes of decision, or involved patients in totally new aspects of health care delivery processes.[25] Other innovations have.

THE PATIENT AS PROVIDER

As chapter 3 discussed, one impact of an increase in the stage of knowledge is to change the way in which decisions are made and problems are solved. In particular, increased knowledge stage allows problems that once required unstructured trial-and-error problem solving by an expert to be solved by less expert decision makers applying simplified rules (see chapter 4, figure 4-2). Health problems that once required a doctor for their solution no longer do. By applying rules, or using technologies that incorporate such rules, patients can do for themselves things that once required interaction with the professions of the health care delivery system. Less tacit knowledge is needed to solve some problems.[26] New technologies and services not only allow patients to do better what they have always done, but also (for better or for worse) allow patients to take on a whole new role—that of the provider of their own health care.

Such a role transition, from customer to part-time worker, is not unique to health care delivery. Other service industries have also entrained customers to actively participate in their operational processes. Automatic teller machines (ATMs), for instance, not only offer bank customers the convenience of twenty-four-hour access to cash; they also involve customers directly in some of the bank's internal service operations—in this case, cash dispensing and balance transfers—that were previously exclusively undertaken by tellers.[27] Many service industries use the Internet to achieve the same thing, reasoning that it is cheaper to have the customer do something for himself or herself (for example, an ATM transaction costs only 36¢, compared with $1.15 for a teller-assisted transaction).[28]

Of course, not all diseases or health problems allow the patient to have direct involvement in the delivery of their own care. The nature and extent of the patient's participation in his or her own care varies on a spectrum from recipient to controller, as shown in table 7-1. At one end of the spectrum is the severely ill patient who is often not much more than the passive recipient of the care others provide. When the patient is unconscious, others make and execute all the critical decisions for him or her; the patient is effectively the "vessel" in which the health problem being solved is contained. The patient neither makes the diagnosis nor selects and executes the treatment.

Historically, the patient's predominant role in the care process was to be the complier. The physician made all the important decisions—diagnosis and treatment selection—and the patient's participation was limited to complying with the treatment regimen (usually enshrined on a piece of paper handed to the patient by the physician at the conclusion of the consultation) by taking the prescribed medicine.[29] In this model the patient was deeply involved in the care process—albeit with variable performance—as the executor of the clinician's decisions.[30] More recently, as described above, the patient has had a growing role in deciding among competing treatment options, especially when no one option clearly trumps another, such as in the case of a woman with breast cancer who must decide between mastectomy and lumpectomy with radiation. In this case, often because the therapies themselves are hospital based, the patient has a lesser role in treatment execution.

TABLE 7-1

Patient participation in the care process

	Receipt	Compliance	Monitoring	Adjustment	Control
Diagnosis	No	No	No	No	**Yes**
Treatment selection	No	No	No	No	**Yes**
Dose modification	No	No	No	**Yes**	**Yes**
Treatment execution	No	**Yes**	**Yes**	**Yes**	**Yes**
Treatment monitoring	No	No	**Yes**	**Yes**	**Yes**
Diabetes example	Inpatient on starvation diet	Comply with prescribed insulin dose	Measure serum glucose	Adjust insulin dose and diet	

In some circumstances, most notably certain chronic diseases, the patient's role has extended beyond merely complying with the clinician's medication orders, to monitoring the effect of the treatment once executed. Thus, for example, asthmatic, diabetic, and hypertensive patients were asked to keep symptom logs or measure key physiological parameters such as peak flow, serum glucose, and blood pressure. As treatment algorithms were developed, patients were also able to make adjustments to their own medication doses based on what they observed when they monitored these parameters. Asthmatic and diabetic patients now adjust their therapies by making reference to action plans and insulin sliding scales, respectively.

Finally, for a limited range of conditions and problems, patients are in complete control of their own health care process. They not only select and implement treatments, but they also make the preceding diagnoses. Seasonal allergies are perhaps the best, but by no means the only, example of this in the United States. Patients diagnose the symptoms of this condition themselves, purchase medications over the counter, deliver the medications, and monitor the outcome. A positive outcome is final confirmation that the diagnosis and treatment choice were correct. Similarly, recent availability of oral contraceptives, ovulation tests, and pregnancy tests has allowed sophisticated fertility management to become the sole domain of the woman herself. The trend toward increasing total control of the care process is fostered by the increased over-the-counter (OTC) availability of medications that were previously available only by prescription.[31] In taking the medication, the patient is formally testing his or her own diagnostic hypothesis and making treatment decisions accordingly.

In the examples and table above, different conditions or different problems are at different points on the spectrum of patient participation—trauma to the left, seasonal allergies to the right. However, the spectrum represented in table 7-1 also has a temporal aspect to it. That is, as the stage of knowledge for any one condition or problem increases, patient participation in the care process for that disease can change. The history of diabetes treatment (see chapter 4) provides a good example of this phenomenon (bottom row in table 7-1). At the turn of the twentieth century, when the best treatment available was an inpatient starvation diet, the patient's role in the care process was as a recipient of care. Because insulin, discovered in 1921, was a protein that could only be delivered by injection, patients immediately became an integral participant in the care process, being the only "worker" who could practically deliver the therapy long term. But although home testing was feasible even before insulin's discovery, and was made easier with the introduction of Benedict's test in 1914, the patient did not have a major role in managing the insulin treatment beyond self-administration. Instead, patients brought the results of home (urine) glucose tests to their doctors, who adjusted the insulin dosage for them. With the advent of reliable home serum glucose monitoring (1961), improved patient education, and the development of dosage algorithms (sliding scales), the patient's role evolved from not only monitoring the therapy to also making critical day-by-day adjustments in insulin dose. Thus over the twentieth century, the patient's operational role in the care process has undergone a gradual transition toward ever-greater participation in the integral details of the care process. As the stage of knowledge has increased for any given condition or health problem, patients have been able to participate in more and more aspects of the health care process.[32] The increasing stage of knowledge and the concomitant development of highly specified rules make the knowledge for solving health problems more accessible to less highly trained health care "workers." Because greater knowledge specificity makes decisions more rules based, decision makers do not need the wealth of subtle and ambiguous content knowledge that an expert uses to make clinical judgments and decisions to resolve an unstructured or ill-defined health problem. The net effect is to transfer decision rights from the expert to the less expert. So not only is there a flux of patient health problems from iterative to sequential care processes (see chapter 4), but there is an analogous phenomenon in the roles of the participants in the process.

CONDITIONS FAVORING INCREASED PATIENT
INVOLVEMENT IN THE CARE PROCESS

However, this phenomenon—the transfer of decision rights with an increasing stage of knowledge—doesn't happen equally, or at the same rate, in all diseases. Diabetes and the other chronic diseases in which there are high levels of patient participation share some important characteristics that enable this progression and that are not shared by other diseases or health problems. The examples of those diseases in which patients participate as cocaregivers (such as asthma, diabetes, congestive heart failure, and seasonal allergies) suggest that even with concrete instructions and exact specification of expected outcomes of interventions (for example, as in the case of the hypertension management guidelines discussed in chapter 1), two other conditions—relating to the outcome and the intervention—are necessary for patients to easily take a significant operational role in the delivery process and the clinical management of their disease as they are in the chronic diseases above. Together, these two conditions make it easier for the patient to engage in iterative problem solving in exactly the same ways as clinicians.

First, the diseases above all have a distinct outcome or clinical marker that a patient may easily observe and manage so that the patient can, in effect, manage the disease or problem by managing the marker. This may be a clinical parameter that it is tightly tied to, or that is the basis of, the disease (such as serum glucose). It may also be an intermediate outcome (such as HbA_{1C}), or an end outcome or symptom that is strongly tied to the state of the disease (for example, the symptoms of seasonal allergies). The marker must be sensitive to changes in the intervention. Diabetes's two markers, for example, vary meaningfully over short periods of time (hour to hour in the case of glucose, and over one to two weeks for HbA_{1C}) in response to insulin, thereby allowing the patient to assess the effect of their interventions. Changes in care can be tested against changes in the markers.

Second, they have a mechanism that allows patients to exercise control over the disease or problem. For a patient to take increasing control over his or her disease with ease, in the manner of diabetes, the primary intervention that influences the outcome or clinical parameter must be rapidly acting and have a strong dose-response relationship (such as is the case with insulin therapy). Moreover, meaningful secondary variables—such as diet, exercise, or exposure to dust and pollens—must be observable (by the patient) and under the patient's control. Such is not the case for all diseases. Warfarin, for example, is an oral anticoagulant taken chronically by patients at risk of a stroke. Superficially, it might seem that patients could easily manage their own blood clotting in the same way that diabetic patients manage their insulin—checking their clotting times and adjusting their warfarin doses and diets accordingly.[33] However, several characteristics of warfarin and its metabolism may make it a more challenging intervention for patients to manage. The biology of warfarin, unlike that of insulin, is such that there is a long lag time and an unpredictable relationship between an individual dose of the drug and the effect this dose has on an individual's clotting.[34] Moreover, many other things—for example, some foods and other drugs—influence warfarin's impact on blood clotting.[35]

In circumstances where these conditions are met, the tight feedback loop involving an effective intervention, a well-specified decision rule, and a sensitive marker allows some patients with well-described chronic diseases to perform structured experiments on their own disease. The outcomes of these personal experiments are twofold: first, the patient gains control over the disease; and second, he or she learns about the disease as it is manifest in his or her body. The net result is to increase the stage of knowledge as it relates to the disease manifest in the individual person. That is, structured patient experiments with primary variables (such as insulin) can allow patients to isolate and test the impact of other variables (such as diet and the amount and timing of exercise) on their disease. Such variables are neither well understood by, nor measurable by, nor under the direct control of the patient's physician, and are not the subject of highly specified rules in the same way as is insulin. Over time, patients become experts in their own disease and develop their own patterns and rule sets relating to these other variables, and have the potential to operate at a higher stage of knowledge than even their clinical experts (with respect to the disease manifest in them). Thus patients are not confined to participating in the care process in the role of novice, applying simple rules, but eventually can develop their own clinical judgment and expertise about themselves and their own disease.

Thus far, comparatively few diseases and problems are at the extreme right-hand side of the spectrum represented in table 7-1. However, several industry forces make it possible that over time some more diseases and problems will be manageable by the patient operating as his or her caregiver in the way described above. First, improved point-of-care testing has the potential to increase the number of outcomes that patients could manage. For example, patient self-monitoring of blood pressure has been enabled by the development of more reliable home blood pressure–monitoring equipment. Cholesterol measurement from a single-drop blood specimen raises the possibility that hyperlipidemic patients will be able to manage their disease in a similar fashion to diabetics. The fields of genomic and molecular medicine offer the promise of new and more sensitive clinical markers and thus more and better diagnostic tests. Second, new device technologies embed highly specified protocols in their software. These automate complex decisions and allow less highly trained people to undertake complex tasks. For instance, new portable defibrillators—which are capable of both making a diagnosis and delivering a therapy—allow any passerby to intervene to aid a collapsed patient. And new-generation blood glucose monitors can provide explicit advice to diabetic patients. And third, a new generation of targeted medicines, to which these markers are sensitive, would increase patients' control over their disease.

These technological forces may increase the number of diseases and problems amenable to patient monitoring and adjustment. But for patients to be truly in control (as in the examples cited above, in which patients provide their own care, even without reference to a health professional), other societal changes would be necessary. Tests and therapies must be legally available to the patient "over the counter." Although regulators' future views on the advisability of increased OTC availability are uncertain, the recent trend has been toward increased availability. Some drugs, until recently thought of as prescription-only—for example, H2-receptor antagonists such as cimetidine, and, in England, the cholesterol-lowering agent simvastatin (Zocor)—are now available over the counter.[36] Finally, younger generations are rapidly becoming accustomed to exercising greater control over many aspects of their daily lives and doing things for themselves—for example, managing their investments and retirement savings, booking their travel, and managing their bank accounts. As these generations age, they may think it only natural to deliver some of their own health care with little or minimal recourse to a health professional.

The foregoing has focused on the technological capability and legal authority of the patient to take a significant caregiving role in the process of care. It has said nothing about patients' willingness to do so. In fact, the evidence suggests that patients will vary significantly in their appetite for this role. The experience of other service industries in which coproduction is an important feature of the service is that, in addition to varying in their capabilities (such as skills, knowledge, resources, and sense of self-efficacy), customers vary in their preferences for delivering some of their own service and the effort they are willing and able to expend.[37]

In health care, patients vary in both their capabilities for self-care (for example, their sense of self-efficacy, or the "confidence to carry out a behavior necessary to reach a desired goal") and the kind of role they want to take in the health care process.[38] Several simple taxonomies exist to describe the range of ways in which patients wish to interact with their care providers and the process of care. One, for example, describes patient decision-making preferences and divides patients into three categories depending on how engaged they are with decision making relating to their own care: "deferrers," "delayers," and "deliberators."[39] *Deferrers* apply an implicit decision rule: seek the advice of an expert and then follow their recommendation. *Delayers* typically consider more than one option but quickly make a choice without actively seeking much information from either a doctor or other sources. And *deliberators* actively gather information from multiple sources, weigh the pros and cons, and assume some responsibility for the decision. Another taxonomy sorts patients by the nature of their relationship with their physician: paternalistic, informative, interpretive, and deliberative.[40] And yet another, devised at the time of the Internet bubble, divides patients' attitudes to physicians and the information they provide into "accepting" of the information the physician provides, "informed" by supplemental information, "involved" and seeking much more information, and "in control," diagnosing themselves before seeking a physician's opinion.[41] The point, of course, of these taxonomies is that patients are distributed in their attitudes toward their health providers and their role in their own health care. For instance, a 2001 Boston Consulting Group survey found that the distribution was accepting (11 percent), informed (57 percent), involved (23 percent), and in control (9 percent).[42] Only a proportion of patients will want an increased role in their own care process and as their own caregiver in spite of the extent to which improvements in technology or changes in regulation make such an increased role possible.

Note that the preceding paragraphs have adopted a cautious tone. Regardless of whether they are willing or able to take on new roles as their own caregivers, or are in fact advantaged by doing so, patients are increasingly empowered to do so by new technologies that incorporate improved medical knowledge and allow them to take over some functions that were previously reserved for clinical professionals. Nonetheless, patients and providers are a long way from determining an optimal balance of activities for each constituent, and this will likely vary from disease to disease as well as patient to patient. In spite of this, demand for self-management tools is growing, and in limited ways the "outsourcing" of some care processes or portions of a care process to the patient is already happening.[43] Not only are the roles and responsibilities of physician and nonphysician caregivers important design considerations for the care process and the delivery organization, but so too is the role of the patient. The patient's "job description" is becoming an important component of the human resource planning that goes into the design of an operating system.

In spite of the wide distribution in patient preferences, the leading group of patients—those seeking or accepting of a larger role in their own care process—is already having an impact on the structure of the delivery sector by creating a market for a range of new products and services.

MARKET EVOLUTION AND THE INCREASING DIVERSITY OF HEALTH CARE DELIVERY ORGANIZATIONS

Over recent years, both the retail and the wholesale health care services markets have changed considerably. In the former, a whole new range of consumer goods and services seek to serve the needs of patients who are more active in their own care. These include new "intelligent" devices (such as Web-enabled pillboxes), new generations of old devices (e.g., glucose monitors in a cell phone), and new services (e.g., telemonitoring services that both alert patients and provide advice). Furthermore, some services previously available only to physicians are now available to patients. For example, some national laboratories are making their tests available directly to the consumer without requiring a physician's order. Hence diabetic patients can send off a blood sample and get an HbA_{1C} determination.

The value propositions these new goods and services make to patients vary. In-store clinics, for example, provide, among other things, diagnosis confirmation. That is, the patient seeking care at an in-store clinic already has a reasonable idea of his or her diagnosis and seeks both confirmation of that hypothesis and treatment. Other services offer various combinations of surveillance and alerting, either by monitoring parameters of chronic diseases (such as heart rate and rhythm or serum glucose) or by scanning healthy patients for undetected disease (for example, retail CT-scanning businesses). Yet other services offer information, either general (for example, general or disease-specific Web sites and online communities run by provider organizations or advocacy groups) or specific (through electronic physician consultations). And still others provide therapies themselves to a retail market (for example, laser eye surgery and alternative health providers).

Similarly, diversification has also occurred in "wholesale" services—services that either provide venues in which physicians treat their patients or work in conjunction with established professionals or insurers to provide components of a patient's total care needs. Specialty surgical hospitals, ambulatory care centers, infusion centers, hospices, and long-term care facilities have all experienced significant growth in recent years, as have chronic disease management and disease prevention services. And all these new services are supported by entrepreneurs providing business support services, such as outsourced billing, electronic health records, and materials management.

What is notable about these new consumer and wholesale services is that they are predominantly highly focused, typically on a specific single dimension—for example, a patient group, a process, an intervention, a piece of infrastructure, or a disease. By concentrating on only one market niche, they are able to employ a single operating system. The efficiencies they have realized through such focus (improved operational performance and reduced capital needs) have helped them take business from diversified providers, such as general services hospitals and primary practitioners, which typically employ a single operating system to address the needs of multiple conditions and patient groups and therefore have a much less favorable cost structure. Moreover, not only are these niche providers' businesses centered on a single operational model, but they also are frequently focused on the management of less complex conditions (the left side of the distribution represented in figure 7-1) that can be managed with a sequential care process (see chapter 5, table 5-2). Entrepreneurs, naturally, target the most profitable segments of a heterogeneous patient population. Fewer entrepreneurs address the needs of patient groups with complex, uncertain, or multiple conditions that require iterative processes and expensive infrastructure. In general, these patients are being left to the diversified health care providers— physicians and hospitals.

The net result of the growth in specialized service providers is the gradual diversification and fragmentation of the market for health care services— especially for those that address single simple conditions with sequential care processes. Primary care provides an example of this fragmentation (see table 7-2). Primary care predominantly comprises the eight general activities shown in the left-hand column of table 7-2, and primary care physicians have typically used a single, general-purpose, operating system to provide these services, in which they perform most of the work and direct the rest. However, as the right-hand column illustrates, niche providers are competing with primary practitioners for individual components of their service. Entrepreneurs, in a predictable process of innovation, focus on a particular activity

FIGURE 7-1

A spectrum of health services

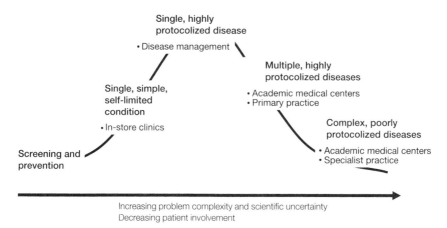

Note: For illustration, figure 7-1 represents the distribution of problem complexity and uncertainty as normal. In fact, the distribution is likely significantly right skewed; see L. A. Green et al., "The Ecology of Medical Care Revisited," *New England Journal of Medicine* 344 (2001): 2021–2025.

and build a service and business model uniquely configured for it.[44] Those providers have built specific care platforms for a particular category of service: prevention, screening, diagnosis of acute, self-limited illness, and so on.[45] Each provider in the right-hand column exploits the benefits of operational focus (in which "simplicity, repetition, experience, and homogeneity of tasks breed competence") by standardizing decisions and activities within the limits of the available evidence and avoiding the additional costs inherent in providing a diversified service.[46] In many cases, they provide a service of equal (and occasionally better) quality more efficiently and less expensively. This phenomenon is not limited to primary care: general hospitals are under attack from for-profit investor-owned specialist hospitals that focus on a limited range of highly standardized procedures; physician specialists compete with nonphysicians over the right to prescribe for less complex cases; consumers have access to ever-wider Web-based information, decision aids, and nonphysician expertise; and so on.

   Although this trend may improve the quality and efficiency of each of the particular services, it exacerbates a particularly thorny problem. Health care services are not necessarily independent; the clinical or informational

TABLE 7-2

Components of primary care

Components of primary care	Innovations in practice
Prevention	Lifestyle management companies (e.g., smoking cessation companies), personal trainers, gyms, Weight Watchers, etc.
Screening	Centralized single-condition screening services (e.g., Swedish mammography program)
Diagnosis and treatment of acute, non-life-threatening, self-limiting diseases	In-store clinics
Diagnosis and treatment of acute serious illness	Emergency rooms, hospitalists (inpatient)
Management of chronic stable conditions	Disease management companies, provider-based disease management programs
Diagnosis and treatment of exacerbations of chronic conditions	Hospitalists
Navigation and advocacy for complex (multiple, interacting) diseases	Care coordinators
Palliative care	Palliative care (hospice) companies and organizations

outcomes of one may be an essential input into another, and sequence and timing can matter greatly. A fragmented market for health care services—if it fractures feedback loops within an episode of care or meaningful connections between episodes of care—potentially impedes care processes. This is much less of an issue in the hospital-within-a-hospital model (see chapter 5), in which both services, although somewhat independent, are specifically designed to operate together.

The coordination and integration of multiple services for the same patient, either concurrently or over long periods of time, is an important determinant of quality and safety as well as a significant operational challenge.[47] Studies suggest that failure of coordination of activities and transfer of critical information between doctors (doctor to doctor, diagnostic service to doctor, hospital to primary physician, etc.), and between doctors and patients, is already a significant problem.[48] As the broader market for health services further fragments, who should be responsible for coordinating care and how this should be achieved remains uncertain. In previous generations, when diseases were acute and therapies fewer, there was less to coordinate, and the primary care practitioner took this role. But with the advent of multiple therapies and chronic diseases, this work has become a significant additional burden for primary practitioners, who face an increasing workload, a lack of interoperable information systems, and a fragmented care delivery system.[49]

Several approaches to coordination currently exist, many focused on practitioners and health care delivery organizations; although at the moment, none clearly dominates. One approach, centered on the primary care practitioner, proposes revising the primary practice as the "medical home," a model of primary practice in which a "basket" of medical services are centralized and coordinated and integrated.[50] This model emphasizes the integration of practice information systems, a broader range of office staff to support a team approach to care, and evidence-based guidelines to support both responsive and prospective care. Other approaches include electronic referrals and practice-based coordination by advanced practice nurses.

Alternatives, less reliant on the practitioner and focused more on the patient, include new roles and new technologies. For example, *care coaches* are volunteers (often survivors) or professionals whose role is to help patients navigate their way through the multiple components of the health care delivery system during an episode of disease such as cancer. Coaches can help patients manage their information, interpret it, evaluate their options, and identify and access resources. The American Cancer Society, for example, trains volunteers to support patients diagnosed with breast cancer. Personal health records (PHRs) and secure patient portals have some of the same aims. By allowing patients to establish, maintain, and query their own medical record, PHRs facilitate the patient taking over some of the work of coordination. One ultimate goal of a PHR is to allow the patient to proactively evaluate his or her own record, looking for patterns in the data that would suggest further actions, such as screening tests or alternative therapies that should be considered (by utilizing an evidence-based rules engine embedded in the software).

Although, currently, there is little evidence of the acceptability or effectiveness of new consumer-focused services or approaches to coordination, what is clear is that many of them presume a new role for a more active, educated, and empowered consumer. They also presume a competent consumer. For example, in offering a "diagnosis confirmation" service, in-store clinics have assumed that patients have already made appropriate diagnoses and triage decisions for themselves. Similarly, the growth in over-the-counter medications explicitly assumes that patients are more than competent to handle these drugs. What remains unclear, however, is the appropriate allocation of risk (both financial and medicolegal) between a patient and a provider when the patient is more deeply involved in the coproduction of his or her own care process. In the past, the health risks of medication noncompliance were the patient's, but the financial risks went to the insurer. Health savings accounts have reallocated some of the financial risk back to the consumer, but even when a patient plays the role of a key health care "worker," the medicolegal risk may stay with the doctor and the health care delivery organization. For instance, Boston's CRICO, the medicolegal insurer for the Harvard Medical Institutions, reports that in circumstances where patients have failed to attend appointments for screening tests, the provider organization has nonetheless been found liable for subsequent undetected cancers.[51] Hence health care delivery organizations are in a difficult position. They can afford neither to ignore the increasing involvement of the patients they serve as coproducers in their own health care nor to distance themselves from patients who choose to be less involved. Where appropriate (e.g., in primary care), their process designs have to account for varying styles and levels of patient involvement.

CONCLUSION: ACCOMMODATING AND DESIGNING NEW ROLES

Typically, only some roles are explicitly planned in a care delivery organization. Few doctors, employed or not, have their work defined by an explicit job description. Instead, an unwritten compact usually shapes what they expect of the systems for delivering care with which they interact, and local regulations and payment arrangements define their scopes of practice and range of available tools.[52] Yet, independent of regulation, the same forces influencing care processes, operating systems, and managerial purviews have the potential to reshape the roles of all the participants in the care process—doctors, patients, and the many nonphysician clinicians who contribute to care delivery systems—and are already reshaping the market for health care services that is the context in which these practitioners work.

The continual flux of the knowledge for health care both allows and in fact forces an ongoing redefinition of who is to use that knowledge and how it is to be used, through revising the participants' capabilities, rights, responsibilities, and roles. These revised roles are an important input into the design of an operating system such as those discussed in chapters 5 and 6. Moreover, not only do current practitioner roles need to be specified relative to new care processes and operating systems, but entirely new roles (perhaps "system architect," for example) need to be developed and reimbursed. Roles require as much attention to design as all the other aspects of operating systems for care delivery and for learning. And because both how the scientific and organizational knowledge for care will evolve, and which new health problems will develop, remains uncertain, these roles may change repeatedly. Hence, irrespective of the current state of the local scope of practice regulations, no role design—who is to do what and when—can be safely regarded as fixed in the medium and long term. Role redesign is an ongoing managerial task as who is able to, who wants to, and who is permitted to do what continue to change.

Although the evolving knowledge for care allows and forces important new roles for health practitioners, few health care delivery organizations or national-level health systems adequately prepare their workforces for these new roles. Few professional schools provide any managerial training for undergraduate nurses or doctors. Although "team-based care" is commonly referenced both at conferences and in the literature, little investment is made in preparing individual clinicians for teamwork. And patients are often forced to take on the work of care, either decision making or task execution, without adequate support or preparation. Designs for care require attention not only to human resource deployment but also to development (as Istituto Clinico Humanitas demonstrates), patient education, and the careful integration of the roles of employed and nonemployed health care "workers." Without industry- and organization-level investment in staff development, managers' degrees of freedom in designing care are significantly limited.

8

Designing Care

The preceding three chapters have described some of the design parameters for, and an approach to, the day-to-day management of organizations that provide patient relief: operating systems for improving the performance of care delivery and operating systems for learning during care delivery. Both are designed to account for the nature of care and the various processes by which it is delivered, and both require and exploit new roles of patients and caregivers alike. But these designs have thus far been treated separately—delivery as distinct from innovation and learning. In reality, both are necessary for the successful delivery of health care.

How are the performance of current processes and the creation of better ones for the future to be managed simultaneously in an already complex environment? The operating systems for delivery and learning discussed in the previous chapters are designed and managed in very different ways. In particular, although they both account for, exploit, and manage variation in the processes by which health problems are solved for individual patients, they take very different approaches to practice variation. In the former, the design of the operating system that executes care is matched to the nature of the care process—iterative or sequential—with the aim of reducing variation or, in the case of the hospital-within-a-hospital model, corralling that variation which does remain to one part of the operating system specifically designed to accommodate it. It aims to improve patient outcomes by better executing on known "best care." In the latter, variation in the outcomes of the daily experiments of patient care is the essential driver of the innovation and learning the operating system is specifically designed to capture. This operating system aims to improve outcomes by creating and capturing new knowledge about what is best care and how to best execute it. How can these approaches to delivery and learning be reconciled?

INTEGRATING PERFORMANCE
AND INNOVATION

In fact, the two approaches to variation taken by the care systems discussed in chapters 5 and 6—minimize and exploit, respectively—are not necessarily at odds with one another. Rather, they are complementary and come together in an important way. That variation which remains after the operating system for care delivery has controlled as much as possible is treated as a signal by the operating system for learning. The operating systems for delivering care and learning from care are in fact subsystems of a larger system. Together, they make up an operating system for managing care that comprises two linked loops (as shown in figure 8-1) that function as a delivery cycle and a learning cycle. At the intersection of the two loops, linking them together, are the core processes of care—the decisions and tasks of daily patient care—iterative and sequential. This care management model integrates the various structures, capabilities, and actions that were discussed in previous chapters, and illustrates the work required to manage care and control complex health care delivery organizations.

FIGURE 8-1

A design for managing the delivery of care

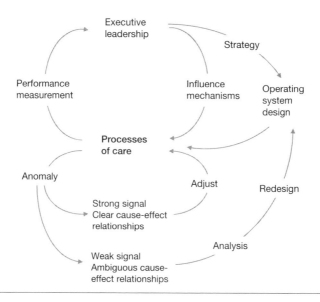

Figure 8-1 represents the relationships between, and interactions among, the four elements of a system for delivering health care: knowledge, care process, organization, and practitioner. Note that the term *managing* in this context means much more than controlling care—"management" in the sense of exercising production control—as is the primary goal of the tools described in chapter 1. It includes designing, managing, and redesigning the function of, and relationships among, the four components of a system for delivering health care. And it requires a set of interacting capabilities that are represented in figure 8-1.

The top loop in figure 8-1 represents the operating system for delivering care—in effect, the mechanism by which the health care delivery organization's strategy is executed. It is the system that applies current evidence to solve individual patients' problems and implements "best care" (evidence-based medicine). The configuration of the operating system—both "software" and "hardware"—is matched to the process of care. Current best evidence about how to solve specific problems is embedded both in the protocols guiding clinical decisions and in the design of the operating system that supports these clinical processes. Different clinical processes generate different measurements with which managers evaluate the organization's ability to effectively solve patients' health problems and thereby execute managerial control—iterative processes evaluated by outcome measures, and sequential processes by process measures. And managers execute control over the production system by adjusting (financial and nonfinancial) incentives, establishing behavioral boundaries, creating supporting structures and business processes, and making strategic investments in human and technical capital, all predicated on the nature of the underlying process for solving the patient's health problem.

The bottom loop in figure 8-1 represents the operating system for learning—for creating new evidence from routine practice (evidence-creating medicine). Anomalies or deviations from what is expected are the signals that trigger short-term process and operating system adjustments (where signals are strong and cause and effect relationships are clear and well understood) and longer-term analysis and formal testing (where signals or their meaning are ambiguous). The anomaly that triggers the learning cycle is in fact any unexpected event, either positive (an unexpectedly good outcome, such as Dr. Sheskin's observation of the positive effect of thalidomide on leprosy) or negative (such as an error). Clinical managers use the output of this learning system in the bottom loop to inform improved designs of the operating system for care delivery (the top loop in figure 8-1). Over time, improvements in the protocols or the supporting operating system reduce the variation in the delivery cycle.

Hence, the two loops—a delivery cycle and a learning cycle—act in concert to simultaneously optimize the implementation of the current best understanding of health problems and their solution, create the next generation of knowledge required to solve problems, and embed that new knowledge into clinical practice. In combination, the two cycles function to make the health care delivery organization a self-improving system. The point of integration is the care process—hence the importance of understanding the process's true nature. The delivery cycle is triggered through performance measurement, and the learning cycle by the observation of an anomaly.

SIX CAPABILITIES

An integrated design for care delivery and learning from care, depicted in figure 8-1, depends on six key capabilities (see table 8-1). Each is essential for organizations that manage care. Individual care delivery organizations may vary in the ways they develop these capabilities or the specific tools they choose to effect them, but ultimately they all must have these capabilities.

TABLE 8-1

Capabilities for design and management of systems for delivering health care

Capability	Characteristics
Operating capability	Internally aligned operating system configured to meet the needs of the target population (externally aligned)
Performance measurement	Balance of process and outcome measures
Production control	Financial and nonfinancial incentives and sanctions that influence provider behavior
Anomaly detection	Supportive culture and multiple methods capable of detecting signals of varying strengths
Analysis	Qualitative and quantities analysis of small and large data sets and multiple experimental methods (hypothesis generating and hypothesis confirming)
Adjustment and redesign	Short-term response to individual problems and long-term operating system redesign

1. Operating Capability

The first component is an operating capability: an operating system in which the hardware and software are explicitly configured (and aligned) to match the nature of the clinical work it is intended to support (see chapter 5). This operating system or systems will represent the local balance of more custom and standard care (with associated iterative and sequential processes, respectively), depending on the particular needs of the population being served. A focused provider serving a homogeneous community with well-characterized single conditions is more likely to have a single operating system, whereas several operating systems in parallel are more suited to complex, diversified health care delivery organizations serving multiple constituencies with multiple, complex, and uncertain clinical conditions.

2. Performance Measurement

Care delivery organizations need a capacity for performance measurement and management oversight and control that relies heavily on measurements derived from the process of care. These can be process measures (e.g., was the patient tested for HbA_{1C}), intermediate outcome measures (such as the level of HbA_{1C} or the percentage of patients with HbA_{1C} less than 8 percent or greater than 9.5 percent in a defined practice panel), or outcome measures (e.g., short- and long-term diabetic complication rate), and may be both clinical and service measures. As previously discussed, where the stage of knowledge is high and the care process is sequential, the measures tend to be process measures—compliance rates with specified protocols. When the health care process is iterative, such a reductivist approach to process management is infeasible—individual decisions or actions cannot be relied upon to consistently lead to a specific health outcome—and so management oversight must depend on utilization measures and risk-adjusted outcome measures.

At Intermountain Healthcare the appropriate measures for each clinical condition are identified by the development teams as part of protocol development—drawing on both current published scientific evidence and clinicians' own experience. The majority of Intermountain's care management measures are developed in-house and directly relate to the care the organization actually delivers—of the 204 measures in use by the clinical programs in 2008, only 50 were derived from external sources, such as the Centers for Medicare and Medicaid Services (CMS), The Joint Commission, or the National Committee for Quality Assurance (NCQA). These measures express the institution's causal hypotheses about which outcomes matter and which elements of the care process and the associated supporting operating systems drive those outcomes, either positively or negatively. Thus they form the basis of the performance measurement system for each clinical process; they are, in effect, the practical manifestation of the "model of cause" (see chapter 5). That is, the measures that managers use to assess the organization's clinical success are developed by the clinical teams themselves. The care processes, business processes, and associated measures represent more than any individual clinician's experience and knowledge relating to a health problem; they are the sum total of the institution's knowledge and experience. Moreover, these measurements can be (and are at Intermountain) integrated with measures of financial performance to create a balanced scorecard.[1] This model of management of a care delivery organization gives attention not only to measures of financial health (for example, return on investment, revenue, or cost per case) or global measures of operational performance (such as average length of stay, patient satisfaction, mortality or infection rates), but also to detailed measures of clinical performance (such as rates of compliance with specific protocols and detailed disease-specific risk-adjusted outcome rates).

3. Production Control (Mechanisms of Influence)

The third component is a diverse portfolio of mechanisms for influencing the clinical process (that is, for exercising production control), usually through influencing practitioner behavior. This often includes, but is not limited to, financial incentives for physicians and executives. Such are typically related to global financial performance and, more recently, to performance for specific clinical conditions through pay-for-performance contracts with health insurers. Beyond incentives, tools that improve physicians' and nurses' working life, by making it easy for them to practice their chosen professions, are also an important mechanism for implementing and modifying clinical processes. These include tools that "make it easy to do it right," most of which attend to physician workflow in some way, and many rely on information systems.[2] They either link tasks usually associated with one another, reduce paperwork through default text and documents, decrease reliance on memory by making protocols available at the time of care (e.g., computerized reminders, checklists, and standard order sets), or expedite decision making by increasing access to critical patient information and current evidence (for example, electronic medical record, "just-in-time" knowledge delivery, and critical results paging).[3]

Many techniques to smooth clinical work do not rely on information systems. Seattle's Virginia Mason Medical Center (VMMC), for example, has applied techniques drawn from the Toyota Production System, such as value stream mapping, to simplify and eliminate many unnecessary physician and nurse tasks.[4] Virginia Mason also pays close attention to clinicians' physical environment. Clinical care areas are designed to reduce clutter, reduce patient and staff walking distances, and ensure that critical drugs and equipment are always available. These small-scale physical redesigns use Toyota's principle of 5S (sort, simplify, sweep, standardize, and self-discipline) to organize a complex workplace. The net result—a smooth workflow—aids process control at VMMC.[5]

4. Anomaly Detection

A fourth component is a set of mechanisms to aid in the detection of anomalies in clinical processes. Anomalies are of several different types and strengths, and may be positive or negative: problems in task execution (or unexpected "obstacles that thwart expected work processes"), unexpected events (e.g., foam strikes) or process steps (e.g., outpatient care of moderately ill pneumonia patients who are usually treated as inpatients), and unexpected outcomes of tasks executed correctly (e.g., the effect of thalidomide on leprotic skin lesions) or incorrectly (i.e., an error).[6] Because they must be capable of surfacing anomalies of differing signal strengths, various detection methods are needed, each appropriate for a different type of signal (see chapter 6, table 6-1). Where signals are strong and easily detected by individuals, formal and informal reporting systems—such as communication channels for reporting unexpected observations ("hotlines") and incident-reporting systems—suffice. In the Toyota Production System, the andon cord (a cord running above the work station that, when pulled, initiates music and a flashing light that signal that the worker has encountered a problem) is a simple tool that allows a car assembly worker to alert team leaders of an anomaly. Weaker signals, however, require deliberate amplification, either by reducing the background noise that might submerge a signal through standardization of clinical practices, or by creating specific structures or processes that seek and amplify signals—such as deliberate surveillance for key sentinel events ("never events"), control charts, regular analyses of aggregate variance data, team meetings to review outcomes, and a culture that supports speaking up.[7] As discussed in chapter 6, the latter is extremely important. Managers' acceptance of the possibility that a failure might occur, and receptivity to observations that might portend such a failure, is an essential element in a capability for signal detection.

Not only do managers need to create a culture of speaking up; they also need to be willing to support the subsequent costs of increased signal detection.[8] Anomalies vary in the strength of the signal and the underlying cause-effect relationship, and also in their potential significance and the response they engender. The risk of deliberately amplifying anomalies is that some of the signals will turn out to be false alarms—false positives, or true positives with no real meaning or importance. Although some anomalies do justify "stopping the line," the majority of the times an andon cord on the Toyota production line is pulled, the line is not stopped. Moreover, many anomalous observations, such as the unusually large piece of foam being shed from the ascending *Columbia* or the unexpected transfer of a heart failure patient from the nurse-practitioner to the cardiologist in Duke's heart failure clinic, represent ambiguous threats—signals that may, or may not, portend future harm.[9] And analyzing each to determine its significance can be costly, especially in the short term, because so many will ultimately be found to be insignificant.

5. Analysis

Thus, because signals vary in their strength and significance, the fifth necessary capability is one for analysis. Mechanisms that help surface anomalies need to be linked to mechanisms for analyzing the anomalies, making meaning of them, and sorting the significant from the inconsequential. Differing signal strengths and different levels of risk will require different approaches to analysis. Strong signals and tight cause-effect relationships lend themselves to immediate analysis—often by an individual worker—of the single observation. Such is the case when an andon cord is first pulled in a car assembly plant. They can also lend themselves to simple tests of an intervention. Weak signals or loose or unclear cause-effect relationships require statistical analysis of large databases, as in the case of pneumonia treatment at Intermountain. Without its capability for analyzing a large database and deliberately examining unexplained and anomalous practice variation, analysts at Intermountain would not have identified an alternative way of caring for moderately ill pneumonia patients. And when a signal, weak or strong, might portend a significant risk, it should initiate a "brief but intense period of heightened inquiry, experimentation, and problem solving," often utilizing rapid cycle experimentation and hypothesis generating, and open-ended experimental methods, rather than hypothesis-confirming controlled trials.[10] Hence a health care delivery organization has to develop and maintain a portfolio of different analytic skills that include individuals' expertise in problem solving, team-based rapid cycle experimentation, and large database analysis.

Although examining anomalies can be expensive, the cost of developing skills in analysis and response may be justified, not just because any individual anomaly might contain a nugget of new insight, or a real threat might be thwarted; but because as organizations identify and evaluate more anomalies, they develop their capabilities—they learn and get better at recognizing true signals and threats. Hence, over time, the threshold for initiating an evaluation, and consequently the proportion of meaningful anomalies detected, may rise, thereby reducing the overall costs. Moreover, each time a team in an organization evaluates an anomaly, it practices the skills required to effectively and efficiently evaluate and respond. Thus, in the long term, the cost to evaluate an anomaly and the number of anomalies reduces.

6. Adjustment and Redesign

Sixth, organizations need the capability to respond to what they learn, both by making short-term process adjustments and, in the longer term, by reconfiguring the operating system to better support clinical processes.[11] This capability comprises several elements. Many responses depend on individual action. Short-term fixes are usually undertaken by individual workers responding to their own observations and diagnoses in real time. In fact, professionals are trained to (and lionized for their ability to) manage "unexpected," yet well-characterized, clinical problems such as anesthetic or surgical complications and cardiac arrests. They do so by drawing upon their own personal libraries of "precomplied responses" and routines.[12] Individuals also solve more-mundane problems in their daily work, such as the absence of needed equipment or information, most frequently by creating their own unique workarounds (for example, by hoarding equipment or sending two or three copies of a laboratory request). However, although such responses are often locally effective and solve the immediate problem, they often do nothing to prevent recurrence (sometimes termed *second-order problem solving*).[13] Just the opposite—firefighting (acutely addressing individual problems as if they were unique) often gets in the way of permanent solutions by sapping resources for long-term improvement.[14]

Individuals make and test permanent adjustments and improvements to local processes and systems—either to accommodate a particular anomaly or prevent its recurrence, or to elevate a problem to a level in the organization at which a permanent solution of the problem can be created—much less frequently.[15] In recognition of this fact, a health care delivery organization needs a mechanism for rapidly mobilizing an institutional response to an anomaly. Pulling the andon cord in a Toyota assembly plant immediately brings an experienced problem solver (or group of problem solvers) to assist at the site of the problem. The equivalent at Seattle's VMMC is its *patient safety alert*. In response to a safety alert sounded by a clinician (for example, an actual or near medication or surgical error), senior managers mobilize a team to undertake an immediate root cause analysis and design a permanent fix. In 2005 VMMC experienced an average of thirty-two patient safety alerts a month, each of which taking from forty-eight hours to two weeks to resolve.[16] For example, VMMC's response to a retained sponge incident was to sideline the surgeon, the operating room team, and the operating room for forty-eight hours until the cause of the error was identified and remedied.

Such problem-solving teams may be ad hoc, their composition depending on the nature of the anomaly; or they may be specifically created teams that are intended as problem-solving resources. These "rapid response teams" are configured not to execute known solutions to known problems (as are cardiac arrest teams) but to rapidly solve new problems, some of which no one may have previously encountered. They are analogous to the "Tiger Teams" that flight director Gene Kranz famously mobilized during the Apollo 13 crisis—teams drilled in strategies for rapid problem solving. The importance of rapid response teams is that they represent a pre-prepared capability for responding to an anomaly. That is, the organization does not wait for an anomaly to occur before creating a response capability; it presumes that anomalies in care processes will occur and develops a response mechanism—both the resource and the process for activating it—in advance.[17]

Equally, a care delivery organization needs to be practiced at long-term process and operating system redesign. These skills are hard to acquire rapidly in the crisis moments after a significant anomaly has surfaced. Intermountain Healthcare and the Virginia Mason Medical Center have taken different approaches to explicitly developing this capability. In the former, several structures, including the permanent development teams and guidance councils (see chapter 6) are the locus of expertise in designing and redesigning clinical processes and their supporting operating systems; and these groups develop and use a range of influence mechanisms to embed their new designs into the fabric of the organization. Moreover, IHC's Institute for Health Care Delivery Research—the group responsible for most of the data collection, reporting, and statistical analyses (see chapter 6)—also serves as a resource for new process and operating system designs. VMMC, in contrast, has established a highly distributed process for repeated operating system redesign: the Rapid Process Improvement Workshop (RPIW), a structured five-day team-based redesign event run by an individual unit. During an RPIW, the unit aims to eliminate waste, improve processes, and increase efficiency and productivity in a specific process. Each RPIW has the same format: define the existing process; establish measures and targets; observe, measure, and critique the existing process; develop and experiment with an improved process; and implement. VMMC has run hundreds of RPIWs—over four hundred between 2002 and 2007—and often runs multiple RPIWs within the same unit and on similar topics. As a result, processes and operating systems are continually being redesigned.

ETHICAL CONSIDERATIONS: THE EXPERIMENTAL NATURE OF CARE

The operating system and capabilities described above, designed to integrate performance and innovation, together leverage the certainty and manage the uncertainty of health care. In fact, the state of medical knowledge is such that it is not possible to manage care without addressing the inherent uncertainty in what to do for a patient and how to do it. The above operating system explicitly exploits the experimental nature of care by capturing the learning from the hundreds of small-scale focused tests of medical knowledge and system design in day-to-day care. But this raises an important issue: the ethics of experimentation.

Experimentation has always been at the heart of medical care, and is central to the approach to managing care discussed earlier. The routine care of an individual patient, especially for those patients with conditions or combinations of conditions that remain inadequately understood and poorly described, often has a large experiential component to it. In particular, iterative clinical processes are essentially experimental, albeit in a constrained and structured way. And long-term performance improvement in the above model depends on learning from the individual patient experiments that are the substance of day-to-day care. Moreover, it is not just day-to-day care that is experimental. Organizational improvement is also experimental. No organization successfully designs an operating system the first time. All real-world service organizations experiment repeatedly before coming to an operating system design that creates real value for their customers. But most service organizations do not put their customers at risk when they develop and test new operational models. They can either undertake such experiments "offline" in an experimental facility or in simulation, far away from their customers, or create well-controlled experimental environments, as, for example, did Bank of America when it created a specific branch to test new ideas.[18]

Frequently, health care organizations can do neither. Both learning from routine practice and the explicit testing of new ways of organizing care processes and operating systems occur "on the shop floor" in real organizations caring for real patients. But many of the experiments upon which insights from practice are based do not occur under the auspices of an Institutional Review Board (IRB), with the oversight and patient protections that these bodies bestow. None of the examples of insights derived from, and innovations made in, routine care that were described in chapter 6 involved either individual patient consent or an IRB. Although these issues are not considerations for other industries' attempts to improve operational performance, in health care they beg the question of the ethical obligations of the health care managers (whether clinically trained or not). Should the innovations discussed in chapter 6 have been treated as research? Are the experiments in daily care or organizational performance improvement "research," and to what extent do the obligations of a researcher apply to managers overseeing systems that support everyday experimentation in routine care or creating new and improved health care systems?

In fact, bioethicists have wrestled with questions of the relationship between management, improvement, and research, and the implications for managers, in recent years. A common starting point is the consideration of what constitutes research. Federal regulations define research as "a systematic investigation, including research development, testing and evaluation, designed to develop or contribute to generalizable knowledge."[19] (Inherent in this definition is the notion that patients in a research study expect no personal benefit from participation, and that any insights gained will be applied to future patients.[20]) The importance of this determination derives from what follows. An improvement initiative—for instance, a rapid cycle test, a system redesign, a deliberate process evaluation—treated as research will require review by an IRB before it is initiated, and that review may demand specific patient consent and written documentation, a process that has the potential to not only slow improvement efforts but serve as a disincentive to even starting them.[21]

Criteria for determining whether the activities of patient care or quality improvement are research vary, and include the intent for generalizability, the extent of deviation from "standard care," and whether the activity involves explicit patient recruitment.[22] Because of the difficulty of applying these criteria in practice, Casarett et al. have proposed a simple two-stage test for determining what improvement activities should be considered research and therefore accorded all the associated protections and oversight. These authors suggest first determining whether "the majority of patients are not expected to benefit directly from the knowledge to be gained." If this is the case, the initiative should be reviewed and regulated as research. If the majority of patients are likely to benefit directly, a second test is applied: would participants "be subjected to additional risks or burdens beyond usual clinical practice to make its results generalizable?"Again, if this is the case, the initiative should be treated as research.

According to Casarett et al.'s test, the experimentation in daily care—in particular, that inherent in iterative care processes, is not research, because its sole intent is to benefit that patient, and only that patient; and no additional risks are conferred in order to make new knowledge generalizable, even though there may be risks inherent in the care itself (for example, those related to adjustment of insulin dosing in an intensive care unit; see chapter 6). Moreover, short-term process adjustments in response to observed anomalies (see figure 8-1) are not research, because they, too, typically are for the benefit of the index patient and do not add risk for the purpose of generalizability.

If, however, the experiments of routine care generate insights that do require further testing in order to understand their significance, then that further testing may be research if seeking generalizability creates additional risk. Hence, a physician's use of thalidomide to aid a patient's sleep that resulted in the chance observation of this drug's effect on leprotic skin lesions is not research, but, by today's standards, the use of this drug for the purpose of testing its effect on leprosy in future patients is. Similarly, monitoring databases for unexpected (and possibly adverse) events—such as the outpatient treatment of pneumonia patients—is not research, since this activity is likely to directly benefit the patients involved and does not confer any additional risks. But a subsequent trial of outpatient treatment of community-acquired pneumonia would be research. From this perspective, larger health care systems are at an advantage. Systems such as Intermountain have the resources internally to mount the further research needed to make meaning of an observed anomaly (in Intermountain's case, the Institute for Health Care Delivery Research), and do not have to apply for external funding to support these analyses.

Irrespective of whether the experiments of the type discussed above should be considered research, and therefore beget a set of ethical obligations, health care managers (once again, whether clinically trained or not) are obligated to ensure that experiments are of good quality: that the experiments are rigorous and the learning system well designed and well managed. Experiments that, as a result of their poor design, are unlikely to yield useful information are harder to justify. Thus, when processes are "noisy" as a result of high levels of random variation, meaningful anomalies that occur during routine patient care are less likely to be observed, responded to, and learned from. The same is true when organizational cultures do not support speaking up or no processes exist for identifying and responding to anomalies. We cannot immediately change the experimental nature of much of routine health care—it is, after all, the nature of care—but we can improve the quality of those experiments, the likelihood that they will yield useful lessons, and our ability to act upon those lessons. Creating health care delivery organizations that capture and implement learning could be seen as an ethical obligation.

DESIGNING CARE

This chapter has described a model of care management that integrates reliably delivering what we know with learning about what we don't know. The delivery cycle marries the organization's strategy in its market or community with its internal operations for executing that strategy—reflected in its choices of clinical processes and associated operating systems. The learning cycle realizes performance improvement by exploiting the experimental nature of day-to-day care and captures the incremental improvements these experiments have the potential to generate. Both cycles accommodate the underlying nature of care processes that vary on a spectrum from sequential to iterative, depending on the particularities of the disease and the current state of scientific understanding.

Importantly, the key elements of the model represented in figure 8-1 are the capabilities required to manage care and the relationships among them. Developing a care delivery organization that delivers care and learns requires cultivating these six core capabilities. But organizations will differ in how they approach developing these capabilities and the specific tools they use to manifest them. For instance, different organizations will chose to influence care processes in different ways, depending, among other things, on the values of the organization and the specific resources available. What is important is that an organization can effectively influence the care process and the clinical behavior of employed and nonemployed physicians. Similarly, although there are many ways to ensure that anomalies are surfaced and analyzed, and each organization will marshal its available resources differently, ultimately the organizations that will be successful will be those that can most effectively learn from their own experience, however they chose to realize this goal.

Furthermore, organizations will tend to use whatever structures and processes they already have to support these capabilities. For example, in Boston's Massachusetts General Hospital's redesign, the long-term analytic capability is provided by a primary care research group that has been in existence for many years; the signal detection system relies, among other things, on modifications to the hospital's existing incident-reporting system; and its approach to influencing processes draws heavily (although not exclusively) on its new pay-for-performance contracts. Although these resources are not new, the hospital made use of them and some new resources when it reorganized them in 2007 into an integrated system like that in figure 8-1.

Many organizations already have some or all of the above capabilities in place but have not configured them in a mutually reinforcing system for managing and improving care.[23] Designing care does not have to await an infusion of new resources, unlikely in the current environment both within the United States and outside it. Rather, it is primarily a matter of configuring existing resources and matching operating systems to patient needs— evaluating the needs of the population being served, specifying the mechanism by which the organization adds value to those patients, designing and implementing operating systems, and configuring delivery and improvement cycles to meet those needs.

Although resources and capabilities may already be in place in many health care delivery organizations, most of these organizations were not explicitly designed to deliver care. Rather, they just developed—created to aggregate key resources needed in care provision. However, health care has become so complex—scientifically, technologically, organizationally, and socially—that organizations and processes not specifically designed and managed to account for this complexity as they create patient relief will ultimately disappoint. Organization is needed, and organizations need to perform well in order to realize the best possible clinical outcome.

Herein is the future work of the health care manager and a substantial part of any future health care reform. This work is, to a large degree, independent of how policy makers approach financing and reimbursing health care. Although financing and reimbursement changes may provide further incentives for change in health care delivery, a predominant focus on financing may be a distraction from the need for substantial reconfiguration of health care delivery organizations. The practical challenge is that this work needs to be undertaken in thousands of hospitals, physician practices, and nursing facilities all over the nation. The approach to managing care represented in figure 8-1 is relevant to both the health care delivery organization as a whole (for example, an entire hospital or physician practice) and to individual units within a larger organization (for example, a clinical service). The model applies equally to the design and management of an individual department in a diversified hospital. Moreover, because the knowledge for care is in continual evolution, designing care is a never-ending process that in the long term requires the development of new skill sets for both clinicians and managers.

CONCLUSION

At its heart, health care is the application of a general body of knowledge to the needs of a specific patient. For centuries this knowledge was generally regarded as the property of the healing professions and the individual clinician, not the health care delivery organization. Managerial practice too treated this knowledge as an attribute of the provider, thus focusing on the resources clinicians used as they provided care and on the hotel functions of inpatient institutions. That is, there was a deliberate demarcation between management practice, focused on business processes, and clinical practice, focused on the activities and decisions of diagnosis and treatment.

However, health care delivery has been undergoing a gradual but important change. Patient care, once the domain of the individual practitioner, is becoming the domain of the care delivery organization. The mission of these organizations is shifting. As science, technology, care processes, and care teams have become more complex and diverse, the way in which the activities of care are organized and the institutional context in which they occur have become an increasingly important determinant of the effectiveness and efficiency of that care. Thus the object of management has changed. In response to these changes, health care managers have started attending to the management of the care as well as the management of the institutions in which the care takes place.

The tools used for managing care have largely focused on getting clinicians to do what was known, thus treating the knowledge for care as scientific, static, and a property of the professions and the individual professionals.

Consistent with this view of the knowledge for care, management tools such as practice guidelines, performance measurement and reporting, and financial performance incentives for physicians have predominated.

This approach to the management of the care itself has, however, failed to account for several significant changes in the nature of the knowledge for care and the way it is applied in practice to patient health problems. These changes include increasing knowledge specificity and the standardized sequential care processes this has allowed; the experimental nature of some care and the iterative process this requires; the dynamic relationship between iterative and sequential care processes; the interplay between scientific and organizational knowledge in care delivery; and the organization's role in developing and maintaining the knowledge for care, both scientific and organizational.

Accounting for these requires a fundamentally different approach to managing care. Operating systems and processes must be deliberately designed to realize great medical outcomes; past experience suggests that they cannot be presumed to reliably result from existing organizational and operational arrangements. Underpinning these designs is the need for health care delivery organizations to develop their own knowledge bases for solving health problems. And a capacity for learning—creating and disseminating the scientific and organizational knowledge for care—must be deliberately designed. Contrary to individual learning, organizational learning does not happen naturally.

Given the organization's key role in reliably creating cures and preventing errors, the question is not whether to create organizations capable of providing patient relief, but how. Performance improvement in health care delivery ultimately means the better application of medical knowledge and must address three key underlying problems: not knowing what to do, not doing what we know, and not doing it well. This is predominantly a management problem. It cannot, in the final analysis, be achieved by policy means acting at a distance. Policy interventions, such as new financing and payment models or health plan contracts, can only provide an incentive for change. Nor is it simply a matter of adopting wholesale a successful management model from another industry. It is more difficult than this. For improved performance to be realized, managers acting locally need to design processes and organizations that are more effective at executing on the knowledge for care.

Although the previous chapters have described some principles for designing care, and several specific designs, they have deliberately not specified a dominant design, arguably because none exists. Local conditions—for example, patient needs, regulatory constraints, human and technological resources—vary to such an extent that each organization, even when applying the same principles, will likely arrive at a different operating system design. Instead, this book has focused on the design principles of and capabilities for two key operating systems that need to be deliberately designed if they are to perform optimally: the operating system for delivering the care that we know, and an operating system for creating new knowledge about which care to deliver in the future and how to better deliver it. Central to understanding how to design processes and operating systems is an understanding of the nature of clinical processes and the relationship between the medical knowledge, care processes, organizations, and practitioners.

The book has also focused on the dynamic relationship between the above two operating systems. Because each of the four components of a system for delivering health care continues to change, ongoing redesign—that both reacts to, and creates, new knowledge and then implements it in the care of the next patient—will be a constant feature of managers' and clinicians' working lives. Understanding the relationship between the four components, and between the operating systems for delivering care and learning from care, will be essential for care delivery organizations as they think through how they will approach care in the future and how they will cope with this constant change. The capacities to do the redesign work, and to accept the results of the redesign, are perhaps the most important capability an organization can have and value.

The imperative for this design work is more than either the financial pressure under which most national health systems currently find themselves or the avalanche of distressing data demonstrating suboptimal quality. It is embedded in the personal patient stories such as that expressed in the quote by the late Avedis Donabedian, one of the foremost thinkers about the quality of health care, with which this book begins. In the face of such sentiments by someone who knew health care so well—as a professional, a scholar, and a patient—business as usual is hard to see as a viable option for the future; without deliberate design, health care delivery organizations will continue to disappoint.

Notes

Introduction

1. F. Mullan, "A Founder of Quality Assessment Encounters a Troubled System Firsthand," *Health Affairs* 20, no. 1 (2001): 137–141.

2. By "health care delivery system" or "a system for delivering health care," I mean here any integrated grouping of the processes, practitioners, and organizations that act together to bring relief to patients. Such systems may be small and local "microsystems"—see E. C. Nelson et al., "Microsystems in Health Care: Part 1. Learning from High-Performing Front-Line Clinical Units," *Joint Commission Journal on Quality Improvement* 28, no. 9 (2002): 472–493—or larger regional or national health care systems.

3. M. R. Chassin, "Is Health Care Ready for Six Sigma Quality?" *Milbank Quarterly* 76 (1998): 565–591.

4. G. A. Lin et al., "Frequency of Stress Testing to Document Ischemia Prior to Elective Percutaneous Coronary Intervention," *JAMA* 300, no. 15 (2008): 1765–1773.

5. Institute of Medicine, *To Err Is Human: Building a Safer Health System* (Washington, DC: National Academy Press, 2000).

6. Chassin, "Is Health Care Ready?"

7. G. D. Bryant and G. R. Norman, "Expressions of Probability: Words and Numbers," *New England Journal of Medicine* 302 (1980): 411.

8. D. M. Eddy, "Variations in Physician Practice: The Role of Uncertainty," *Health Affairs* 3 (1984): 74–89.

9. F. G. Donini-Lenhoff and H. L. Hedrick, "Growth of Specialization in Graduate Medical Education," *JAMA* 284 (2000): 1284–1289.

10. Note that the nursing and allied health professions have undergone a significant evolution over the course of the twentieth century. For example, nurses are no longer "handmaidens" who simply execute doctors' orders. The nursing profession has developed its own detailed body of knowledge about disease and treatment, which is an important input into the care process.

11. By "health care manager," in what follows I mean individuals, clinically trained or not, who take a role in designing, managing, and improving clinical operations and performance.

12. R. L. Wears and M. Berg, "Computer Technology and Clinical Work: Still Waiting for Godot," *JAMA* 293, no. 10 (2005): 1261–1263; and S. R. Barley, "Technology as an Occasion for Structuring: Evidence from Observations of CT Scanners and the Social Order of Radiology Departments," *Administrative Science Quarterly* 31, no. 1 (1986): 78–109.

13. A. C. Edmondson, R. M. J. Bohmer, and G. P. Pisano, "Disrupted Routines: Team Learning and New Technology Adaptation," *Administrative Science Quarterly* 46 (2001): 685–716.

Chapter 1

1. A. Brandt and D. Sloane, "Of Beds and Benches: Building the Modern American Hospital," in *The Architecture of Science*, eds. P. Gallison and E. Thompson (Cambridge, MA: MIT Press, 1999), 281–308.

2. T. A. Brennan and D. M. Berwick, *New Rules: Regulation, Markets and the Quality of American Health Care* (San Francisco: Jossey-Bass, 1996), 23.

3. Ibid., 37.

4. K. N. Lohr, *Medicare: A Strategy for Quality Assurance*, vol. 1 (Washington, DC: National Academy Press, 1990).

5. The JCAHO's name has subsequently been changed to The Joint Commission. R. H. Palmer and M. M. E. Adams, "Quality Improvement/Quality Assurance Taxonomy: A Framework," in *Putting Research to Work in Quality Improvement and Quality Assurance*, eds. M. L. Grady, J. Bernstein, and S. Robinson (Washington, DC: Department of Health and Human Services Agency for Health Care Policy and Research, July 1993), AHCPR Publication No. 93-0034.

6. A similar observation had been made several decades earlier in England, when Glover noted variation in tonsillectomy rates in 1938. See J. A. Glover, "The Incidence of Tonsillectomy in School Children," *Proceedings of the Royal Society of Medicine, England* 31, no. 10 (1938): 1219–1236.

7. J. Wennberg and A. Gittelshon, "Variations in Medical Care Among Small Areas," *Scientific American* 246 (1982): 120–129.

8. Ibid.

9. Notably, most of the inquiry into these issues has made the implicit assumption that the observed variation is primarily related to the behavior of physicians, not patients.

10. C. M. Winslow et al., "The Appropriateness of Performing Coronary Artery Bypass Surgery," *JAMA* 260 (1988): 505–509; and M. R. Chassin et al., "Does Inappropriate Use Explain Geographic Variations in the Use of Health Care Services?" *JAMA* 258 (1987): 2533–2537.

11. D. M. Eddy, "Variations in Physician Practice: The Role of Uncertainty," *Health Affairs* 3 (1984): 74–89.

12. R. S. Stafford and D. E. Singer, "National Patterns of Warfarin Use in Atrial Fibrillation," *Archives of Internal Medicine* 156 (1996): 2537–2541; S. B. Soumerai et al., "Adverse Outcomes of Underuse of Beta-Blockers in Elderly Survivors of Acute Myocardial Infarction," *JAMA* 277 (1997): 115–121; and R. S. Stafford, D. Saglam, and D. Blumenthal, "National Patterns of Angiotensin-Converting Enzyme Inhibitor Use in Congestive Heart Failure," *Archives of Internal Medicine* 157, no. 21 (1997): 2460–2464. Rates have improved somewhat since these studies were conducted.

13. P. A. Scott et al., "Prevalence of Atrial Fibrillation and Antithrombotic Prophylaxis in Emergency Department Patients," *Stroke* 33, no. 11 (2002): 2664–2669.

14. E. A. McGlynn et al., "The Quality of Health Care Delivered to Adults in the United States," *New England Journal of Medicine* 348 (2003): 2635–2645.

15. T. A. Brennan et al., "Incidence of Adverse Events and Negligence in Hospitalized Patients: Results of the Harvard Medical Practice Study I," *New England Journal of Medicine* 324 (1991): 370–376.

16. The Institute of Medicine (IOM) distinguished guidelines from medical review criteria, which it defined as "systematically developed statements that can be used to assess the appropriateness of specific health care decisions, services and outcomes." Institute of Medicine, *Clinical Practice Guidelines: Directions for a New Program*, eds. M. J. Field and K. N. Lohr (Washington, DC: National Academy Press, 1990); and Institute of Medicine, *Guidelines for Clinical Practice: From Development to Use*, eds. M. J. Field and K. N. Lohr (Washington, DC: National Academy Press, 1992).

17. Records of the Boston Dispensary, Harvard Medical Library in the Francis A. Countway Library of Medicine, box 1.

18. A. H. Morris, "Treatment Algorithms and Protocolized Care," *Current Opinion in Critical Care* 9 (2003): 236–240.

19. Morris cites the Ovid definitions of a guideline and a protocol: "a systematic statement of policy rules or principles," and "precise and detailed plans for the study of a medical or biomedical problem and/or for a regimen or therapy," respectively.

20. D. L. Sackett et al., "Evidence-Based Medicine: What It Is and What It Isn't," *BMJ* 312 (1996): 71–72.

21. J. A. Muir Gray, *Evidence-Based Healthcare* (Edinburgh: Churchill Livingstone, 2001).

22. These data were gathered from the Web site for Ovid, a commercial database company whose products include the clinical and general science database Medline. Ovid, "Database Products and Services: Medline," March 19, 2002, http://www.ovid.com/products/databases/database_info.cfm?dbID=53.

23. This number (10,000 publications from randomized controlled trials published in Medline per annum) comes from M. R. Chassin, "Is Health Care Ready

for Six Sigma Quality?" *Milbank Quarterly* 76 (1998): 565–591. Ten thousand is the number added in 1995. In 2006 this number was 16,000.

24. McGlynn et al., "The Quality of Health Care Delivered to Adults in the United States," *New England Journal of Medicine*.

25. E. A. McGlynn et al., "The Quality of Health Care Delivered to Adults in the United States" (working paper WR-174-1, RAND, Santa Monica, CA, March 2006).

26. Greg Pawlson, MD, MPH, executive vice president of the National Committee for Quality Assurance (NCQA), personal communication with author, September 2007.

27. M. B. Rosenthal et al., "Pay for Performance in Commercial HMOs," *New England Journal of Medicine* 355 (2006): 1895–1902.

28. M. B. Rosenthal et al., "Paying for Quality: Providers' Incentives for Quality Improvement," *Health Affairs* 23, no. 2 (2004): 127–141.

29. G. B. Risse, *Mending Bodies, Saving Souls: A History of Hospitals* (New York: Oxford University Press, 1999), 495.

30. In the nineteenth and twentieth centuries, the daily ward round was an event both patients and staff awaited with anxious trepidation. See Risse, *Mending Bodies, Saving Souls*.

31. M. B. Rosenthal et al., "Early Experience with Pay-for-Performance: From Concept to Practice," *JAMA* 294 (2005): 1788–1793.

32. M. K. Wynia et al., "Medical Professionalism in Society," *New England Journal of Medicine* 341, no. 21 (1999): 1612–1616; Hippocrates, *Epidemics*, bk. 1, sect. 5; and the Hippocratic Oath.

33. R. Simons, *Levers of Control: How Managers Use Innovative Control Systems to Drive Strategic Renewal* (Boston: Harvard Business School Press, 1995).

34. G. Szulanski and S. Winter, "Getting It Right the Second Time," *Harvard Business Review*, January 2002, 64–69.

35. E. S. Fisher et al., "Hospital Readmission Rates for Cohorts of Medicare Beneficiaries in Boston and New Haven," *New England Journal of Medicine* 331 (1994): 989–995.

36. J. E. Wennberg, J. L. Freeman, and W. J. Culp, "Are Hospital Services Rationed in New Haven or Over-Utilized In Boston?" *Lancet* 1 (1987): 1185–1189.

37. Roemer's finding ultimately came to bear his name. Roemer's "law" stated that a bed built is a bed filled. See M. I. Roemer, "Bed Supply and Hospital Utilization: A Natural Experiment," *Hospital* 35 (1961): 37–40; and J. E. Wennberg, "Unwarranted Variations in Healthcare Delivery: Implications for Academic Medical Centres," *BMJ* 325 (2002). 961–964.

38. These are not simply restrictions that outside parties place on physicians and care delivery organizations. Managers within care delivery organizations use the same tools internally. See E. A. Kerr et al., "Managed Care and Capitation in California: How Do Physicians at Financial Risk Control Their Own Utilization?" *Annals of Internal Medicine* 125 (1995): 500–504.

39. M. O. Mundinger et al., "Primary Care Outcomes in Patients Treated by Nurse Practitioners or Physicians: A Randomized Trial," *JAMA* 283 (2000): 59–68.

40. W. A. Ghali et al., "Statewide Quality Improvement Initiatives and Mortality After Cardiac Surgery," *JAMA* 277 (1997): 379–382.

41. This phenomenon is known as the volume outcome hypothesis. See A. M. Epstein, "Volume and Outcome: It Is Time to Move Ahead," *New England Journal of Medicine* 346 (2002): 1161–1164.

42. N. A. Omoigui et al., "Outmigration for Coronary Bypass Surgery in an Era of Public Dissemination of Clinical Outcomes," *Circulation* 93 (1996): 27–33; and J. Green and N. Wintfeld, "Report Cards on Cardiac Surgeons: Assessing New York State's Approach," *New England Journal of Medicine* 332 (1995): 1229–1232. For a thorough and thoughtful review of these issues, see D. M. Shahian et al., "Cardiac Surgery Report Cards: Comprehensive Review and Statistical Critique," *Annals of Thoracic Surgery* 72 (2001): 2155–2168.

43. The extent to which public reporting in fact influences provider selection has been questioned. A survey of five hundred cardiac patients who had undergone coronary artery bypass graft (CABG) surgery in Pennsylvania found that only 12 percent were aware of the existence of surgeon- and hospital-specific mortality data before undergoing surgery, and less than 1 percent knew the correct standing of their hospital; see E. Schneider and A. M. Epstein, "Patient Use of Public Performance Reports: A Survey of Patients Undergoing Cardiac Surgery," *JAMA* 279 (1998): 1638–1642. Similarly, the same performance data had little credibility among cardiovascular specialists and did not appear to influence their referral patterns. In a parallel survey of Pennsylvania cardiologists, 87 percent indicated that the report had minimal to no influence on their referral recommendations. Only 10 percent discussed provider-specific mortality rates with CABG-eligible patients prior to referral; see E. C. Schneider and A. M. Epstein, "Influence of Cardiac-Surgery Performance Reports on Referral Practices and Access to Care: A Survey of Cardiovascular Specialists," *New England Journal of Medicine* 335, no. 4 (1996): 251–256.

44. T. H. Lee, D. F. Torchiana, and J. E. Locke, "Is Zero the Ideal Death Rate?" *New England Journal of Medicine* 357 (2007): 111–113.

45. L. L. Leape et al., "Systems Analysis of Adverse Drug Events," *JAMA* 274 (1995): 35–43.

46. J. Chen et al., "Do 'America's Best Hospitals' Perform Better for Acute Myocardial Infarction?" *New England Journal of Medicine* 340 (1999): 286–292.

47. D. M. Berwick, A. B. Godfrey, and J. Roessner, *Curing Health Care: New Strategies for Quality Improvement* (San Francisco: Jossey-Bass, 1991); and D. M. Berwick, "Continuous Improvement as an Ideal in Health Care," *New England Journal of Medicine* 320 (1989): 53–56.

48. G. Laffel and D. Blumenthal, "The Case for Using Industrial Quality Management Science in Health Care Organizations," *JAMA* 262 (1989): 2869–2873.

49. The National Academy of Engineering (NAE)/IOM report, *Building a Better Delivery System: A New Engineering/Health Care Partnership* (Washington, DC: National Academies Press, 2005), describes an engineering technique called quality functional deployment (QFD), which has a similar goal. In QFD the key determinants of the performance of a product or service are identified, and key steps required to make those determinants happen are put in place.

50. C. J. McDonald, "Protocol-Based Reminders, the Quality of Care and the Non-Perfectability of Man," *New England Journal of Medicine* 295 (1976): 1351–1355.

51. R. M. Dawes, *Rational Choice in an Uncertain World* (San Diego: Harcourt Brace Jovanovich, 1988).

52. G. Millar, quoted in "Doctors and Electronic Records," *All Things Considered*, National Public Radio, July 17, 2000.

53. T. H. Davenport and J. Glaser, "Just-in-Time Knowledge Delivery Comes to Knowledge Management," *Harvard Business Review*, July 2002, 107–111.

54. T. Fujimoto, *The Evolution of a Manufacturing System at Toyota* (New York: Oxford University Press, 1999).

55. M. Balconi, "Tacitness, Codification of Technical Knowledge and the Organization of Industry," *Research Policy* 31 (2002): 357–379.

56. Furthermore, increasing expectations of payers, regulators, and the public for high-quality and efficient patient care and reliable outcomes have put a premium on process control.

57. M. McCarthy, "Can Car Manufacturing Techniques Reform Health Care?" *Lancet* 367 (2006): 290–291.

58. D. Blumenthal and C. Kilo, "A Report Card on Continuous Quality Improvement," *Milbank Quarterly* 76, no. 4 (1998): 625–648.

59. S. M. Shortell, C. L. Bennett, and G. R. Byck, "Assessing the Impact of Continuous Quality Improvement on Clinical Practice: What It Will Take to Accelerate Progress," *Milbank Quarterly* 76, no. 4 (1998): 593–624.

60. Ibid.

61. M. Arndt and B. Bigelow, "The Implementation of Total Quality Management in Hospitals: How Good Is the Fit?" *Health Care Management Review* 20, no. 4 (1995): 7–14.

62. The power imbalance between physicians and hospitals is exacerbated in the United States by the fact that American physicians bill for their services separately from the hospital and are therefore more financially independent than salaried physicians.

63. M. Murray and D. M. Berwick, "Advanced Access: Reducing Waiting and Delays in Primary Care," *JAMA* 289 (2003): 1035–1040.

64. V. Fuhrmans, "Withdrawal Treatment: A Novel Plan Helps Hospital Wean Itself off Pricey Tests—It Cajoles Big Insurer to Pay a Little Bit More for Cheaper Therapies," *Wall Street Journal*, January 12, 2007.

65. L. Casalino et al., "External Incentives, Information Technology, and Organized Processes to Improve Health Care Quality for Patients with Chronic Diseases," *JAMA* 289 (2003): 434–441.

66. Rosenthal et al., "Pay for Performance in Commercial HMOs."

67. This history is drawn from R. M. J. Bohmer, J. D. Street, and L. Feldman, "The Evolution of Treatment: The Case of Diabetes," Case 302-023 (Boston: Harvard Business School, 2003).

68. A process measure related to diabetes (rate of retinal examinations) was included in the first generation of the HEDIS (Health Effectiveness Data and Information Set) effectiveness-of-care measures.

Chapter 2

1. D. G. Altman, "Poor-Quality Medical Research," *JAMA* 287 (2002): 2765–2767.

2. Ibid.

3. L. Mariani and E. Marubini, "Content and Quality of Currently Published Phase II Cancer Trials," *Journal of Clinical Oncology* 18 (2000): 429–436.

4. J. P. A. Ioannidis, "Contradicted and Initially Stronger Effects in Highly Cited Clinical Research," *JAMA* 294 (2005): 218–228.

5. B. C. Martinson, M. S. Anderson, and R. de Vries, "Scientists Behaving Badly," *Nature* 435 (2005): 737–738.

6. The Office of Research Integrity reported results of similar magnitude in its report *Observing and Reporting Suspected Misconduct in Biomedical Research* (Rockville, MD: Office of Research Integrity, 2008).

7. Altman, "Poor-Quality Medical Research."

8. S. M. McGuigan, "The Use of Statistics in the British Journal of Psychiatry," *British Journal of Psychiatry* 167 (1995): 683–688.

9. See Altman, "Poor-Quality Medical Research," and others.

10. V. M. Montori et al., "Users' Guide to Detecting Misleading Claims in Clinical Research Reports," *BMJ* 329 (2004): 1093–1096.

11. A. Chan et al., "Empirical Evidence for Selective Reporting of Outcomes in Randomized Trials: Comparison of Protocols to Published Articles," *JAMA* 291 (2004): 2457–2465.

12. In a result that seems consistent with Martinson's findings, Chan et al. also reported that 86 percent of the trialists contacted initially denied the existence of unreported outcomes.

13. R. Moynihan et al., "Coverage by the News Media of the Benefits and Risks of Medications," *New England Journal of Medicine* 342 (2000): 1645–1650.

14. L. M. Schwartz, S. Woloshin, and L. Baczek, "Media Coverage of Scientific Meetings: Too Much Too Soon?" *JAMA* 287 (2002): 2859–2863.

15. J. P. Kassirer, *On the Take: How Medicine's Complicity with Big Business Can Endanger Your Health* (Oxford: Oxford University Press, 2005).

16. H. E. Stelfox et al., "Conflict of Interest in the Debate over Calcium-Channel Antagonists," *New England Journal of Medicine* 338 (1998): 101–106.

17. G. Harris and A. Berenson, "10 Voters on Panel Backing Pain Pills Had Industry Ties," *New York Times*, February 25, 2005.

18. R. P. Dellinger et al., "Surviving Sepsis Campaign Guidelines for Management of Severe Sepsis and Septic Shock," *Critical Care Medicine* 32 (2004): 858–873; errata: 1448, 2169–2170.

19. P. Q. Eichacker, C. Natanson, and R. L. Danner, "Surviving Sepsis: Practice Guidelines, Marketing Campaigns, and Eli Lilly," *New England Journal of Medicine* 355 (2006): 1640–1642.

20. E. A. McGlynn et al., "The Quality of Health Care Delivered to Adults in the United States: Appendix" (working paper WR-174-1, RAND, Santa Monica, CA, March 2006).

21. K. G. Shojania, B. W. Duncan, K. M. McDonald, and R. M. Wachter, eds., *Making Health Care Safer: A Critical Analysis of Patient Safety Practices* (Rockville, MD: Agency for Healthcare Research and Quality, 2001). Patient safety practices are defined by the authors as "processes or structures whose application reduces the probability of adverse events resulting from exposure to the health care system across a wide range of diseases and procedures."

22. What is most distressing about the RAND results is that even these simple "good practices" are not routinely followed. Researchers found that the compliance rates with the two examples cited were 56.18 and 38.09, respectively.

23. D. M. Mirvis, "Managed Care, Managing Uncertainty," *Archives of Internal Medicine* 157 (1997): 385–388.

24. G. D. Bryant and G. R. Norman, "Expressions of Probability: Words and Numbers," *New England Journal of Medicine* 302 (1980): 411.

25. Ibid.

26. M. D. Cabana et al., "Why Don't Physicians Follow Clinical Practice Guidelines? A Framework for Improvement," *JAMA* 282, no. 15 (1999): 1458–1465.

27. F. J. Fowler et al., "Comparison of Recommendations by Urologists and Radiation Oncologists for Treatment of Clinically Localized Prostate Cancer," *JAMA* 283 (2000): 3217–3222.

28. Ibid.

29. Although this is the hope and promise of genomic medicine. Recently, genetic testing has helped us better understand, and predict, responses to drugs such as warfarin (for anticoagulation) and gefitinib (in lung cancer).

30. C. M. Coley et al., "Early Detection of Prostate Cancer. Part I: Prior Probability and Effectiveness of Tests. The American College of Physicians," *Annals of Internal Medicine* 126 (1997): 394–406; and "Early Detection of Prostate Cancer. Part II: Estimating the Risks, Benefits, and Costs," *Annals of Internal Medicine* 126 (1997): 468–479.

31. R. C. Bast and G. N. Hortobagyi, "Individualized Care for Patients with Cancer—A Work in Progress," *New England Journal of Medicine* 351, no. 27 (2004): 2865–2867.

32. S. Paik et al., "A Multigene Assay to Predict Recurrence of Tamoxifen-Treated, Node-Negative Breast Cancer," *New England Journal of Medicine* 351, no. 27 (2004): 2817–2826.

33. Y. Caraco, "Genes and the Response to Drugs," *New England Journal of Medicine* 351, no. 27 (2004): 2867–2869.

34. Paik et al., "A Multigene Assay to Predict Recurrence."

35. E. M. Wagner, "Meeting the Needs of Chronically Ill People," *BMJ* 323 (2001): 945–946.

36. M. E. Tinetti et al., "Potential Pitfalls of Disease-Specific Guidelines for Patients with Multiple Conditions," *New England Journal of Medicine* 351, no. 27 (2004): 2870–2874.

37. C. Boyd et al., "Clinical Practice Guidelines and Quality of Care for Older Patients with Multiple Comorbid Diseases: Implications for Pay for Performance," *JAMA* 294 (2005): 716–724.

38. J. E. Wennberg, "Unwarranted Variations in Healthcare Delivery: Implications for Academic Medical Centres," *BMJ* 325 (2002): 961–964.

39. F. J. Fowler et al., "Symptom Status and Quality of Life Following Prostatectomy," *JAMA* 259, no. 20 (1988): 3018–3022.

40. S. Saigal et al., "Differences in Preferences for Neonatal Outcomes Among Health Care Professionals, Parents, and Adolescents," *JAMA* 281, no. 21 (1999): 1991–1997.

41. I am indebted to Dr. Al Mulley Jr. for this distinction. Dr. Mulley adds a third class of "stochastic" uncertainty—simple chance, representing the fact that any individual patient represents a point on a distribution of outcomes—to this classification.

42. Note that economists distinguish between uncertainty and risk. In the former, the probabilities (or shapes of the probability distributions) of two outcomes are known, but the outcome for the individual is not known *ex ante*. Well-studied interventions are associated with no less risk than less well-studied interventions, but the risk is better quantified. In the latter, not only are the probability distributions not known, but neither are the possible outcomes.

43. R. P. Feynman, "Report of the Presidential Commission on the Space Shuttle Challenger Accident, Appendix 2," http://history.nasa.gov/rogersrep/v2appf.htm.

44. M. A. Roberto, R. M. J. Bohmer, and A. C. Edmondson, "Facing Ambiguous Threats," *Harvard Business Review*, November 2006, 106–113.

Chapter 3

1. The term *health care process* is defined here as that set of tasks and decisions that takes as its "input" a sick patient (plus capital, labor, and raw materials) and creates a value-added "output"—namely, a patient whose health is improved (see chapter 5).

2. The term *operating system* is used more broadly to describe that set of people, policies, and organizational procedures that supports the core health care process.

3. M. H. Bazerman, *Judgment in Managerial Decision Making* (New York: Wiley, 2002); and G. P. Pisano, "Learning Before Doing in New Process Technology," *Research Policy* 25 (1996): 1097–1119.

4. The problem-solving method of health care is thus a form of the scientific method, although its goal is to solve individual patient problems rather than identify universal laws. It is also essentially the same as the "plan-do-check-act" cycle of continuous improvement. However, in the case of health care, it is the core production process that is structured this way, rather than the process that is used to *improve* the production process in other industries.

5. Patients and physicians often differ over when a problem is to be considered "solved." The physician is often concerned about what a condition is not (e.g., the chest pain is not due to cardiac ischemia), while the patient is concerned about what the condition is. The result is that the internist may be quite satisfied that he or she has ruled out all of the most pernicious causes of the patient's symptomatology, yet the patient's desire for a specific diagnosis is left unmet. Gregg Meyer, senior vice president for quality and safety, Massachusetts General Hospital, personal communication with author, 2008.

6. Note that diagnosis and treatment is possible even in the absence of an exact biological cause. For most of the history of medicine, problems were solved without being fully understood. Even today some diseases are diagnosed and treated even though the exact root cause remains unknown. Syndrome diagnoses, for example, are groups of symptoms and signs that are associated with specific outcomes and responses to treatment but for which the underlying cause remains obscure.

7. In fact, the time between the first observation of a new disease and an understanding of its causes and course has shortened dramatically. For example, the first cases of AIDS were described in June 1981, but the HIV virus was not characterized until two years later. In comparison, the lag between the description of the first cases of SARS, in February 2003, and the characterization of the virus was a matter of months. Problems in medicine do not stay new for long.

8. D. M. Gaba, "Human Error in Dynamic Medical Domains," in *Human Error in Medicine*, ed. M. S. Bognor (Hillsdale, NJ: Lawrence Erlbaum Associates, 1994), 197–224.

9. The principle of Occam's razor—that, all things being equal, the simplest solution (i.e., that requiring the fewest assumptions) is the best—also applies to medical diagnosis.

10. D. M. Eddy, "Variations in Physician Practice: The Role of Uncertainty," *Health Affairs* 3 (1984): 74–89.

11. Where an experiment is "an operation carried out under controlled conditions in order to discover an unknown effect or law, to test or establish a hypothesis,

or to illustrate a known law," or "the process of testing" (*Merriam-Webster's Collegiate Dictionary*, 10th ed., s.v. "experiment"). Another dictionary definition is "a test under controlled conditions that is made to demonstrate a known truth, examine the validity of a hypothesis, or determine the efficacy of something previously untried" (*American Heritage Dictionary of the English Language*, 4th ed.).

12. E. von Hippel and M. J. Tyre, "How Learning by Doing Is Done: Problem Identification in Novel Process Equipment," *Research Policy* 24 (1995): 1–12.

13. J. F. Nunn, *Ancient Egyptian Medicine* (Norman: University of Oklahoma Press, 1996; Red River edition, 2002).

14. D. A. Garvin, *Learning in Action: A Guide to Putting the Learning Organization to Work* (Boston: Harvard Business School Press, 2000), 149.

15. Ibid.

16. J. P. Kassirer, "Our Stubborn Quest for Diagnostic Certainty: A Cause of Excessive Testing," *New England Journal of Medicine* 320, no. 22 (1989): 1489–1491.

17. Ibid.

18. Institute of Medicine, *Saving Women's Lives: Strategies for Improving Breast Cancer Detection and Diagnosis* (Washington, DC: National Academies Press, 2004).

19. K. Gupta et al., "Patient-Initiated Treatment of Uncomplicated Recurrent Urinary Tract Infections in Young Women," *Annals of Internal Medicine* 135, no. 1 (2001): 9–16.

20. E. Rosenthal, "Girl Is First to Survive Rabies Without a Shot," *New York Times*, November 25, 2004.

21. Von Hippel and Tyre, "How Learning by Doing Is Done"; and H. A. Simon, "The Structure of Ill-Structured Problems," *Artificial Intelligence* 4 (1973): 181–201.

22. K. A. Sepkowitz, "AIDS—The First 20 Years," *New England Journal of Medicine* 344, no. 23 (2001): 1764–1772.

23. Ibid.

24. M. E. Tinetti et al., "Potential Pitfalls of Disease-Specific Guidelines for Patients with Multiple Conditions," *New England Journal of Medicine* 351, no. 27 (2004): 2870–2874.

25. As Simon notes, "much problem solving effort is directed at structuring problems, and only a fraction of it at solving problems once they are structured." Simon, "The Structure of Ill-Structured Problems," 187.

26. Here the term *knowledge* is used to mean the level of understanding of the relationship between cause and effect, input and output.

27. R. E. Bohn, "Measuring and Managing Technological Knowledge," *Sloan Management Review* 36, no. 1 (1994): 61–73; and R. E. Bohn and R. Jaikumar, "The Structure of Technical Knowledge in Manufacturing" (working paper 93-035, Harvard Business School, Boston, 1992).

28. Bohn, "Measuring and Managing Technological Knowledge."

29. See, for example, M. Polanyi, *The Tacit Dimension* (Garden City, NY: Doubleday, 1966).

30. I. Nonaka, "The Knowledge-Creating Company," *Harvard Business Review*, November–December 1991, 96–104.

31. Eddy, "Variations in Physician Practice."

32. Chapter 4 discusses the potential for each cycle to also generate new general information about the capabilities of the clinician and the delivery organization and occasionally about the disease itself.

33. In the operations literature, this is referred to as *jumbled flow* and is characteristic of a job shop.

34. R. Austin and L. Devin, *Artful Making: What Managers Need to Know About How Artists Work* (Upper Saddle River, NJ: Financial Times Prentice Hall, 2003).

35. K. B. Clark and T. Fujimoto, *Product Development Performance: Strategy, Organization, and Management in the World Auto Industry* (Boston: Harvard Business School Press, 1991).

36. G. P. Pisano, *The Development Factory: Unlocking the Potential of Process Innovation* (Boston: Harvard Business School Press, 1997).

Chapter 4

1. For further detail, see R. M. J. Bohmer, J. D. Street, and L. Feldman, "The Evolution of Treatment: The Case of Diabetes," Case 302-023 (Boston: Harvard Business School, 2003).

2. C. M. Christensen, "Patterns in the Evolution of Product Competition," *European Management Journal* 15 (April 1997): 117–127.

3. Ibid.

4. E. P. Joslin, *A Diabetic Manual for the Mutual Use of Doctor and Patient*, 7th ed. (Philadelphia: Lea & Febiger, 1941), 11.

5. E. P. Joslin, *Diabetes Manual for the Doctor and Patient*, 9th ed. (Philadelphia: Lea & Febiger, 1953), 70.

6. L. P. Krall, ed., *Joslin Diabetes Manual*, 11th ed. (London: Harry Klimpton Publishers, 1978), 222.

7. DCCT Research Group, "The Effect of Intensive Treatment of Diabetes on the Development and Progression of Long-Term Complication in Insulin-Dependent Diabetes Mellitus," *New England Journal of Medicine* 329, no. 14 (1993): 977–986.

8. R. Pérez-Peña, "Diabetic Brothers Beat Odds with Grit and Luck," *New York Times*, February 5, 2006.

9. Committee on Quality of Health Care in America, Institute of Medicine, *Crossing the Quality Chasm* (Washington, DC: National Academy Press, 2001).

10. D. C. Classen et al., "The Timing of Prophylactic Administration of Antibiotics and the Risk of Surgical-Wound Infection," *New England Journal of Medicine* 326, no. 5 (1992): 281–286.

11. See, for example, S. J. Spear, "Fixing Health Care from the Inside, Today," *Harvard Business Review*, September 2005, 78–91.

12. Note that it is possible to solve a problem without a complete understanding of the cause of the problem or the reason that the solution works, a state of affairs that has existed in medicine for most of the last several thousand years. For example, at a 1987 conference on AIDS, Dr. Maurice Hilleman, the developer of the mumps, measles, chicken pox, pneumonia, and meningitis vaccines, said in reference to the prospects for the development of an AIDS vaccine (and only partly in jest), "I think the big problem of trying to get up here and talk about how vaccines work is that we don't know a damn thing about how they work. In the old days, you know, we used to try to solve problems without understanding them and it was great. This is the first time we've ever had need to understand anything and I'm sorry I couldn't talk about how vaccines work because I don't know." "Pioneering Vaccine Researcher Hilleman Dies," National Public Radio, April 12, 2005.

13. R. Cowan, P. A. David, and D. Foray, "The Explicit Economics of Knowledge Codification and Tacitness," *Industrial and Corporate Change* 9, no. 2 (2000): 211–253.

14. M. Balconi. "Tacitness, Codification of Technological Knowledge and the Organization of Industry," *Research Policy* 31 (2002): 357–379.

15. A. C. Edmondson, A. B. Winslow, R. M. J. Bohmer, and G. P. Pisano, "Learning How and Learning What: Effects of Tacit and Codified Knowledge on Performance Improvement Following Technology Adoption," *Decision Sciences* 34, no. 2 (Spring 2003): 197–223.

16. K. G. Vosburgh and R. S. Newbower, "Moore's Law, Disruptive Technologies, and the Clinician," in *Medicine Meets Virtual Reality 02/10*, eds. J. D. Westwood et al. (Amsterdam: IOS Press, 2002), 8–13.

17. J. L. Willems et al., "The Diagnostic Performance of Computer Programs for the Interpretation of Electrocardiograms," *New England Journal of Medicine* 325, no. 25 (1991): 1767–1773.

18. Vosburgh and Newbower, "Moore's Law, Disruptive Technologies."

19. The implications of this characteristic of the knowledge bases for health care are discussed more fully in chapter 5.

20. R. Porter, *The Greatest Benefit to Mankind: A Medical History of Humanity* (New York: W. W. Norton, 1998), 369.

21. Ibid.

22. P. R. Carlile and C. M. Christensen, "Practice and Malpractice in Management Research" (unpublished manuscript, January 6, 2005).

23. I. Nonaka and H. Takeuchi, *The Knowledge-Creating Company: How Japanese Companies Create the Dynamics of Innovation* (New York: Oxford University Press, 1995), 66–67.

24. C. H. Hennekens and J. E. Buring, *Epidemiology in Medicine* (Boston: Little, Brown, 1987), chap. 2.

25. Ibid.

26. Ibid., 18.

27. R. E. Bohn, "Measuring and Managing Technological Knowledge," *Sloan Management Review* 36, no. 1 (1994): 61–73.

28. Edmondson, Winslow, Bohmer, and Pisano, "Learning How and Learning What."

29. Cowan, David, and Foray, "The Explicit Economics of Knowledge."

30. A. L. Tucker, I. M. Nembhard, A. C. Edmondson, and R. M. J. Bohmer, "Managing the Learning Challenge: Understanding Improvement Processes for Knowledge Creation and Knowledge Dissemination in Health Care Delivery" (unpublished data).

31. L. Berger, "Cancer Care Seeks to Take Patients Beyond Survival," *New York Times*, May 22, 2007.

32. R. M. Hamm, "Clinical Intuition and Clinical Analysis: Expertise and the Cognitive Continuum," in *Professional Judgment: A Reader in Clinical Decision Making*, eds. J. Dowie and A. Elstein (Cambridge: Cambridge University Press, 1988).

33. C. Christensen, R. M. J. Bohmer, and J. Kenagy, "Will Disruptive Innovations Cure Health Care?" *Harvard Business Review*, September–October 2000, 102–117. Note that although it has happened sufficiently to suggest the possibility of widespread certainty in health care (see chapter 1), this progression, from unstructured problem solving to rules application, can be irregular and episodic, can occur at different rates for different diseases, and is by no means inevitable.

34. Balconi, "Tacitness, Codification of Technological Knowledge."

35. B. E. Landon et al., "Physician Clinical Performance Assessment: Prospects and Barriers," *JAMA* 290, no. 9 (2003): 1183–1189.

36. Ibid.

37. P. Benner, *From Novice to Expert: Excellence and Power in Clinical Nursing Practice* (Menlo Park, CA: Addison-Wesley, 1984).

38. Ibid.

Chapter 5

1. R. D. Hayes and S. C. Wheelwright, "Link Manufacturing Process and Product Life Cycles," *Harvard Business Review*, January–February 1979, 2–9.

2. J. A. Fitzsimmons and M. J. Fitzsimmons, *Service Management*, 4th ed. (Homewood, IL: Irwin McGraw-Hill, 2004).

3. R. M. Henderson and K. B. Clark, "Architectural Innovation: The Reconfiguration of Existing Product Technologies and the Failure of Established Firms," *Administrative Science Quarterly* 35 (1990): 9–30.

4. R. M. J. Bohmer, "The Rise of In-Store Clinics: Threat or Opportunity?" *New England Journal of Medicine* 356, no. 8 (2007): 765–768.

5. Government Accountability Office, *Specialty Hospital Moratorium*, GAO-05-647R (Washington, DC: May 19, 2005), http://www.gao.gov/new.items/d05647r.pdf.

6. S. Kershaw, "Drugstore Clinics Spread, and Scrutiny Grows," *New York Times*, August 23, 2007.

7. C. R. Horsburgh, "Healing by Design," *New England Journal of Medicine* 333, no. 11 (1995): 735–740.

8. R. Hayes et al., *Operations, Strategy and Technology: Pursuing the Competitive Edge* (Hoboken, NJ: Wiley, 2005).

9. Note that this is a choice, not a mandate. Whether managers choose to standardize, and what and how much they standardize, will depend on, among other things, their beliefs about the stage of knowledge relating to that process and the extent to which this knowledge justifies the standardization, and their appetites for managing exceptions that do not fit well with the standard process.

10. B. E. Landon et al., "Physician Clinical Performance Assessment: Prospects and Barriers," *JAMA* 290, no. 9 (2003): 1183–1189.

11. L. Esserman, MD, director, Carol Franc Buck Breast Care Center, University of California, San Francisco Medical Center (UCSF), personal communication with author, April 2008.

12. For further detail, see R. M. J. Bohmer, G. P. Pisano, and N. Tang, "Istituto Clinico Humanitas (A)," Case 603-063 (Boston: Harvard Business School, 2002); R. M. J. Bohmer, "Istituto Clinico Humanitas (B)," Case 604-096 (Boston: Harvard Business School, 2004); and R. M. J. Bohmer, "Istituto Clinico Humanitas (C): Pronto Soccorso," Case 607-022 (Boston: Harvard Business School, 2006). Note that the case examples used in this book are meant not as recommendations of best practice, but as illustrations of particular design principles.

13. Since opening, ICH has expanded the range of services it offers to include electrophysiology, dialysis, radiotherapy, rheumatology, and trauma. It opened a full-scale emergency room in 2003.

14. The Veterans Health Administration recently found itself in a similar situation of misalignment precipitated by a change in target population. Initially well designed to meet the needs of an aging population of veterans with predominantly chronic diseases, it recently found itself challenged by the very different needs of young Iraq War veterans, for which its operating system was ill configured.

15. I am indebted to my friend and colleague Amy Edmondson, who makes an analogous distinction between managing for execution and managing for learning. See A. C. Edmondson, "The Competitive Imperative of Learning," *Harvard Business Review*, July–August 2008, 60–67.

16. To use a biological analogy, each new species has evolved to occupy a specific niche in the environment of health care services.

17. The classes of medical work presented in this table are intended to be neither exhaustive nor mutually exclusive. Elsewhere, David Lawrence and I have termed these operating systems *care platforms*. See R. M. J. Bohmer and D. M. Lawrence, "Care Platforms: A Basic Building Block for Care Delivery," *Health Affairs* 27, no. 5 (2008): 1336–1340.

18. For some of these new health care service businesses, the operating system and the organization are equivalent. Moreover, some prescriptions for health care

reform center on organizational forms that imply an operating system, such as focused factories and integrated delivery units. But most provider organizations comprise multiple operating systems, and the issue is how to manage these concurrently.

19. *Critical access hospital* is a designation by the Centers for Medicare and Medicaid Services for rural hospitals with up to twenty-five beds.

20. To use a metaphor from the new-product development literature, the early stages of a patient's care (the left-hand side of figure 5-3) can be thought of as a small-scale design process, and the latter stages (the right-hand side of figure 5-3) as the execution of that design. And the operating systems that support design (diagnostic decision making) and execution (treatment) are not necessarily the same.

21. S. J. Spear, "Fixing Health Care from the Inside, Today," *Harvard Business Review*, September 2005, 78–91. At the time of the now infamous death of Betsy Lehman, the *Boston Globe*'s health reporter, from an overdose of cyclophosphamide at the Dana-Farber Cancer Institute, there were thirty-six different ways in which this drug could be delivered in this hospital; Sylvia Bartell, director of pharmacy, Dana-Farber Cancer Institute, personal communication with author, 1999.

22. Government Accountability Office, *Specialty Hospitals: Information on National Market Share, Physician Ownership, and Patients Served*, GAO-03-683R (Washington, DC: April 18, 2003), http://www.gao.gov/new.items/d03683r.pdf; and Bohmer, "The Rise of In-Store Clinics."

23. R. M. J. Bohmer, "Medicine's Service Challenge: Blending Custom and Standard Care," *Health Care Management Review* 30, no. 4 (2005): 322–330.

24. W. Skinner, "The Focused Factory," *Harvard Business Review*, May–June 1974, 113–120.

25. Huckman and Zinner provide a good review of this issue and literature. R. S. Huckman and D. E. Zinner, "Does Focus Improve Operational Performance? Lessons from the Management of Clinical Trials," *Strategic Management Journal* 29 (2008): 173–193.

26. C. P. McLaughlin, S. Yang, and R. van Diederonck, "Professional Service Organizations and Focus," *Management Science* 41 (1995): 1185–1193.

27. For further detail, see R. M. J. Bohmer and L. R. Feldman, "The Duke Heart Failure Program," Case 604-033 (Boston: Harvard Business School, 2003). Note that the case examples used in this book are meant not as recommendations of best practice, but as illustrations of particular design principles.

28. Intermountain Healthcare's Brent James, MD, executive director of the Institute for Health Care Delivery Research, articulates the underlying design principle this way: "Design for the usual, manage the unusual." Personal communication with author, 2002. Note that beneath this principle is Intermountain's presumption that much routine care, in fact, can be standardized.

29. A. Edmondson, "Speaking Up in the Operating Room: How Team Leaders Promote Learning in Interdisciplinary Action Teams," *Journal of Management Studies* 40, no. 6 (September 2003): 1419–1452.

30. M. A. Roberto, R. M. J. Bohmer, and A. C. Edmondson, "Facing Ambiguous Threats," *Harvard Business Review*, November 2006, 106–113.

31. Here the term *frame* refers to a mental structure—a set of tacit beliefs and assumptions—that helps individuals make sense of a complex reality. J. E. Russo and P. J. H. Schoemaker, *Decision Traps: Ten Barriers to Brilliant Decision-Making and How to Overcome Them* (New York: Doubleday, 1989).

32. A. C. Edmondson, M. A. Roberto, R. M. J. Bohmer, E. M. Ferlins, and L. R. Feldman, "The Recovery Window: Organizational Learning Following Ambiguous Threats," in *Organization at the Limit: Lessons from the Columbia Disaster*, eds. W. Starbuck and M. Farjoun (Malden, MA: Blackwell Publishing, 2005), 220–245.

33. For more details, see *The Columbia Accident Investigation Board (CAIB) Report* (Washington, DC, August 26, 2003); and R. M. J. Bohmer, M. A. Roberto, and A. C. Edmondson, "The *Columbia*'s Final Mission," Case 304-090 (Boston: Harvard Business School, 2004).

34. Roberto, Bohmer, and Edmondson, "Facing Ambiguous Threats."

35. It also might not have. Notably, managers at NASA thought that this was not so, and that the terrible outcome was not preventable; Sheila Widnall, member, Columbia Accident Investigation Board, interview with author, May 21, 2004.

36. Edmondson, Roberto, Bohmer, Ferlins, and Feldman, "The Recovery Window."

37. M. P. Young et al., "Inpatient Transfers to the Intensive Care Unit: Delays Are Associated with Increased Mortality and Morbidity," *Journal of General Internal Medicine* 18 (2003): 77–83.

38. B. Sachs, "A 38-Year-Old Woman with Fetal Loss and Hysterectomy," *JAMA* 294 (2005): 833–842.

39. In the analysis of the case, the attending obstetrician implied that junior medical staff did not feel comfortable expressing that they were worried; Sachs, "A 38-Year-Old Woman," 834.

40. Note that the frequency with which an individual clinic or organization will identify patients needing transfer from one operating system to another will depend in part on the nature of the population being served and in part on the institution's beliefs about how much routine care it prefers to standardize, and its capability for identifying and dealing with transfers.

41. R. Bellomo et al., "A Prospective Before-and-After Trial of a Medical Emergency Team," *MJA* Rapid Online, August 18, 2003, http://www.mja.com.au/public/issues/179_06_150903/bel10089_fm.html.

42. Salt Lake City's Intermountain Healthcare also attempts integration but, in contrast to many other organizations, aims to insert islands of customization into an otherwise standardized process (see chapter 6).

43. For further detail, see R. M. J. Bohmer, F. W. McFarlan, and J. Adler-Milstein, "Information Technology and Clinical Operations at Beth Israel Deaconess Medical Center," Case 607-150 (Boston: Harvard Business School, 2007). Note that

the case examples used in this book are meant not as recommendations of best practice, but as illustrations of particular design principles.

44. V. W. Slack, *Cybermedicine: How Computing Empowers Doctors and Patients for Better Heath Care* (San Francisco: Jossey-Bass, 1997).

45. It has been estimated that 27 percent of clinical decisions are made in the absence of the complete medical record; G. Millar, MedicaLogic, quoted in "Doctors and Electronic Records," *All Things Considered*, National Public Radio, July 17, 2000.

46. L. Poissant et al., "The Impact of Electronic Health Records on Time Efficiency of Physicians and Nurses: A Systematic Review," *Journal of the American Medical Informatics Association* 12 (2005): 505–516.

47. In essence, the BIDMC has invested a lot of effort in understanding the work of care that it is designing an IT system to support.

48. J. Metzger and J. Fortin, *Computerized Physician Order Entry in Community Hospitals; Lessons from the Field* (California HealthCare Foundation, June 2003); and L. Gater, "CPOE—Building Electronic Safeguards," *Radiology Today* 6, no. 12 (2005): 18. Kaiser Permanente struggled for ten years to implement its electronic medical record; David Lawrence, chairman emeritus, Kaiser Permanente, personal communication with author, March 2007. Intermountain Healthcare has been developing its information system for forty years and its standardized approach to care management for ten years (see chapter 6), and is still only partway through its program.

49. One reason doctors don't follow guidelines is that they don't agree with them or don't think that they are applicable to the specific patient currently under treatment (see chapter 2).

50. I am indebted to John Glaser, CIO of Partners HealthCare System, for this taxonomy.

51. Utah's Intermountain Healthcare addresses this issue by making the in-house process for developing such rules highly transparent (see chapter 6).

52. Upton defines flexibility as "the ability to change or react with little penalty in time, effort, cost or performance"; D. M. Upton, "The Management of Manufacturing Flexibility," *California Management Review* 36 (1994): 72–89.

Chapter 6

1. Of course, this is more than enough—it is, after all, the primary goal of care.

2. A. L. Tucker and A. C. Edmondson "Why Hospitals Don't Learn from Their Failures: Organizational and Psychological Dynamics That Inhibit System Change," *California Management Review* 45 (2003): 55–72.

3. A. A. Daemmrich, "A Tale of Two Experts: Thalidomide and Political Engagement in the United States and West Germany," *Social History of Medicine* 15, no. 1 (April 2002): 137–158.

4. The case of thalidomide was a very important event in the history of drug regulation, particularly influencing the development of the FDA.

5. W. G. McBride, "Thalidomide and Congenital Abnormalities," *Lancet* 2 (1961): 1358.

6. N. Raje, "Thalidomide—A Revival Story," *New England Journal of Medicine* 341 (1999): 1606–1609.

7. J. Sheskin, "Thalidomide in the Treatment of Lepra Reactions," *Clinical Pharmacology and Therapeutics* 6 (1965): 303–306. Sheskin confirmed thalidomide's role by substituting other drugs or placebos, and then reintroducing the drug and noting that it was the thalidomide that was most reliably associated with clinical remission.

8. H. M. Connolly et al., "Valvular Heart Disease Associated with Fen-fluramine-Phentermine," *New England Journal of Medicine* 337 (1997): 581–588.

9. Ibid.

10. H. J. DeMonaco, A. Ali, and E. von Hippel, "The Major Role of Clinicians in the Discovery of Off-Label Drug Therapies," *Pharmacotherapy* 26, no. 30 (2006): 323–332.

11. The authors differentiated truly new uses from those already known by the drug's discoverer, but not included in an application to the FDA for authorization to cite that use in labeling, by checking each drug's original patent. If the use was known by the drug's discoverer (as evidenced by the original patent), but not included in the FDA application, it was classified as a "central" rather than "field" discovery.

12. Interestingly, thirty-two of the eighty-six new uses for drugs registered that year were for thalidomide.

13. G. P. Pisano, R. M. H. Bohmer, and A. C. Edmondson, "Organizational Differences in Rates of Learning: Evidence from the Adoption of Minimally Invasive Cardiac Surgery," *Management Science* 47 (2001): 752–768.

14. A. H. Morris et al., "Randomized Clinical Trial of Pressure-Controlled Inverse Ratio Ventilation and Extracorporeal CO2 Removal for Adult Respiratory Distress Syndrome," *American Journal of Respiratory and Critical Care Medicine* 149 (1994): 295–305; published erratum appears in *American Journal of Respiratory and Critical Care Medicine* 149, no. 3 (1994): 838. Interestingly, the highly stabilized conventional therapy was significantly more effective (at reducing mortality) than was $ECCO_2R$, the new experimental therapy.

15. For further detail, see R. M. J. Bohmer and E. M. Ferlins, "Clinical Change at Intermountain Healthcare," Case 607-023 (Boston: Harvard Business School, 2006).

16. G. Van den Berghe et al., "Intensive Insulin Therapy in Critically Ill Patients," *New England Journal of Medicine* 345 (2001): 1359–1367.

17. In fact, liver failure patients were not included in the original Van den Berghe study.

18. DCCT Research Group, "The Effect of Intensive Treatment of Diabetes on the Development and Progression of Long-Term Complication in Insulin-Dependent Diabetes Mellitus," *New England Journal of Medicine* 329, no. 14 (1993): 977–986.

19. Dr. Terry Clemmer, head of the LDS ICU, commented, "We are not trying to control the doctors, we are trying to get the doctors to control the system." Personal communication with author, February 2006.

20. Further detail, including the protocols and severity criteria, is contained in Bohmer and Ferlins, "Clinical Change at Intermountain Healthcare."

21. Connolly et al., "Valvular Heart Disease Associated with Fenfluramine-Phentermine."

22. R. M. J. Bohmer, D. F. Torchiana, and J. Newell, "The Effect of Decreasing Length of Stay on Discharge Destination and Readmission After Coronary Bypass Operation," *Surgery* 132 (2002): 10–16.

23. G. R. Venning, "Validity of Anecdotal Reports of Suspected Adverse Drug Reactions: The Problem of False Alarms," *BMJ* 284 (1982): 249–252.

24. Ibid., 251.

25. J. K. Aronson, "Anecdotes as Evidence," *BMJ* 326 (2003): 1346.

26. H. G. Welch and J. Mogielnicki, "Presumed Benefit: Lessons from the American Experience with Marrow Transplantation for Breast Cancer," *BMJ* 324 (2002): 1088–1092.

27. Ibid.

28. Ibid.

29. B. Levitt and J. G. March, "Organizational Learning," *Annual Review of Sociology* 14 (1988): 319–340.

30. Ibid., 326.

31. T. Greenhalgh, "Narrative Based Medicine in an Evidence Based World," *BMJ* 318 (1999): 323–325.

32. D. L. Sackett et al., "Evidence Based Medicine: What It Is and What It Isn't," *BMJ* 312 (1996): 71–72.

33. D. M. Berwick, "Disseminating Innovations in Healthcare," *JAMA* 289 (2003): 1969–1975.

34. E. A. Balas and S. A. Boren, "Managing Clinical Knowledge for Health Care Improvement," in *Yearbook of Medical Informatics: Patient-Centered Systems*, eds. J. H. Van Bemmel and A. T. McCray (Stuttgart: Schattauer, 2000), 65–70.

35. D. A. Davis et al., "Changing Physician Performance: A Systematic Review of the Effect of Continuing Medical Education Strategies," *JAMA* 274 (1995): 700–705; M. B. Rosenthal et al., "Early Experience with Pay-for-Performance: From Concept to Practice," *JAMA* 294 (2005): 1788–1793; A. R. Jadad et al., "Methodology and Reports of Systematic Reviews and Meta-analyses: A Comparison of Cochrane Reviews with Articles Published in Paper-Based Journals," *JAMA* 280 (1998): 278–280; and J. P. A. Ioannidis, J. C. Cappelleri, and J. Lau, "Issues in Comparisons Between Meta-analyses and Large Trials," *JAMA* 279 (1998): 1089–1093.

36. R. Bohmer and A. Edmondson, "Organizational Learning in Health Care," *Health Forum* (March–April 2001): 32–35.

37. Note that the case examples used in this book are meant not as recommendations of best practice, but as illustrations of particular design principles.

38. See R. M. J. Bohmer and A. C. Edmondson, "Intermountain Health Care," Case 603-066 (Boston: Harvard Business School, 2002).

39. B. C. James, "Making It Easy to Do It Right," *New England Journal of Medicine* 345 (2001): 991–993.

40. In fact, the very opposite is true. Managers at Intermountain are concerned when they see compliance rates that are too close to 100 percent. As Brent James, MD, executive director of Intermountain Healthcare's Institute for Health Care Delivery Research, notes, "No protocol fits *every* patient, and no protocol perfectly fits *any* patient." Brent James, personal communication with author, July 2002.

41. In autopsy studies, about 10 percent of autopsies find "missed diagnoses that would have resulted in a change in therapy and might have prolonged survival if identified earlier"; see K. G. Shojania and E. C. Burton, "The Vanishing Nonforensic Autopsy," *New England Journal of Medicine* 358 (2008): 873–875.

42. M. P. Young et al., "Inpatient Transfers to the Intensive Care Unit: Delays Are Associated with Increased Mortality and Morbidity," *Journal of General Internal Medicine* 18 (2003): 77–83.

43. A. Edmondson, "Framing for Learning: Lessons in Successful Technology Implementation," *California Management Review* 45 (2003): 34–54; and A. C. Edmondson, R. M. J. Bohmer, and G. P. Pisano, "Disrupted Routines: Team Learning and New Technology Implementation in Hospitals," *Administrative Science Quarterly* 46 (2001): 685–716.

44. Edmondson, Bohmer, and Pisano, "Disrupted Routines"; and Pisano, Bohmer, and Edmondson, "Organizational Differences in Rates of Learning."

45. R. M. J. Bohmer et al., unpublished findings from the Managing Medical Innovation Study, 2001.

46. Steve Colvin, MD, chairman, Department of Cardiothoracic Surgery, New York University Medical Center, personal communication with author, August 16, 2002 (Dr. Colvin is now deceased).

47. A. Edmondson, "Psychological Safety and Learning Behavior in Work Teams," *Administrative Science Quarterly* 44, no. 4 (1999): 350–383.

48. A. C. Edmondson, R. Bohmer, and G. P. Pisano, "Speeding Up Team Learning," *Harvard Business Review*, October 2001, 125–134; and A. C. Edmondson, M. Roberto, and A. L. Tucker, "Children's Hospital and Clinics (A)," Case 302-050 (Boston: Harvard Business School, 2001).

49. A. C. Edmondson, G. P. Pisano, R. M. J. Bohmer, A. B. Winslow, "Learning How and Learning What: Effects of Tacit and Codified Knowledge on Performance Improvement Following Technology Adoption," *Decision Sciences* 34 (2003): 197–223.

50. Ibid.

51. One important implication of this is that the spread of explicit knowledge is typically faster (and more uniform) than that of tacit knowledge. Rates of performance improvement across organizations are much more heterogeneous when that improvement relies on tacit knowledge than when it depends on the spread of explicit knowledge; see Edmonson, Pisano, Bohmer, and Winslow, "Learning How and Learning What."

52. A. L. Tucker, I. M. Nembhard, and A. C. Edmondson, "Implementing New Practices: An Empirical Study of Organizational Learning in Hospital Intensive Care Units," *Management Science* 53 (2007): 894–907.

Chapter 7

1. F. G. Donini-Lenhoff and H. L. Hedrick, "Growth of Specialization in Graduate Medical Education," *JAMA* 284 (2000): 1284–1289; and E. Ginsberg, quoted in K. Shine, "Health Care Quality and How to Achieve It" (2001 Robert H. Ebert Memorial Lecture, Milbank Memorial Fund, New York City, 2002).

2. The economic value of such family caregiving is substantial. One report estimated it to be $196 billion in 1997; see P. S. Arno, C. Levine, and M. M. Memmott, "The Economic Value of Informal Care Giving," *Health Affairs* 18, no. 2 (1999): 182–188.

3. L. L. Leape et al., "Systems Analysis of Adverse Drug Events," *JAMA* 274 (1995): 35–43; and J. Chen et al., "Do 'America's Best Hospitals' Perform Better for Acute Myocardial Infarction?" *New England Journal of Medicine* 340 (1999): 286–292.

4. R. S. Huckman and G. P. Pisano, "The Firm Specificity of Individual Performance: Evidence from Cardiac Surgery," *Management Science* 52 (2006): 473–488.

5. Ginsberg, quoted in Shine, "Health Care Quality and How to Achieve It"; and E. J. Emanuel, "Changing Premed Requirements and the Medical Curriculum," *JAMA* 296 (2006): 1128–1131.

6. Note that management skill in this context is distinct from business skill.

7. W. E. Sasser, R. P. Olsen, and D. D. Wyckoff, *Management of Service Operations* (Boston: Allyn & Bacon, 1978), chap. 7.

8. R. Simons, *Levers of Organization Design: How Managers Use Accountability Systems for Greater Performance and Commitment* (Boston: Harvard Business School Press, 2005).

9. A. C. Edmondson, R. M. J. Bohmer, and G. P. Pisano, "Disrupted Routines: Team Learning and New Technology Implementation," *Administrative Science Quarterly* 46 (2001): 685–716; and A. C. Edmondson, R. M. J. Bohmer, and G. P. Pisano, "Speeding Up Team Learning," *Harvard Business Review*, October 2001, 125–134.

10. S. J. Spear, "Fixing Health Care from the Inside, Today," *Harvard Business Review*, September 2005, 78–91.

11. To this point, of course, physicians legitimately argue that it is hard for them to take a system view when they are held legally accountable as individuals.

12. N. Edwards, M. J. Kornacki, and J. Silversin, "Unhappy Doctors: What Are the Causes and What Can Be Done?" *BMJ* 324 (2002): 835–838.

13. T. M. Waters et al., "Factors Associated with Physician Involvement in Care Management," *Medical Care* 39, Supplement (2001): I-79–I-91.

14. R. J. Baron and C. K. Cassel, "21st Century Primary Care: New Physician Roles Need New Payment Models," *JAMA* 299 (2008): 1595–1597.

15. While 98 percent, 92 percent, and 89 percent of primary care physicians (PCPs) in the Netherlands, New Zealand, and the United Kingdom report using electronic medical records in their practices, only 28 percent of American PCPs do so; see C. Schoen et al., "On the Front Lines of Care: Primary Care Doctors' Office Systems, Experiences, and Views in Seven Countries," *Health Affairs* 25 (2006): w555–w571.

16. L. R. Burns et al., "Physician Commitment to Organized Delivery Systems," *Medical Care* 39, Supplement (2001): I-9–I-29; and S. M. Shortell et al., "Physician-System Alignment: Introductory Overview," *Medical Care* 39, Supplement (2002): I-1–I-8.

17. L. R. Burns and R. W. Muller, "Hospital-Physician Collaboration: Landscape of Economic Integration and Impact on Clinical Integration," *Milbank Quarterly* 86, no. 3 (2008): 375–434.

18. Shortell et al., "Physician-System Alignment."

19. Burns and Muller, "Hospital-Physician Collaboration."

20. R. E. Bohn and R. Jaikumar, *From Filing and Fitting to Flexible Manufacturing*, Foundations and Trends in Technology, Information and Operations Management, vol. 1, no. 1 (Hanover MA: Now Publishers, 2005), 1–120; and R. E. Bohn, *From Art to Science in Manufacturing: The Evolution of Technical Knowledge*, Foundations and Trends in Technology, Information and Operations Management, vol. 1, no. 2 (Hanover MA: Now Publishers, 2005), 121–202.

21. Bohn and Jaikumar, *From Filing and Fitting.*

22. They also take back control at key times, such as in a crisis, as in the famous case of United Airlines Flight 232, which, in 1989, having lost its hydraulics, was manually steered by differentially speeding and slowing its engines (resulting in the saving of 185 lives).

23. K. M. Harris et al., "Buyers Health Care Action Group: Consumer Perceptions of Quality Differences," in *Consumer-Driven Health Care: Implications for Providers, Payers and Policymakers*, ed. R. Herzlinger (San Francisco: Jossey-Bass, 2004), 475–486.

24. J. H. Hibbard and J. J. Jewett, "Will Quality Report Cards Help Consumers?" *Health Affairs* 16, no. 3 (1997): 218–228.

25. Decision aids such as these tend to improve patients' satisfaction with their decisions and their understanding of their risks but do not necessarily influence their

decisions; see J. E. Joy, E. E. Penhoet, and D. B. Pitetti, *Saving Women's Lives: Strategies for Improving Breast Cancer Detection and Diagnosis* (Washington, DC: National Academies Press, 2005).

26. M. Balconi, "Tacitness, Codification of Technological Knowledge and the Organization of Industry," *Research Policy* 31 (2002): 357–379.

27. The term *coproduction* has been used to describe the customer's participation in the provider's operations.

28. Y. Moon and F. X. Frei, "Exploding the Self-Service Myth," *Harvard Business Review*, May–June 2000, 26–27.

29. To this extent, health care has long involved coproduction. That is, it is the patient who is predominantly responsible for executing the primary care physician's decision.

30. Note that customer coproduction is not necessarily cheaper. When consumers are involved in creating a service, they can introduce additional variability that may increase the service provider's costs; see F. X. Frei, "Breaking the Trade-off Between Efficiency and Service," *Harvard Business Review*, November 2006, 92–101. For example, patients' compliance with medication is a significant problem inasmuch as noncompliance reduces a therapy's effectiveness. In one study, nearly half the patients who were prescribed a long-term cholesterol-lowering drug were not taking it a year later; see S. E. Andrade et al., "Discontinuation of Anti-Hyperlipidemic Drugs—Do Rates Reported in Clinical Trials Reflect Rates in Primary Care Settings?" *New England Journal of Medicine* 332 (1995): 1125–1131.

31. E. P. Brass, "Changing the Status of Drugs from Prescription to Over-the-Counter Availability," *New England Journal of Medicine* 345 (2001): 810–816.

32. Recall that increasing stage of knowledge means more than simply "we know more about the disease." It means that we know exactly which are the key parameters, how they are related to a diagnosis or an outcome, and exactly how to influence them.

33. Some foods interfere with the metabolism of warfarin and thus influence the drug's action.

34. The extent to which such variation is genetically determined is slowly being elucidated, but this new knowledge has not yet generated a dosing schedule of the kind used for insulin. At the moment, it informs a general guidance that "patients of Asian, European, and African ancestry require, on average, lower, intermediate, and higher doses of warfarin, respectively"; see S. B. Shurin and E. G. Nabel, "Pharmacogenomics—Ready for Prime Time?" *New England Journal of Medicine* 358 (2008): 1061–1063.

35. Ideally, interventions that patients take an increased role in managing would have a reasonably wide margin of safety (low cost of error, particularly overdose), as is the case with asthma medications. Although insulin overdose is potentially very dangerous, patients can often recognize the symptoms of overdose in time to intervene to prevent harm.

36. "Statins: Affair of the Heart," *Guardian*, May 15, 2004.

37. Frei, "Breaking the Trade-off Between Efficiency and Service."

38. T. Bodenheimer et al., "Patient Self-Management of Chronic Disease in Primary Care," *JAMA* 288 (2002): 2469–2475.

39. P. Pierce, "Deciding on Breast Cancer Treatment: A Description of Decision Behavior," *Nursing Research* 42, no. 1 (1993): 22–28.

40. E. Emanuel and L. Emanuel, "Four Models of the Physician-Patient Relationship," *JAMA* 267 (1992): 2221–2226. In the *paternalistic* relationship, the physician presents selective information to encourage the patient to consent to certain procedures that the physician considers best, and the patient complies. In the *informative* relationship, the physician provides all the relevant evidence and information to the patient, and the patient chooses. In the *interpretive* model, the physician focuses on eliciting the patient's values and uses these to help the patient select appropriate choices. And in the *deliberative* relationship, the physician helps the patient choose the most appropriate values to guide decision making. Physicians not only provide information but also can direct and influence the values of the patient, indicating why some may be more worthwhile than others.

41. D. Lovich, M. Silverstein, and R. Lesser, *Vital Signs: The Impact of E-Health on Patients and Physicians* (Boston: Boston Consulting Group, February 2001).

42. Ibid.

43. M. J. Barrett, *Patient Self-Management Tools: An Overview* (Oakland: California HealthCare Foundation, 2005).

44. C. M. Christensen, R. M. J. Bohmer, and J. Kenagy, "Will Disruptive Innovations Cure Health Care?" *Harvard Business Review*, September 2000, 102–117.

45. R. M. J. Bohmer and D. M. Lawrence, "Care Platforms: A Basic Building Block for Care Delivery," *Health Affairs* 27, no. 5 (2008): 1336–1340.

46. W. Skinner, "The Focused Factory," *Harvard Business Review*, May–June 1974, 113–120. Standardizing decisions and activities is made easier by the narrower range of services provided in each category; see Bohmer and Lawrence, "Care Platforms."

47. L. A. Petersen et al., "Does Housestaff Discontinuity of Care Increase the Risk for Preventable Adverse Events?" *Annals of Internal Medicine* 121, no. 11 (1994): 866–872.

48. T. Bodenheimer, "Coordinating Care—A Perilous Journey Through the Health Care System," *New England Journal of Medicine* 358 (2008): 1064–1071.

49. Ibid.

50. "The Future of Family Medicine: A Collaborative Project of the Family Medicine Community," *Annals of Family Medicine* 2 (2004): S3–S32. The term *medical home* was coined by the American Academy of Pediatrics.

51. Luke Sato, MD, chief medical officer, CRICO/RMF, personal communication with author, March 2008.

52. Edwards, Kornacki, and Silversin, "Unhappy Doctors."

Chapter 8

1. R. S. Kaplan and D. P. Norton, "The Balanced Scorecard: Measures That Drive Performance," *Harvard Business Review*, January–February 1992, 71–79.

2. B. C. James, "Making It Easy to Do It Right," *New England Journal of Medicine* 345 (2001): 991–993.

3. T. H. Davenport and J. Glaser, "Just-in-Time Knowledge Delivery Comes to Knowledge Management," *Harvard Business Review*, July 2002, 107–111. The design of such computer-based workflow support tools is critical. As James notes, computerized systems "must present the right information, in the right format, at the right time, without requiring special effort." Physicians have neither the time nor the inclination to "learn to use a series of disconnected computer systems," particularly if they are "at odds with physicians' concept of the medical record or sense of autonomy in decision making"; see James, "Making It Easy to Do It Right."

4. In *value stream mapping*, those tasks that add customer value are differentiated from those that add no value, and only the former are linked into a new process.

5. For further detail, see R. M. J. Bohmer and E. M. Ferlins, "Virginia Mason Medical Center," Case 606-044 (Boston: Harvard Business School, 2005).

6. A. C. Edmondson, "Learning from Failure in Health Care: Frequent Opportunities, Pervasive Barriers," *Quality and Safety in Health Care* 13, Supplement II (2004): ii3–ii9.

7. For example, during the adoption of a new device and technique for minimally invasive cardiac surgery at NYU Medical Center, the entire surgical team—surgeons, nurses, and technicians—met at the end of the working day each time the new technique was used on a case that day. The purpose of these meetings—in effect, "after action reviews"; see D. A. Garvin, *Learning in Action: A Guide to Putting the Learning Organization to Work* (Boston: Harvard Business School Press, 2000)—was to identify what went well and badly, and to plan changes that should be made to the conduct of the very next case.

8. Anomalies are already common. Gaba found that in 18 percent of operations, an anesthesiologist will encounter an "unanticipated problem" requiring an intervention, and 3 percent to 5 percent will involve a serious unplanned event requiring a major intervention; see D. M. Gaba, "Human Error in Dynamic Medical Domains," in *Human Error in Medicine*, ed. M. S. Bogner (Hillsdale, NJ: Lawrence Erlbaum Associates, 1994), 197–224. Examining cardiac surgical procedures, Wong et al. found an average of 3.5 (maximum 26) "events with the potential to lead to adverse outcomes" per operation, 32 percent of which the surgeon rated as major; see D. R. Wong, T. J. Vander Salm, I. S. Ali, A. K. Agnihotri, R. M. J. Bohmer, and D. F. Torchiana, "Prospective Assessment of Intraoperative Precursor Events During Cardiac Surgery," *European Journal of Cardio-thoracic Surgery* 29, no. 4 (2006): 447–455.

9. M. A. Roberto, R. M. J. Bohmer, and A. C. Edmondson, "Facing Ambiguous Threats," *Harvard Business Review*, November 2006, 106–113.

10. Ibid. Although morbidity and mortality (M and M) rounds are intended to serve this purpose—structured analyses of individual anomalies—one study suggests they may not be particularly effective, particularly in internal medicine. A study of M and M rounds in internal medicine found that 37 percent of case presentations included an adverse event, and 18 percent an error causing an adverse event (compared with 72 percent and 42 percent, respectively, in surgery M and M rounds). Moreover, only 15.2 percent of the time in internal medicine M and M rounds was given over to audience discussion (versus 36.6 percent in surgery); and when an error was discussed, a specific root cause was identified in 38 percent of internal medicine cases versus 79 percent of surgery cases. See E. Pierluissi et al., "Discussion of Medical Errors in Morbidity and Mortality Conferences," *JAMA* 290 (2003): 2838–2842.

11. Note that these two, short-term adjustment and long-term redesign, are not independent activities. That a process seems to be requiring one short-term adjustment after another may be a sign that a more fundamental redesign is warranted.

12. Gaba, "Human Error in Dynamic Medical Domains."

13. A. L. Tucker and A. C. Edmondson, "Why Hospitals Don't Learn from Their Failures: Organizational and Psychological Dynamics That Inhibit System Change," *California Management Review* 45 (2003): 55–72.

14. R. Bohn, "Stop Fighting Fires," *Harvard Business Review*, July–August 2000, 83–91.

15. In Tucker and Edmondson's study this occurred only 7 percent of the time.

16. Bohmer and Ferlins, "Virginia Mason Medical Center."

17. One of the early implementers of rapid response teams placed a list of criteria for activating the team on the wall in each patient room; see R. Bellomo et al., "A Prospective Before-and-After Trial of a Medical Emergency Team," *Medical Journal of Australia* Rapid Online Publication, August 18, 2003.

18. S. Thomke, "R & D Comes to Services: Bank of America's Pathbreaking Experiments," *Harvard Business Review*, April 2003, 70–79.

19. Department of Health and Human Services, *Protection of Human Subjects*, Code of Federal Regulations, Title 45, Part 46 (1991), § 46.102d.

20. Parenthetically, it is not clear that patients fully appreciate this, even after they have given their "informed consent." One survey of cancer patients who had participated in a clinical trial found that 25 percent of respondents did not recognize that "trials are done mainly to benefit future patients"; see S. Joffe et al., "Quality of Informed Consent in Cancer Clinical Trials: A Cross-Sectional Survey," *Lancet* 358 (2001): 1772–1777.

21. D. Casarett, J. H. T. Karlawish, and J. Sugarman, "Determining When Quality Improvement Initiatives Should Be Considered Research," *JAMA* 283,

no. 17 (2000): 2275–2280; and "Pointy Headed Regulation," editorial, *New York Times*, January 27, 2008.

22. Casarett, Karlawish, and Sugarman, "Determining When Quality Improvement."

23. Hence the importance of the system architect role, discussed in chapter 7.

Index

aberrance. *See* anomaly detection
academic medical centers, 173
accountability, 8–9, 175
   changing physician roles and,
      178–179
   mechanisms for insuring, 164
   pay-for-performance systems and,
      163–164
Accreditation Council for Graduate
      Medical Education (ACGME), 177
ADA (American Diabetes Association),
      47, 94
AIDS epidemic, 78, 79
alignment
   effects of misalignment, 127
   external, 123–125
   in integrated care design, 205
   internal (*see* internal alignment)
   between physician and organization,
      182–184
   systems aligned with goals,
      123–125, 129
ambiguity, 10–11
ambiguous threats, 140–142
American Cancer Society, 197
American Diabetes Association (ADA),
      47, 94
anecdotal evidence, 161–163
anomaly detection
   culture supportive of, 207–208
   role of analysis in, 208–209

short-term process adjustments
      and, 213
   strength of signals of aberrance,
      159–161
   tools for signal detection,
      170–171, 207
   triggering learning cycle, 203–204
Apollo 13 crisis, 210
Aretaeus, 45, 92
asset management, 43

balanced scorecard, 206
Bank of America, 212
benchmarking, 35
best practices, 39–40, 58, 157–158, 163
best-practice transfer, 174
Beth Israel Deaconess Medical Center
      (BIDMC), 143–149
BHCAG (Buyers Health Care Action
      Group), 185
bias
   cognitive, 141, 162–163
   confirmation bias, 141, 162
   in developing medical evidence,
      52–56
   research bias, financial incentives
      and, 55–56
   in results reporting, 52–53
BIDMC (Beth Israel Deaconess
      Medical Center), 143–149

About the Author

Richard M. J. Bohmer, MBChB, MPH, is a New Zealand–trained physician on the faculty of Harvard Business School. He graduated from the Auckland University School of Medicine and has practiced hospital and primary medicine in New Zealand and England. In 1989, he was part of a clinical team that established and ran a surgical hospital in Sudan. He attended the Harvard School of Public Health on a Fulbright Scholarship, graduating in 1993 with a Master's of Public Health in Health Care Management, and joined the HBS faculty in 1997.

At the Harvard Business School, he teaches an MBA course on health care operations management, codirects the MD-MBA program, and is the faculty chair for two executive programs in health care delivery. He teaches and consults on health management issues in numerous locations around the world. Before joining the HBS faculty, Dr. Bohmer was the Clinical Director of Quality Improvement at Massachusetts General Hospital, where he was responsible for planning and implementing the institution's clinical quality-improvement program.

Dr. Bohmer's research focus is on the intersection between medical care and management practice and concentrates on understanding how best to design and manage the process of patient care in order to improve clinical outcomes. He has published in both the management and medical literatures on learning, technology adoption, and operations strategy in health care, and on quality improvement and patient safety.